A Guide to the Police Act

Previous titles in the series

A Guide to the Criminal Justice and Public Order Act 1994
A Guide to the Finance Act 1994
A Guide to the Police and Magistrates' Courts Act 1994
A Guide to the Sunday Trading Act 1994
A Guide to the Trade Marks Act 1994
A Guide to the Finance Act 1995
A Guide to the Pensions Act 1995
A Guide to the Criminal Procedure and Investigations Act 1996
A Guide to the Family Law Act 1996
A Guide to the Finance Act 1996
A Guide to the Housing Act 1996
A Guide to the Crime (Sentences) Act 1997
A Guide to the Finance Act 1997
A Guide to the Finance (No 2) Act 1997

A Guide to the Police Act 1997

Ben Emmerson, LLB
Barrister
Daniel Friedman, BA (Hons), LLM
Barrister

Butterworths
London, Edinburgh, Dublin
1998

United Kingdom	Butterworths a Division of Reed Elsevier (UK) Ltd, Halsbury House, 35 Chancery Lane, LONDON WC2A 1EL and 4 Hill Street, EDINBURGH EH2 3JZ
Australia	Butterworths, SYDNEY, ADELAIDE, BRISBANE, CANBERRA, MELBOURNE and PERTH
Canada	Butterworths Canada Ltd, TORONTO and VANCOUVER
Ireland	Butterworth (Ireland) Ltd, DUBLIN
Malaysia	Malayan Law Journal Sdn Bhd, KUALA LUMPUR
New Zealand	Butterworths of New Zealand Ltd, WELLINGTON and AUCKLAND
Singapore	Butterworths Asia, SINGAPORE
South Africa	Butterworths Publishers (Pty) Ltd, DURBAN
USA	Michie, CHARLOTTESVILLE, Virginia

A CIP Catalogue record for this book is available from the British Library.

ISBN 0 406 89547 3

Printed and bound in Great Britain by Redwood Books, Trowbridge, Wiltshire

For Daniel and Mathew Emmerson

and

Max Friedman (1931–1987)

Preface

The Police Act 1997 aims to create a new constitutional structure which will take policing technology into the 21st century, and enable law enforcement agencies to co-ordinate their efforts to combat organised crime. Part I of the Act puts the National Criminal Intelligence Service onto a statutory footing. Part II brings the Regional Crime Squads together into a single National Crime Squad. In the wake of the House of Lords' decision in *R v Khan (Sultan)* [1997] AC 558, Part III creates a statutory regime for regulating the intrusive surveillance by the police of private property and wireless telegraphy. Part IV gives a statutory basis to the Police Information Technology Organisation which will co-ordinate the incorporation of modern IT facilities into police operations. Part V creates a statutory procedure by which employers will be able to gain access to criminal records and other information concerning prospective employees.

Parts I and II of the Act are already in force (SI 1997/1377). At the time of writing Part III has not been brought into effect. The new Government is still in the process of finalising a code of practice on intrusive surveillance, and the commissioners—who will be responsible for supervising the operation of Part III of the Act—have yet to be appointed. Part IV of the Act is due to come into force in April 1998. For the time being, the existing Police Information Technology Organisation will exist under the auspices of the Home Office Police Science and Technology Unit.

The new Government remains committed to introducing the three types of character certificates that are provided for in Part V. However, at present the Home Office is reconsidering whether a Criminal Records Agency, as envisaged under the Act, is the most appropriate mechanism for providing such certificates.

We would like to acknowlege all those who have contributed to this publication, particularly Butterworths editorial staff, Stephen Uglow and Venous Telford of the University of Kent, and Stephen Cragg and Courtenay Griffiths of 2 Garden Court chambers. Special thanks are due to Joanne Sawyer, Anthony Hudson, Ashley Serr, Katie Ghose, and especially to Anne Shamash, who helped in so many ways.

Ben Emmerson
Daniel Friedman

January 1998

Contents

Table of Statutes

References in the table to *Statutes* are to Halsbury's Statutes of England (Fourth Edition) showing the volume and page number at which the annotated text of the Act may be found. References in the right-hand column are to paragraph numbers.

Table of Cases

K

L

M

O

P

R

1 Introduction

THE AIMS OF THE 1997 ACT

1.1 In introducing the Police Bill in the House of Commons in February 1997, Michael Howard, the Home Secretary, set out the central objectives of the legislation—

> 'Organised crime is nothing new, but it is more sophisticated than ever before. Organised criminals are quick to exploit the opportunities provided by the ease of modern travel and modern communications. They operate across police force boundaries and national boundaries. They use the latest technology. They create large and complex businesses, part legal and part illegal, to launder the proceeds of their crimes. The Government are determined to ensure that the law enforcement agencies have the tools that they need to fight such crime effectively. They must be able to conduct effective surveillance, to obtain reliable intelligence and to target major crime in a co-ordinated way. The Bill will help them to achieve that'.[1]

Lord Browne-Wilkinson saw things from a slightly different perspective. Whilst acknowledging the need for reform, he identified a number of measures in the Bill which had serious implications for civil liberties. 'I am tough on crime', he said, 'but I am steely on freedom'.[2]

1 HC 2R, 12 February 1997, col 345.
2 HL Report, 26 November 1996, col 218.

1.2 Both Michael Howard and Lord Browne-Wilkinson would consider the efficiency and effectiveness of the police to be fundamental to the health of the nation and to the protection of its citizens. However, during the passage of the Police Bill, these individuals and the opinions that lined up behind them, became locked in a debate about whether, in the fight against modern organised crime, the ends necessarily justified the means.

LAW AND ORDER DEBATES SINCE THE 1970s

1.3 The creation of a National Crime Squad and a statutory scheme for justifying unlawful surveillance would have been politically impossible in the 1980s. Early attempts at nationally co-ordinated policing encountered serious political opposition. During the 1984–85 miners' strike, for example, the Association of Chief Police Officers (ACPO) set up a National Reporting Centre (NRC) as a means of co-ordinating a response to the nationwide movements of pickets. ACPO continually emphasised that the NRC was merely a clearing mechanism for allocating mutual aid between police forces. Opponents however characterised the NRC as an embryonic national policing structure, and accused ACPO of acting as a medium for central

Government control of operational policing.[1] Whatever the real function of the NRC, the idea of a national police force became a very entrenched taboo.

1 R Reiner, *Police Constables* (1991) Ch 8; B Loveday, 'Centralised co-ordination: Police Authorities and the Miners' Strike' Political Quarterly (1986), pp 57, 60-73; M Kettle, 'The National Reporting Centre' in M Kettle (ed) *Policing the Miners' Strike.*

1.4 Instead of making efforts to develop a national police force, the Home Office called for more explicit co-ordination between local forces. Douglas Hurd, as Home Secretary, exemplified this view in a speech in April 1989—

> 'There will always be arguments brought forward by friends of the police as well as their critics in favour of a national police force or much bigger regional forces. But, as I have said, the roots of our police forces in their counties and cities is strong, and much has and will be done to keep them strong. It would be quixotic, just when it looks as if we may be turning a corner on crime, if we began to hack at the local connections of the police with some institutional upheaval. Rather we would wish to strengthen the links—for example by building up the special constabulary, and by strengthening the local consultative committees which have now been formally established throughout England and Wales to maintain local understanding and co-operation'.[1]

At ACPO's autumn conference in the same year, Hurd called on chief officers 'to deliver effectively co-ordinated operational action'. Failing this, he implied that the present structure of the police might have to be replaced by either regional forces or a single national force.[2] Regardless of assurances that there was to be no national force, nationwide initiatives gradually came into existence. Most importantly, the Special Branch, the Regional Crime Squads and in 1992, the National Criminal Intelligence Service, all endeavoured to contribute to what ACPO called 'a unity of a more explicit co-ordination.'[3]

1 Parliamentary Research Paper 97/21, p 10.
2 Reiner, *Chief Constables*, op cit, p 31.
3 Op cit.

Management philosophy and the information technology revolution

1.5 The law and order debate intensified in the early 1990s, partly because of rising crime rates and partly because both major political parties chose law and order as a means of establishing their credentials to govern. The system of local policing began to appear both provincial and operationally inadequate to meet the new demands on its resources.

1.6 Recent reforms of the police have borrowed heavily from two dominant trends that are prevalent in the world of industry and business. The first trend embodies a new management ethos that focuses on enhancing organisational cohesion through the adoption of prescribed goals and 'service plans'. The second trend is the global information technology revolution, which dramatically enhances the potential of organisations to analyse and communicate data. These trends have been brought together in the 1997 Act by the creation of three policing organisations with a truly national jurisdiction: the National Criminal Intelligence Service (NCIS), the National Crime Squad (NCS) and the Police Information Technology Organisation (PITO).

The Police and Magistrates' Courts Act 1994

1.7 The key innovation of the Police and Magistrates' Courts Act 1994, Pt I, Ch I, (the 1994 Act),[1] now codified in the Police Act 1996, was to impose the contemporary practices of business and the managerial world onto a police force whose structure had changed little since the nineteenth century. While the need for reform was welcomed by many, there were deep divisions over the policy of forcing the police to adopt the en vogue concepts of 'objectives', 'service plans' and 'performance targets'. In essence, the argument centred on whether it would be more or less in the public interest for police forces to be run like a public limited company. The Government's view prevailed, and the managerial language and structure of the 1994 Act is replicated in the 1997 Act.

1 The 1994 Act implemented changes proposed in the 1993 White Paper, 'Police Reform' (Cm 2281).

1.8 The purpose of the 1994 Act was to redesign, but also to maintain, traditional policing at the local level, and to improve the quality of service.[1] The so-called tripartite principal, whereby the Home Office, Chief Constables and local police authorities share the responsibility for maintaining the police, was central to the Government's commitment to modernising without undermining local autonomy. However, at the time it was widely predicted that provisions which would support greater co-ordination on a national level were still to come.[2] The 1997 Act achieves exactly that.

1 Lord Mackay, HL 2R 18 January 1994, col 458.
2 For details on the 1994 Act, see S Baker and J English, *A Guide to the Police and Magistrates' Courts Act 1994* (1994); T Jones and T Newton, *Policing the Act—Police and Magistrates' Courts Act 1994* (1997).

The Police Act 1997

1.9 The amalgamation of local police initiatives into modern national operations and practices is the key purpose of the 1997 Act, and this purpose manifests itself directly in Parts I and II of the Act. Part I puts the pre-existing National Criminal Intelligence Service (NCIS) onto a statutory footing. Part II creates a new National Crime Squad (NCS) out of the existing Regional Crime Squads. Part III provides a statutory basis for existing intrusive surveillance practices. The remaining provisions of the Act can properly be described as 'operational'. Part IV creates the Police Information Technology Organisation (PITO), with the intention that the information technology revolution can be harnessed for the benefit of national law enforcement strategies. Finally, Part V creates a Criminal Records Agency (CRA) with the purpose of regulating the disclosure of criminal records and criminal intelligence for employment purposes, as well as for voluntary sector appointments.

A national police force?

1.10 The creation of the NCIS and the NCS is in part a consequence of the Home Affairs Committee Report on Organised Crime (1994–95),[1] which concluded that—

> 'if the response to serious crime is to be sharpened and made more effective, the present structure of separate Regional Crime Squads, with no central executive direction, needs to be replaced by a more nationally co-ordinated structure'.[2]

1 Home Affairs Committee, Third Report Session 1994–95, HC 18-I.
2 Ibid, para 105.

1.11 In introducing the Bill, the Government was at pains to stress that it was not their intention to create a national police force.[1] During the Inquiry on Organised Crime, both Albert Pacey, the Director General of the NCIS and Neil Dickens, the National co-ordinator of the Regional Crime Squads (RCS), argued that it would be wrong for the NCIS and the RCS to be joined together, because it would lead to the work of both organisations being devalued. In particular, they argued against a merger, on the ground that it would be seen as a purely police organisation, to the detriment of its relationship with non-police users such as Customs and Excise, the Immigration Service and the Bank of England.[2] In a speech at ACPO's 1996 summer conference, Michael Howard gave assurances that the Government would maintain a multi-agency response and endeavour to strengthen co-ordination. Above all, the NCIS and the NCS were not intended to be a British FBI (a point that was repeated several times during the Parliamentary debates on the 1997 Act).[3]

1 See HL 2R, 11 November 1996, col 789; see also para 2.4.
2 Home Affairs Committee, Third Report Session 1994–95, para 104.
3 Parliamentary Research Paper 97/21, p 15.

1.12 The 1997 Act was thus the culmination of the slow embrace of the idea of national policing that began through the initiatives of ACPO in the 1980s.[1] However, the legislation is a fundamental watershed in that process, because it recognises that the national initiatives of the past have been an inadequate response to the methods used by modern criminal enterprises and because it institutionalises national co-ordination for the future. It remains to be seen whether the current arrangements will turn out to be merely a formal stepping stone towards a single national police organisation with local branches.

1 In a speech in September 1995 the Metropolitan police commissioner, Sir Paul Condon, argued that local police forces ought to be prepared to give up part of their independence to create a 'national strike force' to tackle organised crime. The vested interests of Chief Constables ought not to take precedence over pressing national imperatives. However, the tradition of local policing could and should co-exist with an enhanced national structure; a national agency did not mean 'a national police force', Daily Telegraph, 6 September 1995.

The modern technology of surveillance

1.13 The 1997 Act provides a statutory licence for the use of modern surveillance capabilities by the police. The focus of the legislation, on officers physically interfering with property in order to plant surveillance devices, is however only the tip of the iceberg. There are a number of intrusive surveillance techniques currently available which do not involve any physical interference with property.[1] These will remain unregulated by the new legislation. Nevertheless, the so-called 'bug and burgle' provisions were the source of the fiercest debate, both within and outside Parliament.

1 These include long distance sensitive microphones and laser beam technology. See also Mike Davis, *City of Quartz–Excavating the future of Los Angeles* (1990): an account of policing in Los Angeles which describes how the LAPD are developing a satellite capability that will be able to read car number plates on given streets. See also paras 4.33, 4.45 and 5.16–5.17.

1.14 Although the interception of telephone and postal communications is already governed by legislation,[1] the use of electronic devices by the police to record communications on private property remained subject only to Home Office Guidelines. This was almost certainly contrary to the European Convention on

Human Rights[2] and had been the subject of criticism by the House of Lords.[3] The Government responded by introducing proposals to govern surveillance actions by the police in respect of property. In stark contrast to other legislation that deals with covert surveillance, the original proposals contained no system of prior independent authorisation for such action. The decision whether to sanction intrusive surveillance was to remain with the police themselves. Following extensive pressure in the House of Lords and the media, amendments to the Bill were passed which require certain types of surveillance to have the prior approval of an independent commissioner, who has the rank of a High Court judge or above. However, in circumstances where it is not reasonably practicable to obtain such approval, authorisations can be implemented without approval for up to 72 hours. Part III of the 1997 Act has undoubtedly extended police powers in a way in which no other piece of legislation has done since the Police and Criminal Evidence Act 1984 (PACE). The fact that intrusive surveillance can be authorised to deal with matters that would not constitute an arrestable offence under s 24 of PACE is one indication of the breadth of the new powers. Moreover, the warrant procedures contained in PACE may be circumvented by new powers allowing the police to make covert entries and to search premises and seize documents.

1 Interception of Communications Act 1985; Security Service Act 1996.
2 *Malone v United Kingdom* (1984) 7 EHRR 14.
3 *R v Khan (Sultan)* [1997] AC 558.

Police Information Technology

1.15 The creation of PITO is essential to the operation of the 1997 Act. Many of the structural changes that the Act introduces are dependent upon information technology (IT). The IT revolution is already in the process of profoundly transforming both what is normal, and what is possible, in our everyday lives. It therefore seems surprising that PITO will ostensibly have no direct involvement in police operations.[1] The influence of IT is such that the demarcation between major police operations and the IT facilities upon which they rely will become increasingly difficult to maintain. The reality of the contribution that PITO will make to police operations was brought home by comments made by Sir Michael Marshall, Chairman of the All-Party Parliamentary Information Technology Group, during the Parliamentary debates—

> 'I believe that the battle against crime in the twenty-first century will be fought over information technology'.[2]

1 See para 5.12.
2 HC 2R, 12 February 1997, col 424.

Access to personal information

1.16 For some time it has been recognised that there is a need to create a rationalised system to check the previous convictions of potential employees, especially in circumstances where they would be licensees, would be working with vulnerable persons, or would have access to confidential information. This was the conclusion of the 1993 Green Paper 'Disclosure of Criminal Records for Employment Vetting Purposes',[1] and the 1996 White Paper 'On the Record'.[2] Public anxiety about violent or sexual offenders hiding their background from employers and voluntary organisations reached a new height with the shootings in Dunblane of primary school children in 1996. The Cullen Report on the Dunblane massacre drew attention to this—

> 'The evidence in the Inquiry showed the relative ease with which Thomas Hamilton over many years was able to open a succession of clubs in a number of local authority areas despite persistent complaints and concerns about his behaviour. There was no system in general use for vetting of persons who operated such clubs or for monitoring their conduct'.[3]

1 Home Office, September 1993 (Cm 2319).
2 On the Record (1996) Cm 3308.
3 The Public Inquiry into the Shootings at Dunblane Primary School on 13 March 1996, para 11.2 (Cm 3386).

1.17 However, the 1997 reforms have raised concerns about creating a system that will *continue* to punish people simply because of their criminal pasts. In trying to make provision for paedophiles and fraudsters, the Act has also put into economic jeopardy the significant percentage of the population who have received some kind of non-motoring criminal conviction.[1] The fact that these people will be potentially prejudiced in the labour market carries with it a risk of further offending and appears to overlook Home Office research which establishes that released offenders are more likely to be rehabilitated successfully if they are in work.[2] In his introduction to 'On the Record', Michael Howard stressed the need to—

> 'strike a balance between the rights of some individuals to live down their past crimes and the need to safeguard other individuals, particularly those who, for whatever reason, might be vulnerable to abuse'.

The human rights organisation Liberty (formerly the National Council for Civil Liberties) has strongly criticised the balance struck by the legislation—

> 'Few people would disagree that where an applicant's criminal history is relevant to a licence or job that he or she seeks, there should be some means of ascertaining its accuracy. But conversely, few would contest the principle that where this information is irrelevant, the public interest in safeguarding individual privacy and rehabilitating those who have lived down a criminal past should prevent its disclosure. Liberty's concern is that the Bill strikes the wrong balance between these concerns. Taken as a whole it is difficult to justify the Bill which appears to be using a sledgehammer to crack a nut'.[3]

1 1989 Home Office figures show that 35% of men and 8% of women under the age of 35 have been convicted for non-motoring offences; see HL 2R, 11 November 1996, col 819. See para 6.6.
2 'Protecting the Public: The Government's Strategy on Crime in England and Wales', HMSO (1989).
3 'Police Bill—Liberty Briefing' November 1996.

EUROPEAN CONVENTION ON HUMAN RIGHTS

1.18 In October 1997 the new Labour Government issued a White Paper[1] and a Bill[2] with the intention of directly incorporating the European Convention on Human Rights into UK law. Clause 2 of the Bill obliges any court or tribunal, wherever a question arises in relation to the Convention, to take into account precedents, decisions and advisory opinions, not only of the European Court of Human Rights, but also of the European Commission and the Committee of Ministers. Clause 4 of the Bill allows a court to make a declaration that UK legislation is incompatible with the Convention.[3] Clause 6 would make it unlawful for a public authority to act in a manner which is incompatible with the Convention.

'Public authority' includes any court or tribunal, or any person 'whose functions are of a public nature' (Clause 6(3)(c)). A person who claims that a public authority has acted so as to breach their rights under the Convention will be able to bring proceedings against the authority under the provisions of the proposed legislation. According to the Government—

> 'The time has come to enable people to enforce their Convention rights against the State in the British courts, rather than having to incur the delays and expense which are involved in taking a case to the European Human Rights Commission and Court in Strasbourg and which may altogether deter some people from pursuing their rights . . . Our aim is a straightforward one. It is to make more directly accessible the rights which the British people already enjoy under the Convention. In other words, to bring those rights home'.[4]

1 Rights Brought Home: The Human Rights Bill (Cm 3782).
2 Human Rights Bill [HL] 38, 23 October 1997.
3 Clause 19, requiring a Minister in charge of a Parliamentary Bill to make a statement of its compatibility with the Convention, would have precluded Pt III of the Police Bill being introduced in its original form.
4 Cm 3782, paras 1.18, 1.19.

1.19 If the Government's proposals become law in their current form they will create a context in which many of the powers given to public authorities under the 1997 Act can be closely scrutinised. In particular, the 1997 Act raises important issues with regard to Article 8 of the Convention (the right to privacy), Article 6 (the right to a fair trial) and Article 7 (the right against retroactive penalties). Although these matters are dealt with in greater detail in the main body of this book, some of the Convention issues which the 1997 Act raises include—

(a) the failure to impose data protection obligations on the NCIS, NCS and PITO (Article 8);
(b) the failure to incorporate into the statutory scheme methods of covert surveillance that do not require interference with property (either because of the type of device used or because the owner allows the police to bug his guest or lodger) (Article 8);
(c) the licence to authorise bugging without prior approval, when it would not be reasonably practicable to gain such approval (Article 8);
(d) the failure to impose conditions of relevancy on the CRA and chief officers when compiling character certificates (Article 8);
(e) the retrospective enhancement of the seriousness of a caution, which will now be included in criminal record certificates and enhanced criminal record certificates (Article 7).

1.20 In passing the 1997 Act the previous Government said that the legislation 'would help to protect the public and build a safer Britain'.[1] The new Government, whose front bench gave essential support to the 1997 Act when they were in opposition, now promises legislation that 'will enhance the awareness of human rights in our society'.[2] Under the Human Rights Act it will be for the courts to determine whether a fair balance has been struck between the general interests of the community and the protection of fundamental rights.

1 Baroness Blatch, HL 2R, 11 November 1996, col 789.
2 Tony Blair, Cm 3782.

2 The National Criminal Intelligence Service

INTRODUCTION

2.1 Joint operations between law enforcement agencies in the United Kingdom have not always run smoothly. In recent years reports of deliberate non-co-operation between police and customs officers[1] and the expansion of MI5 into the investigation of serious crime[2] have raised fears that effective use of criminal intelligence was being hampered by demarcation disputes between the various agencies involved. It was partly in response to these concerns that the National Criminal Intelligence Service (NCIS) was created in 1992. The NCIS was established within the Home Office to facilitate the exchange of intelligence between the police, customs and security services, and at the same time to establish a national body which could liaise with other national forces and with the European police organisation (Europol). Its initial remit was to 'gather, collate, evaluate, analyse, develop and disseminate relevant information and intelligence about serious crime and major criminals of a regional, national and international nature in order to assist and promote the efficient and effective use of operational resources and so enable the development of law enforcement agencies'.[3]

1 Baroness Hilton of Eggardon commented that—'We all hope that the regular grinding of gears and total stalling of relations will be a thing of the past' (HL 2R, 11 November 1996, col 828).
2 See the Security Service Act 1989.
3 Home Office (1992) The National Criminal Intelligence Service.

2.2 The creation of the NCIS brought about a major change in the structure and accountability of the agencies concerned, and was perceived by many as the first step towards the creation of a national police force.[1] Originally maintained by direct Home Office funding, the NCIS acquired an annual budget of £29m, and employed 536 staff.[2] It had 1200 informants registered on its databases. Units within the Service included the National Drugs Intelligence Unit, the National Football Intelligence Unit, Interpol, the International Intelligence Branch, the Specialist Crimes Unit (comprising the Kidnap and Extortion Unit, the National Paedophile Index, and the Organised Vehicle Crime section), the Organised Crime Unit and the Economic Crimes Unit (which included the Financial Intelligence and Money Laundering Section, the Gaming and Lotteries Section and the National Office for the Suppression of Counterfeit Currency). By the time of the 1996 annual report the NCIS mission statement had evolved, stating that its core function was 'to assist law enforcement and other relevant agencies by processing intelligence, giving direction, and providing services and strategic analysis to combat serious criminal activity'.[3] Emphasis was placed upon maintaining intelligence databases, avoiding 'duplication of effort' by law enforcement agencies, acting as the lead agency for Interpol and Europol, and processing applications for telephone intercepts under the Interception of Communications Act 1985.[4] In October 1996 the Director General of the NCIS, Albert Pacey, was appointed as the person responsible under the Security Service Act 1989, s 2(2), for co-ordinating police and security service activities so as to enable MI5 to discharge its new role in the prevention and detection of non-political crime.

1 During the second reading of the Bill Lord Rodgers of Quarry Bank described 'an uneasy feeling that the present proposed arrangements will not last and will provide only a half-way house to a British equivalent of the Federal Bureau of Investigation' (HL 2R, 11 November 1996, col 800).
2 NCIS Annual Report 1995–96.
3 Ibid.
4 Ibid.

2.3 Certain sources of criminal intelligence are, by their very nature, vulnerable to inaccuracy, so that the creation of a public body with the express function of disseminating intelligence information as widely as possible obviously requires the most careful regulation. It was thus a cause of real concern amongst civil liberties groups that the NCIS was brought into existence and permitted to become fully operational with no statutory basis, and without Parliamentary debate. Liberty (formerly, the National Council for Civil Liberties) and others continued to call for the powers of the organisation to be delineated by an Act of Parliament. That is what the Police Act 1997, Pt I, set out to achieve.

2.4 By placing the NCIS on a statutory footing the 1997 Act reflects many of the institutional arrangements which were already in place. But it also makes a number of significant changes, particularly in the areas of funding, supervision and accountability. In introducing the legislation, the Home Office Minister in the House of Lords, Baroness Blatch, explained that although organised crime required a national response, it was not the Government's intention to establish a national police force. The NCIS and its companion body the National Crime Squad (NCS)[1] were to be maintained within the existing tripartite framework of control consisting of a partnership between local authorities, police forces and the Home Secretary—

> 'We are not proposing a British equivalent of the FBI. There will be no 'federal crimes' over which the new organisations will have exclusive jurisdiction. The public will continue to report all crimes to their local police forces. There will be no direct recruitment of police officers to either body: police officers will continue to be seconded or recruited from police forces.'[2]

In order to allay fears about the formation of a national police force, the Government chose to adopt the legal fiction that neither the NCIS or the NCS are to be recognised as police forces in their own right.

1 See Ch 3.
2 HL 2R, 11 November 1996, col 789.

2.5 The first important change to the NCIS concerns its funding. Prior to the Act, the organisation was maintained directly from the Home Office Vote. Its substantial running costs are now to be met from local police authority budgets by direct levy (or 'top-slicing' as it has come to be known). The second major change is the establishment of a statutory supervisory body, the NCIS Service Authority, comprising senior police and customs officers, Home Office representatives, local police authority members and independent members. The Act prescribes a complex system of allocated places which reflects the interests of the agencies concerned. The inclusion of local police authority representatives in the core membership of the Authority ensures a limited measure of democratic accountability, particularly in the area of funding.[1] But, as the Opposition pointed out during debates,[2] police authority representatives are unlikely to be in a position to influence policy within the NCIS because the entire framework of the legislation vests effective control firmly with the Secretary of State. During the passage of the Bill, a number of amendments were moved which aimed to reduce the powers of the Home Secretary to intervene directly in the running of the Service[3] but these amendments were all resisted.

1 See para 2.38.
2 The Opposition spokesman Lord McIntosh of Haringey criticised arrangements whereby the Home Secretary retained an 'effective majority' on the Service Authority— 'There can be no doubt that the Secretary of State has the National Criminal Intelligence Service tied hand and foot to his own wishes and to the wishes of central government.' (HL Committee, 26 November 1996, col 124.)
3 See, for example, HL Committee, 26 November 1996, col 123 and 135 et seq.

THE SERVICE AUTHORITY

2.6 The 1997 Act, s 1, creates a body corporate to be known as the NCIS Service Authority whose core functions are—

(a) to maintain the NCIS (s 2(1)),
(b) to secure that it is efficient and effective (s 3(1)),
(c) to publish service plans (s 4(1)),
(d) to publish an annual report (s 5(1)).[1]

The Service Authority is not to be concerned with operational matters,[2] which are the responsibility of the Director General, and the 1997 Act makes express provision for delegation of certain of the Authority's functions.[3] By s 1(2), the NCIS Service Authority is to consist of 19 members, though the Secretary of State retains the right to appoint additional members providing the total number of members remains an odd number (s 1(3)).

1 The Government made it clear during the Committee stage of the Bill that the Secretary of State would ensure that the annual report was laid before Parliament (HL Committee, 26 November 1996, col 158).
2 See eg HL Committee, 19 March 1997, col 889.
3 See s 9(8) and s 44.

Core members

2.7 Ten members of the NCIS Service Authority are to be designated 'core members' which means that they will also serve as core members of the Service Authority for the National Crime Squad (NCS), ensuring that the two organisations are closely co-ordinated (Sch 1, para 1(1)).[1] The Secretary of State is to appoint five of the ten core members in accordance with Sch 1, paras 2, 4, 5. Three of the Secretary of State's appointees are to be independent of the police, the Crown, and the police authorities (Sch 1, para 2(2)) and one of these three is to be appointed as chairman of both the NCIS Service Authority and the Service Authority for the NCS. The power of the Home Secretary to appoint the independent members of the Authority was the subject of particular controversy during the passage of the legislation.[2] Of the remaining two appointments made by the Secretary of State, the first is appointed to represent him in his capacity as police authority for the Metropolitan Police District (Sch 1, para 5), and the second is to be a Crown servant (Sch 1, para 6). Two appointments are to be made by the chief officers of police of forces in England and Wales (Sch 1, para 3(1)). One is to be the chief constable of a force outside London, and the other is to be the Commissioner of either the Metropolitan police or the City of London police (Sch 1, para 3(2)). The remaining three core members are to be appointed by local authority members of police authorities for areas in England and Wales from among their number (Sch 1, para 4).

1 Baroness Blatch, when introducing the Bill, spoke in terms of the need 'to ensure a shared strategic direction' for the two organisations (HL 2R, 11 November 1996, col 789).

2 Baroness Hilton of Eggardon described the use of the term 'independent' in this context as 'puzzling' 'They are perhaps independent of the police service but they are not in any sense independent of the Home Secretary' (HL 2R, 11 November 1996, col 831).

Additional members

2.8 There is nothing to prevent a member of the NCIS Authority who is not a core member from also being a member of the NCS Authority (Sch 1, para 11). However, Sch 1, para 7 provides that additional members of the Service Authority must include—

- (a) the chief constable of a police force in Scotland,
- (b) an officer of at least the rank of deputy chief constable from the RUC,
- (c) two additional members of police authorities from England and Wales,
- (d) one police authority member from Scotland and one from Northern Ireland, and
- (e) two Crown servants and a customs officer appointed by the Commissioners of Customs and Excise.

If the Secretary of State makes an order under s 1(3) increasing the number of members above nineteen, then the delicate ratio of appointments which is established by the Act is to be preserved (Sch 1, para 8). All police authority appointments should, so far as is practicable, reflect the balance of political parties for the time being prevailing among local authority members of police authorities nationally (Sch 1, para 12).

Expenses and voting rights

2.9 The Authority may pay expenses and allowances to members in accordance with rates approved by the Secretary of State, but such payments may not be made to members who are senior police officers, Crown servants or customs officers (Sch 2, para 17). All members of the Authority are generally entitled to vote at any meeting of the Authority, or of a committee of the Authority. There are two exceptions to this principle. Chief constables and senior police officers may not vote on a motion of censure of the Director General or any other member of the NCIS, including any motion on disciplinary action to be taken against him (Sch 2, para 13). In addition, Crown servants appointed by the Secretary of State are not entitled to vote on any issue (Sch 2, para 14).

Co-opted members

2.10 The NCIS Service Authority may co-opt additional members, under s 1(6), subject to disqualification rules (Sch 2, paras 1–3), and to the additional restriction that the Authority may not co-opt a customs officer (Sch 2, para 18(3)). Co-opted members may serve a term not exceeding 12 months, but at the expiry of their period of co-option, they may be further co-opted for a similar period if they remain otherwise eligible for membership (Sch 2, para 18(4)). Co-opted members may be paid expenses, but are to have no voting rights in any meeting of the Authority (Sch 2, paras 18(5), (6)).

Qualification for membership

2.11 Members of either the NCIS or the NCS Service Authority must be aged between 21 and 70 (Sch 2, para 1). Core members must have had their principal place of work or residence in England and Wales during the whole of the twelve months prior to the appointment, and additional members must have had their principal place of work or residence during the same period in the United Kingdom (Sch 2, para 2). Employees of the NCIS or the NCS are disqualified from membership of the relevant Authority, as are bankrupts, persons disqualified from being company directors, and (not surprisingly) those who have been convicted and sentenced to three months imprisonment within five years prior to, or at any time subsequent to, their appointment (Sch 2, para 3).

Terms of office and removal from office

2.12 Terms of office are to be for four years or such shorter term as may be fixed by the person appointing the member (Sch 2, para 8). A member whose term of office expires may be re-appointed provided they are not disqualified, or otherwise ineligible, and provided that they have not been removed from office. The Service Authority may remove any member from office, other than the Chairman, if—

(a) he has been absent for four consecutive months without consent,
(b) he has been convicted of an offence which does not amount to a statutory disqualification,
(c) he is incapacitated through physical or mental illness, or
(d) he is otherwise unable or unfit to discharge his functions.[1]

Members may also be removed by the person who appointed them, or who would be required to appoint a successor (Sch 2, para 8(2)(b)). Thus, the Secretary of State may remove any one of the appointments made by him, and the chief officers of police and relevant police authorities may do likewise. Only the Secretary of State has power to remove the Chairman (Sch 2, para 8(3)).

AIMS AND OBJECTIVES OF THE NCIS

2.13 The 1997 Act, s 2(2), prescribes the general functions of the NCIS as follows—

'(a) to gather, store and analyse information in order to provide criminal intelligence,
(b) to provide criminal intelligence to police forces in Great Britain, the Royal Ulster Constabulary, the National Crime Squad and other law enforcement agencies, and
(c) to act in support of such police forces, the Royal Ulster Constabulary, the National Crime Squad and other law enforcement agencies carrying out their criminal intelligence activities.'

The term 'law enforcement agency' is widely defined to include any government department, the police forces of Jersey, Guernsey and the Isle of Man, or any other person charged with the duty of investigating offences or charging offenders (s 2(3)). It also includes any person engaged outside the United Kingdom in the carrying on of activities similar to any activity carried out by the NCIS Service Authority, the NCIS, a police authority, a police force, the NCS or the NCS Service Authority (s 2(3)). The NCIS is thus authorised to collect and disseminate criminal intelligence to any law enforcement agency anywhere in the world.

EUROPEAN CONVENTION ON HUMAN RIGHTS

2.14 The collection and dissemination of information about an individual without his consent constitutes an interference with the right to privacy contained in Article 8 of the European Convention on Human Rights.[1] In order to be justified under Article 8, such measures must be proportionate to one of the legitimate aims prescribed in Article 8(2)—in this case the prevention of disorder or crime. They must also be 'in accordance with law' which involves a requirement that the rules governing the use of such information be both accessible and precise.[2] Applying these criteria there are three aspects of the functions of the NCIS which give potential cause for concern. The first is the risk that damaging information on an individual may be provided to a foreign state with a record of human rights abuse or oppressive policing methods. This concern was raised in the committee stage of the Bill by Mr Alan Beith, the hon Member for Berwick-upon-Tweed, who pointed out that the wording of s 2—

> '. . . could open the door to co-operation with the most oppressive regimes in the world—those with the most authoritarian and uncontrolled police forces, or with forces that are subject to the control of some element in a deeply divided form of government. It could open the way to intelligence being shared with very insecure organisations whose acquisition of the knowledge from that intelligence could damage our own security and the sources from which the intelligence had come. It could also lead to threats to individuals who are in this country but in whom other governments have an interest, perhaps because they are fugitives from the politics of that country, and might have vulnerable families living there.'[3]

1 *McVeigh v United Kingdom* (1981) 25 DR 15 at 49; *Murray v United Kingdom* (1994) 19 EHRR 193, paras 84, 85; *Leander v Sweden* (1987) 9 EHRR 433. For further discussion of Article 8, see paras 4.1–4.2, 4.11–4.22 and 6.12.
2 *Herczegsalvy v Austria* (1992) 15 EHRR 437 at para 88.
3 HL Committee, 19 March 1997, col 888.

2.15 In order to meet this concern an amendment was tabled which would have required the Service Authority, in discharging its functions, to have regard to the system of justice in any country to which intelligence was to be provided.[1] The amendment was, however, withdrawn following assurances by Mr Timothy Kirkhope, Parliamentary Under-Secretary for the Home Department, that adequate arrangements were already in place to prevent abuse. In particular, the constitution of Interpol, which processes most exchanges of information between law enforcement agencies, specifically requires that mutual assistance should be facilitated 'within the spirit of the Universal Declaration of Human Rights'.[2] At present, exchanges are conducted in accordance with Foreign and Commonwealth Office guidance on the individual country, subject to the discretion of individual liaison officers, who should have a detailed knowledge of the country concerned. That process would continue under the new arrangements. By way of example the Minister pointed out that—

> 'NCIS has refused to exchange information about individuals who have claimed political asylum. Some countries can prosecute individuals for committing an offence in another country, and allegedly bringing discredit to their sovereign country. NCIS does not pass on information in such circumstances, nor does it pass on information when that may lead to a United Kingdom national facing capital punishment.'[3]

1 HL Committee, 19 March 1997, col 888.
2 United Nations Universal Declaration of Human Rights.
3 HL Committee, 19 March 1997, col 890.

2.16 The second problem is that there is no effective means of control over the quality of the intelligence collated and disseminated by the NCIS. The term 'criminal intelligence' is not defined in the 1997 Act, but certainly includes information obtained from criminal informants and other questionable sources. The subject, however, has no right to challenge the accuracy of the information held or disseminated.[1] In contrast to other comparable databases, there is no requirement that the information should be destroyed once it is no longer needed. These complaints are not merely theoretical. Parliamentary briefings on the Bill referred to a specific instance in which three British citizens had been seriously prejudiced by misleading intelligence supplied by the NCIS to the Belgian police.[2] A Labour amendment requiring the appointment of a Commissioner to oversee the quality, accuracy and content of the intelligence held by the NCIS, and to monitor its disclosure and the need for its retention was resisted and subsequently withdrawn.[3]

1 The subject is not allowed to access personal data under the Data Protection Act 1984 if it is held for the purposes of the prevention or detection of crime, or the apprehension or prosecution of offenders, and if access would be likely to prejudice either of these aims (s 28 thereof).
2 The case of Alun, Gwilym and Rhys Boore EC Commission Complaint Nos 94/4998 and 94/4999.
3 HL Committee, 26 November 1996, cols 123 and 135.

2.17 The third area of concern relates to the nature of the offences which will fall within the remit of the NCIS. Section 2 does not confine the activities of the organisation to intelligence concerning serious crime. This stands in contrast to the terms upon which the NCIS was initially established[1] and to its subsequent mission statements.[2] The omission of this qualification, which might be thought inherent in the nature of the organisation, was in fact deliberate. A Labour amendment to confine its functions to 'intelligence necessary for prevention and detection of serious crime' was resisted by the Home Office and subsequently withdrawn.[3] As a result, the legislation permits the compilation of intelligence concerning offences which are in themselves comparatively trivial, but which may be of interest to a law enforcement agency abroad for other reasons, for example because of the identity of the subject. As Baroness Hilton of Eggardon pointed out, it is unsatisfactory that the term 'intelligence' in s 2(2) has been left open to interpretation in this way—

> 'The functions of the NCIS could be subject to individual interpretations and distortions. Because of the powers that NCIS officers will have and the position of the NCIS at the top of the hierarchy of law enforcement agencies, it is important that it should have a very precisely defined function.'[4]

1 See para 2.1.
2 See para 2.2.
3 HL Committee, 26 November 1996, col 144.
4 Ibid.

Annual objectives

2.18 The objectives of the NCIS are to be determined by the Service Authority before the beginning of each financial year (s 3(2)). However, the role of the Authority is heavily circumscribed by s 26 which provides that the Secretary of State may determine objectives for the NCIS by statutory instrument. Before taking this course the Secretary of State is under a duty to consult with the Service Authorities for, and Directors General of, the NCIS and the NCS and with representatives of the chief officers of police, the police authorities and HM Customs and Excise (s 26(2)). Once the Secretary of State has determined objectives for the NCIS, however, the Service Authority is placed under a statutory duty to have regard to those objectives in discharging its functions (s 2(4)(a)). Whilst the Authority may determine additional objectives for the NCIS (s 3), these must 'be so framed as to be consistent' with the objectives determined by the Secretary of State (s 3(3)). In fixing additional objectives the Authority is also placed under a duty to consult with representatives of each of the relevant bodies (s 3(4)).

WORKING METHODS

2.19 Despite its rigid bureaucratic structure, the NCIS's working methods appear to owe their origins to the commercial sector, with results that may seem surprising in view of the sensitivity of its role. Not only is the Service Authority established as a body corporate (s 1(1)),[1] but by virtue of s 20, the Authority may accept gifts and loans from private sources on any terms which it deems appropriate, including gifts which are expressly conditional upon commercial sponsorship of any NCIS activity.[2] Moreover, the Authority may charge for any of its services, on terms which permit intelligence to be sold at a profit (s 19).[3] All these commercial characteristics are, however, in keeping with the managerial principles that were introduced into ordinary policing by the Police and Magistrates' Courts Act 1994, now codified in the Police Act 1996.[4]

1 Local police authorities are also established as bodies corporate.
2 See para 2.41.
3 See para 2.40.
4 Local police authorities are established as corporate bodies under the Police Act 1996, s 3. Under s 93 of that Act, police authorities are also allowed to receive gifts and loans.

Objectives, service plans and performance targets

2.20 Where the Secretary of State has determined an objective under section 26,[1] he may give a direction requiring the Service Authority to set 'performance targets' and impose conditions to which these targets must conform (s 27(1), (2)).[2] The Service Authority is placed under a statutory duty to comply with such a direction, and to take account of the performance targets in discharging its functions (s 2(4)(c), (6)).

1 See para 2.18.
2 The Secretary of State has similar powers under the Police Act 1996, ss 37, 38.

2.21 Section 4 imposes a further duty on the Service Authority to issue a 'service plan' before the beginning of each financial year, setting out the proposed arrangements for the carrying out by the NCIS of its functions during the year. The service plan must include a statement of the Authority's priorities for the year, of the financial resources expected to be available, and of the proposed allocation of those resources. It is also required to give particulars of any objectives established by the Secretary of State pursuant to s 26, any additional objectives determined by the

Authority pursuant to s 3, and any performance targets established by the Authority, whether in compliance with a direction under s 27, or otherwise (s 4(2)). The NCIS Annual Report must include an assessment of the extent to which the service plan for that year has been carried out (s 5(2)).

Duty of the Authority to consult

2.22 The Authority is placed under a continuing duty to consult with police authorities, the NCS Service Authority, the Commissioners of Customs and Excise, and any other persons or bodies which it considers appropriate in order to obtain their views about the Authority and the NCIS (s 41(1)). The Director General is placed under a similar duty to consult with chief officers of police, the Director General of NCS, the Commissioners of Customs and Excise and any other person or body which he considers appropriate (s 41(2)). The Secretary of State however retains a power to intervene if he considers that the consultation arrangements are inadequate (s 41(4), (5)).

Codes of Practice

2.23 Under s 28(1), the Secretary of State may issue codes of practice relating to the discharge by the NCIS Service Authority of its functions. There is an equivalent provision with regard to the NCS Service Authority (s 73).[1] There are no provisions that the codes should be subject to the specific approval of Parliament. Neither is there any provision that a breach of the codes will be admissible as evidence in criminal and civil proceedings, as is the case with breaches of the codes that are issued under PACE, s 69, and under s 101(9) of the 1997 Act (with regard to interference with property).

1 The provisions relating to the Service Authority codes are identical to those of the Police Act 1996, s 39, which relates to ordinary Police Authorities.

2.24 During the Parliamentary debates, the Government resisted attempts to give greater weight to the codes of practice for the Service Authorities. The arguments that ensued revolved around the perceived distinction between the Service Authority and the NCIS itself. The Government emphasised that the codes would be concerned with the financial running of the authorities. Under no circumstances were the Authorities going to be involved in operational matters.[1] The Opposition argued that there were important issues that proper codes could resolve concerning the relationship between the NCIS, the NCS, police forces and other law enforcement agencies around the country.[2] The Government, however, was adamant that it was a matter 'for practitioners and law enforcement agencies to decide their best modus operandi amongst themselves' and that 'it is for them to do so, not for the Home Secretary to prescribe the details of operational matters.'[3]

1 Mr David Maclean (Minister of State for Home Affairs), HC Standing Committee, 25 February 1997, col 9.

2 Alun Michael, ibid, col 9.

3 David Maclean, ibid, col 9.

DIRECTOR GENERAL OF THE NCIS

2.25 The NCIS will be under the direction and control of the Director General (s 10(1)), who will have authority over the police members and civilian employees of the NCIS, and will occupy a central role in co-ordinating the exchange of sensitive criminal intelligence between law enforcement agencies here and abroad. The Director General has the power to conduct joint operations with, and to give and receive manpower and other assistance to and from, any police force in the United Kingdom, including the NCS (ss 22, 23). The Act specifically enables the Secretary of State to authorise the Service Authority to delegate the discharge of its functions to the Director General.[1] The Director General will accordingly have operational responsibility for the central collection and analysis of all criminal intelligence, and for providing intelligence to police forces and other agencies in the United Kingdom and abroad. The importance of this position is underscored by s 12 which provides that the Director General of the NCIS is to be the person responsible under the Security Service Act 1989 for co-ordinating police and security service activities so as to enable MI5 to discharge its new role in connection with the prevention and detection of non-political crime. Section 12 places on a statutory footing a designation which had previously been made by the Secretary of State under s 2(2) of the 1989 Act. In October 1996 the Director General confirmed that he would be 'acting as the central contact point for UK law enforcement agencies which wish to use the Security Service to support particular operations'.[2] A number of MI5 staff are already seconded to the NCIS.

1 See ss 9(8) and 44.
2 Home Office press release 14 October 1996.

2.26 The Director General is to be appointed by a panel of members of the Service Authority from a list of eligible candidates approved by the Secretary of State (s 6(2)). In order to be eligible for the post a candidate must, prior to the appointment, hold—

- (a) the rank of chief constable;
- (b) the rank of Commissioner, Assistant Commissioner or Deputy Assistant Commissioner in the Metropolitan police; or
- (c) the rank of Commissioner in the City of London police;

or he must have been eligible for appointment to one of those ranks.[1]

1 Section 6(3).

2.27 The Director General will be required to have regard to the contents of the service plan established by the Authority[1] in discharging his functions (s 10(2)). He is also required to submit a general report to the Authority and to the Secretary of State concerning the activities of the NCIS as soon as possible after the end of each financial year (ss 11, 32(4)). In addition, the Secretary of State may require the Director General to submit a report at any time on any specified matter connected with the activities of the NCIS (s 32(1)). By s 33 the Director General is put under a duty to provide criminal statistics to the Secretary of State when requested to do so, which are then to be laid before Parliament in the form of a 'consolidated and classified abstract'. This provision, which will also apply to the Director General of the NCS, will support a Home Office commitment to developing accurate data on the figures and geographical distribution of crime. However, the formulation of criminal statistics is not necessarily a politically neutral activity.[4] It remains to be seen how the formation of nationwide policing organisations will alter the way that criminal statistics are compiled and made public, particularly with regard to what activities are included in the category of 'organised crime'.[2]

1 See para 2.21.
2 M Maguire 'Crime, Statistics, Patterns and Trends—Changing Perceptions and their implications', in M Maguire, R Morgan and R Reiner, *The Oxford Handbook of Criminology* (1997), Ch 4.

2.28 The Service Authority has power under s 7(1) of the 1997 Act to remove the Director General by calling upon him to retire in the interests of efficiency and effectiveness. If, after having received representations made by the Director General, the Authority exercises its powers under this section, then, by virtue of s 7(3), the Director General is put under a duty to retire.[1] The direct control of the Secretary of State in the process is maintained by s 29(1) which provides that after appropriate consultation the Secretary of State may require the Authority to call upon the Director General, or any other member of the NCIS appointed directly by the Authority, to retire.[2]

1 See s 38 for the Director General's right to appeal.
2 The Secretary of State has a similar power to require a local police authority to call upon a chief constable to retire in the interests of efficiency and effectiveness (Police Act 1996, s 42).

2.29 The Director General will, by virtue of his post, hold the rank of chief constable regardless of the rank which he held prior to the appointment (s 6(1), (7)). For a variety of operational and legal purposes[1] he is placed into the same position as if he were the chief constable of an ordinary police force. Thus the Director General will be vicariously liable for torts committed by officers of the NCIS in the performance or purported performance of their functions, in the same way as an employer is liable for torts committed by his employees in the course of their employment (s 42(1)).[2] The Director General is to be indemnified from the NCIS service fund[3] against damages or costs incurred as a result of the wrongful acts of his officers (s 42(2)). Any civil proceedings in respect of a claim made by virtue of the Director General's vicarious liability for the acts of his officers are to be brought against the occupant of the post of Director General for the time being (s 42(3)).

1 Including the entering into of mutual aid agreements, see para 2.42.
2 See the Police Act 1996, s 88, which makes identical provision for vicarious liability of chief officers of police. As to the position where mutual aid arrangements are in force, see s 23(4), (5), and para 2.42.
3 See para 2.37.

2.30 By the 1997 Act, s 8, the Director General is obliged to appoint a deputy who will assume all the powers of the Director General—

(a) during any absence, incapacity or suspension from duty of the Director General, or
(b) during any vacancy in the office of the Director General.

In making such an appointment the Director General first has to consult the Service Authority. A person can only be appointed as a Deputy if he holds the rank of chief constable in a police force in Great Britain or in the RUC.

2.31 There are restrictions on designating powers to the Deputy. First, no more than one person can be designated the powers of the Director General at any one time. Secondly, a person who is authorised to exercise the powers of the Director General shall not do so for a continuous period exceeding three months without the consent of the Secretary of State. These restrictions are important, because in the absence of the Director General, the Deputy appointed under s 8 will assume the role of an authorising officer with regard to authorising police interferences with property under the 1997 Act, s 93 (s 94(4)(c)).

THE NCIS STAFF

2.32 The operational staff of the NCIS are classified either as 'police members' or 'employees' (s 9(1)). The Act enables the Secretary of State to authorise the Service Authority to delegate the discharge of its functions to the Director General, including the function of appointing police officers and civilian employees (ss 9(8), 44) and requires the Authority to do so for certain categories of employees.[1]

[1] See para 2.35.

2.33 The provision of police manpower to the NCIS is generally to be achieved by temporary secondment from other forces. The only permanent police members, other than the Director General, are his immediate deputies, ie, officers appointed to the rank of assistant chief constable within the NCIS. Persons appointed to this position must have held the rank of assistant chief constable or commander in the Metropolitan or City of London police forces or have been eligible for appointment to one of those ranks (s 9(3)). The appointment of officers to this rank must be made by the Service Authority directly, and may not be delegated to the Director General (s 9(9)(a)).

2.34 All other police members are engaged on a period of temporary service or secondment (s 9(2)(b)).[1] The Act does not specify a maximum or minimum period of secondment, but provides that all police officers (other than those appointed to the rank of assistant chief constable) cease to be members of the NCIS at the end of their period of temporary service unless they are re-appointed under s 9(7). The temporary secondment of police officers to the NCIS is to be delegated by the Service Authority to the Director General (s 9(8)).

[1] Secondment is governed by the Police Act 1996, s 97.

2.35 The category of 'employees' encompasses all staff who are not police officers, and will therefore include not only civilian staff in the strict sense but also customs officers and members of the security services. Again, the powers of employment and temporary secondment are to be delegated to the Director General (s 9(8)).

2.36 NCIS comprises four divisions as follows—

(a) Headquarters,
(b) UK Division,
(c) International Division, and
(d) Resources Division.

Table 1 shows the current structure of the organisation.

Table 1—Structure of the NCIS

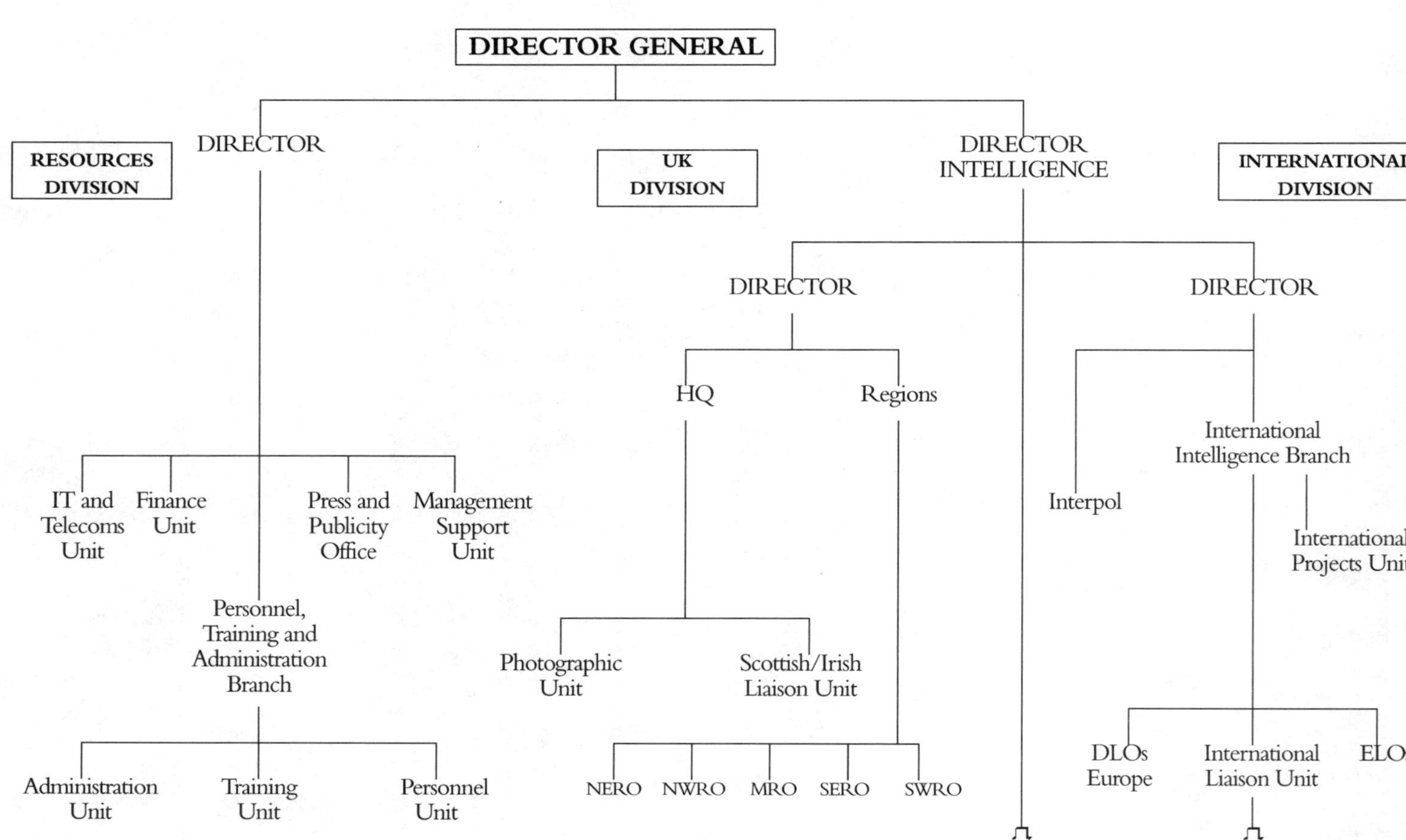

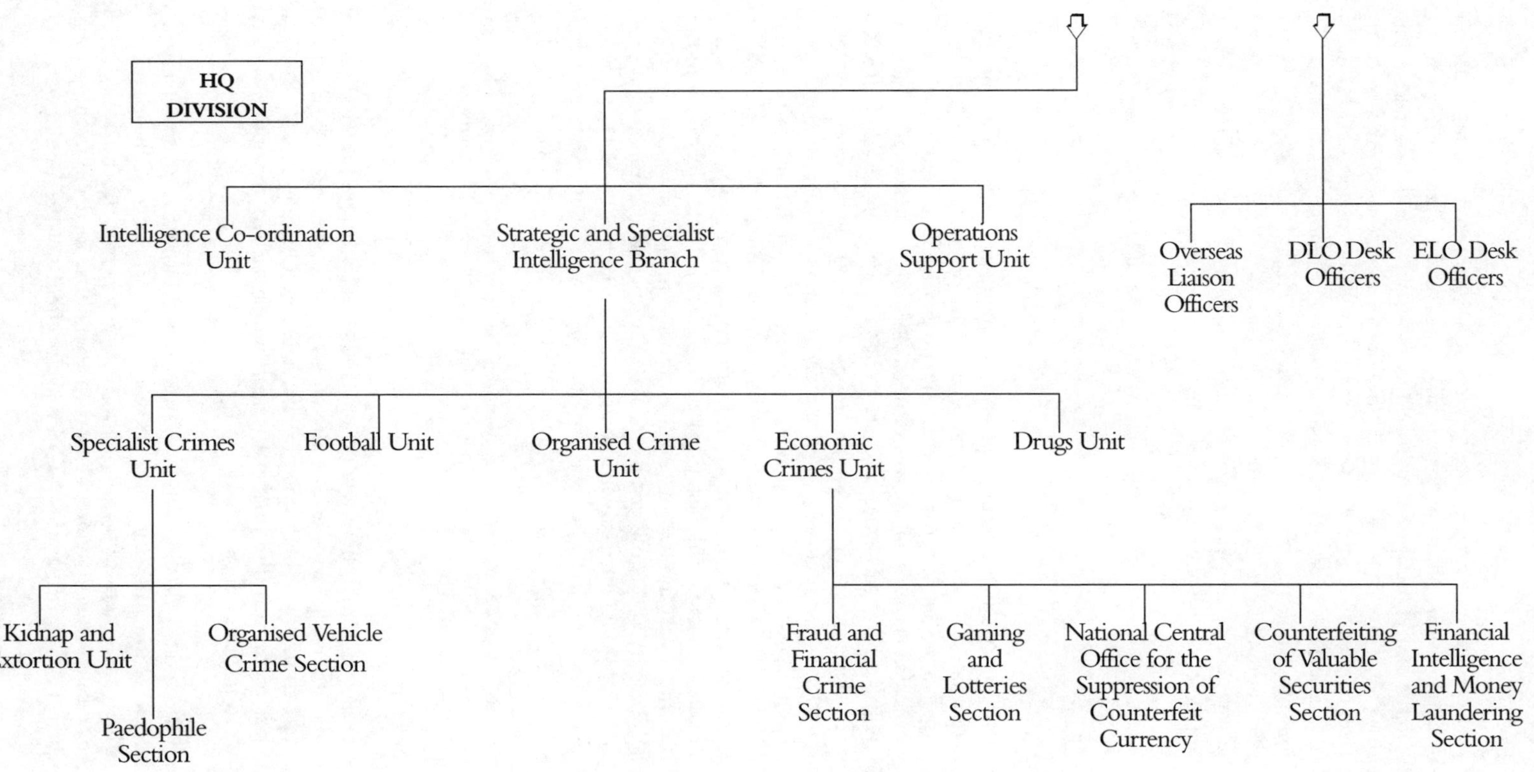
HQ DIVISION
Intelligence Co-ordination Unit
Strategic and Specialist Intelligence Branch
Operations Support Unit
Overseas Liaison Officers
DLO Desk Officers
ELO Desk Officers
Specialist Crimes Unit
Football Unit
Organised Crime Unit
Economic Crimes Unit
Drugs Unit
Kidnap and Extortion Unit
Organised Vehicle Crime Section
Paedophile Section
Fraud and Financial Crime Section
Gaming and Lotteries Section
National Central Office for the Suppression of Counterfeit Currency
Counterfeiting of Valuable Securities Section
Financial Intelligence and Money Laundering Section

FINANCES

2.37 The Service Authority are required by section 16 to establish and maintain a central fund known as the NCIS service fund (s 16(1)). The provision mirrors the requirement of the individual police authorities to establish and maintain a police fund under the Police Act 1996, s 14. All funding received by the Authority, from whatever source, is to be paid into the service fund[1] and all expenditure is to met out of the fund (s 16(2)). The Act provides for four sources of funding—

(a) the issuing of levies to police authorities in England and Wales,[2]
(b) direct funding from the Home Office,
(c) the payment of fees or charges for the provision of services, and
(d) the receipt of gifts or loans including commercial sponsorship.[3]

1 With the exception of sums paid into pension funds which are provided for by s 21.
2 See para 2.38.
3 See paras 2.40 and 2.41.

2.38 Once the statutory scheme is fully operational, the main source of funding for the NCIS will come from a re-allocation of resources from within the existing budgets of police authorities. It is for this reason that the financial memorandum to the Bill described the overall effect on public expenditure as 'broadly cost neutral'. The Service Authority is authorised to issue levies to every police authority in England and Wales, including the Receiver for the Metropolitan police (s 17). Police members of the Authority are excluded from taking part in the decision as to the amount of the levy, which is to be determined by the independent members and police authority members only (Sch 3, para 1(1)).[1] Complex voting procedures ensure that the police authority members hold the final say. The majority of members deciding upon a proposed levy must be police authority members (Sch 3, para 1(2)) and a levy can only be approved if more than half the total number of police authority members support it (Sch 3, para 1(3). The Secretary of State is required to approve the total amount of the levies which the Authority proposes to issue in any financial year (Sch 3, para 2(1)), and where he does not give his approval, the Secretary of State has power to intervene directly and to require the Authority to set such levies as he considers appropriate (Sch 3, para 3).

1 See the comments of Baroness Blatch that 'decisions on the levy should be strongly influenced by locally elected members of the service authorities, as levies will affect local budgets' (HL 2R, 11 November 1996, col 791).

2.39 The Act recognises that there will be a period of delay before the NCIS Service Authority is able to issue levies and it therefore provides that in the interim the organisation may continue to be funded by direct Home Office grants (s 18). Home Office funding is to cease in the financial year in which the first revenue is received from levies issued to police authorities.

2.40 Sections 19 and 20 of the 1997 Act provide for more controversial forms of funding. Under s 19 the Authority may make charges in respect of the provision of any services, or an agreement to provide services, to any person. Charges made under s 19 need not be calculated by reference to the expenditure incurred in the provision of the service (s 19(2)), so that the NCIS may in effect sell the intelligence it has collated to other agencies at a profit.[1]

1 An Authority has similar powers to charge for police services under the Police Act 1996, s 25. As to the discretion to provide services at a charge, or to provide services at all, see *Harris v Sheffield United Football Club* [1987] 2 All ER 838; *R v Chief Constable of Sussex, ex p International Trader's Ferry Ltd* [1997] 2 All ER 65.

2.41 By virtue of section 20, the Authority may accept gifts and loans from private sources on any terms which it deems appropriate. This includes gifts which are expressly conditional upon commercial sponsorship of any NCIS activity. This provision is derived from similar powers in the Police and Magistrates' Courts Act 1994,[1] which permitted the commercial sponsorship of ordinary police activities (best known for the image of police vehicles displaying their sponsor's corporate logos). During the committee stage of the Bill the Minister gave assurances that the Secretary of State would not use his powers under s 26 to determine commercial sponsorship objectives for the NCIS or NCS.[2] He also assured Parliament that the section was not intended to permit the sponsorship of the NCIS itself, but was confined to the sponsorship of particular activities.[3]

1 See the Police Act 1996, s 93. For details on the controversy surrounding the initial development of the gifts and loan principle, see Baker and English *A Guide to the Police and Magistrates' Courts Act 1994* (1994), Ch 10; T Jones and T Newburn *Policing the Act—Police and Magistrates' Courts* (1997), Chs 1, 2.

2 HL Committee, 4 March 1997, col 123.

3 Ibid. As an example the Minister suggested an NCIS forum to discuss money laundering which might be funded by the city banks.

MUTUAL AID AND RELATED ARRANGEMENTS

2.42 Sections 22 to 24 enable the Director General, after appropriate consultation, to enter into agreements with another police force to conduct joint operations, to provide and receive manpower and other resources, and to provide 'special services' as follows—

(a) Section 22 provides that where any police function (including the function of collecting and disseminating criminal intelligence (s 22(3))) can more effectively or efficiently be discharged by members of the NCIS acting jointly with members of a police force, or the NCS, then subject to the approval of the appropriate police authority[1] the Director General may enter into an agreement for that purpose.

(b) Section 23(1) enables the Director General to respond to requests from other chief officers of police to provide constables or other assistance to meet any special demand on the resources of another force. Neither the provision of resources by the NCIS, nor the reciprocal arrangement provided under s 23(2), require the consent of a police authority. Where the Secretary of State considers that the NCIS, the NCS or any police force requires reinforcements which cannot be met by a mutual aid agreement, he may direct the relevant chief officer to provide the necessary resources (s 23(3)). For the purposes of establishing vicarious liability, any police officer who is loaned to another force by the NCIS is deemed to be under the direction and control of the chief officer of the force to which he is loaned (s 23(4)). Similarly, any officer loaned to the NCIS under s 23 is deemed to be under the direction and control of the Director General (s 23(5)).

(c) Section 24 enables the 'provision of special services', which are not defined in the Act. The Director General may provide services to any person, at any premises or in any locality in the United Kingdom, providing those services are consistent with the functions of, and do not prejudice the efficiency and effectiveness of the NCIS. Since policing functions (s 22(3)), and the ordinary intelligence functions of the NCIS are provided for elsewhere in the Act, the effect of s 22 is to give the Director General discretion to provide services of any kind to any agency, whether or not it is a law enforcement agency recognised by the Act. Moreover, there is no requirement for the Director General to seek the approval of the Service Authority or the Secretary of State before providing such a service. This is obviously a wide power and a potentially significant extension of the core functions of the NCIS. Given the power of the Authority to levy charges in respect of its services (s 19),[2] it appears that s 22 would enable the NCIS to sell intelligence to private individuals or agencies, subject of course to the general restriction that the power may not be exercised in a manner which is inconsistent with the functions of the NCIS.

1 The appropriate authority in the case of the National Crime Squad is the NCS Service Authority.
2 See para 2.40.

CONTROL BY THE SECRETARY OF STATE

2.43 Sections 25 to 36 of the 1997 Act set out the role of the Secretary of State in relation to the operation of the NCIS under the heading 'Central supervision and control'. The legislation vests a considerable degree of power in the Home Secretary, not only in relation to the appointment and removal of the Service Authority members and the Director General, but also in relation to the powers of direct intervention in the management of the organisation. It was this aspect of Part I of the Bill which attracted most criticism in the House of Lords debates.[1]

1 Baroness Hilton of Eggardon expressed 'a general worry about the centralisation of power', saying that she was 'concerned that the Home Secretary is reserving for himself such a large element of control in the running of those organisations' (HL 2R, 11 November 1996, col 828). See also notes to para 2.2.

2.44 The Secretary of State is required to exercise his powers 'in such manner and to such extent as appears to him to be best calculated to promote the efficiency and effectiveness of the NCIS' (s 25). Thus, it is for the Secretary of State to appoint five of the ten 'core members' of the Service Authority, including the chairman (Sch 1, paras 2, 4, 5);[1] and to determine the overall number of members of the Authority (s 1(3)).[2] He has power to remove his own appointees (Sch 2, para 8(2)(b)),[3] and it is the Secretary of State alone who may remove the chairman of the Authority (Sch 2, para 8(3)). The Secretary of State also has express power under s 31 to require the Authority to submit a report to him at any time on any matter connected with the discharge of the Authority's functions.

1 See para 2.7.
2 See para 2.6.
3 See para 2.12.

2.45 In relation to the post of Director General, the Secretary of State is required to approve a list of eligible candidates for the post (s 6(2)).[1] Under s 32 he may require the Director General to submit a report to him on any aspect of the activities of the NCIS,[2] and the Director General is placed under a duty to submit his annual report not only to the Authority but directly to the Secretary of State as well (s 32(4)). Although the power to remove the Director General is vested in the first instance in the Authority (s 7(1)),[3] the Secretary of State may require the Authority to call upon the Director General to resign (s 29(1)).[4] Given the breadth of these powers it is perhaps all the more surprising that neither the Secretary of State nor the Service Authority has any role to play in the authorisation of 'special services' under s 24.[5]

1 See para 2.26.
2 See para 2.27.
3 See para 2.28.
4 This power was described by Lord Rogers of Quarry Bank as 'a highly prescriptive requirement which diminishes the independence of each authority' (HL 2R, 11 November 1996, col 828). However the Secretary of State has the same power in relation to the police authority and chief constable of an ordinary police force (Police Act 1996, s 42).
5 See para 2.42(c).

2.46 Of potentially greater significance, the Secretary of State has power under s 26 to determine objectives for the NCIS by statutory instrument,[1] and when he does so the Authority is under a duty to have regard to those objectives in discharging its functions (s 2(4)(a)) and to ensure that any additional objectives are 'so framed as to be consistent' with the objectives determined by the Secretary of State (s 3(3)). Under s 27 he may require the Authority to set 'performance targets' in a prescribed form (s 27),[2] in order to achieve the objectives he has established, and the Authority is placed under a duty to issue a 'service plan' (s 4)[3] setting out those objectives and any performance targets which have been set. Under s 28 the Secretary of State may issue codes of practice relating to the discharge by the Authority of its functions.[4]

1 See para 2.18.
2 See para 2.20.
3 See para 2.21.
4 At the time of writing no code of practice has been issued under s 28.

2.47 Other powers of the Secretary of State include powers to—

(a) require the relevant inspectors of constabulary to carry out an inspection of the NCIS (s 30(1));
(b) direct the Authority to take remedial action in the event of an adverse report (s 30(2));
(c) establish a public or private inquiry into any matter connected with the NCIS (s 34);
(d) make regulations concerning the standard of equipment to be used by the NCIS (s 35);
(e) require the NCIS, and any other police force, including the NCS to use specified facilities or services, if the Secretary of State considers that it would be in the interests of efficiency or effectiveness for them to do so (s 36);

(f) intervene if he considers that the general consultation arrangements established by the Authority and the Director-General under s 41 are inadequate (s 41(4), (5));[1] and

(g) approve or disapprove levies fixed by the Authority under s 17 (Sch 3, para 2(1)).[2]

1 See para 2.22.
2 See para 2.38.

Duty to consult

2.48 The Secretary of State has a duty to exercise his powers so as to promote the efficiency and effectiveness of the NCIS. Questions can therefore be asked in Parliament and in certain instances a failure to exercise the relevant statutory powers could be subject to judicial review proceedings. Moreover, before making an order to determine the objectives of the NCIS under s 26, the Secretary of State is obliged to consult—

(a) the NCS Service Authority,

(b) the Director General of the NCS,

(c) persons whom he considers to represent the interests of the police authorities in England and Wales,

(d) persons whom he considers to represent the interests of the chief officers of police forces in England and Wales,

(e) the NCIS Service Authority,

(f) the Director General of the NCIS (s 71(2)).

A duty to consult involves both carrying out consultations and considering the result of those consultations.[1]

1 *R v Secretary of State for Social Services ex p Association of Metropolitan Authorities* [1986] 1 All ER 164.

DISCIPLINE AND COMPLAINTS

2.49 Section 37 empowers the Secretary of State to issue regulations relating to the conduct of members of the NCIS and the maintenance of discipline. A right of appeal against dismissal is provided by s 38. Complaints from the public are to be handled in a manner which corresponds with a complaint made against a member of an ordinary police force (s 39(1), (2)). The complaints procedure would therefore be limited to the questioning of the conduct of individual officers. A failure of the Director General to exercise proper direction and control on policy grounds, would not be amenable to the complaints procedure.[1] The Act envisages that regulations made by the Secretary of State for this purpose may confer additional functions on the Police Complaints Authority (s 39(2)(c)). The complaints system will apply in the same manner to non-practice employees as it does to police members of the NCIS.

1 A decision by a Director General with regard to operations is unlikely to be subject to judicial review, unless it can be shown to be 'Wednesbury unreasonable'; see *R v Chief Constable of Sussex ex p International Trader's Ferry Ltd* [1997] 2 All ER 65.

INCITEMENT TO DISAFFECTION

2.50 Section 43 creates an offence of incitement to disaffection.[1] Any person who causes, or attempts to cause, or does any act calculated to cause, disaffection among police members of the NCIS (whether permanent or temporary) or induces or attempts to induce any such member to withhold his services is guilty of an offence punishable on indictment with up to two years imprisonment or a fine or both.[2]

1 An identical offence is created in relation to the NCS by s 87 (see para 3.47).
2 The maximum penalty on summary conviction is six months' imprisonment or a fine or both.

2.51 Identically worded offences are created (in relation to ordinary police officers) by the Police Act 1996, s 91, and (in relation to Ministry of Defence police officers) by the Ministry of Defence Police Act 1987, s 6. There is also a statutory precedent in relation to the armed forces, most recently re-enacted in the Incitement to Disaffection Act 1934, s 1. For the offence to be made out it must be proved that the accused knew that the person he incited was a member of the armed forces.[1] Applying this principle to s 34, it would be necessary for the accused to know that the officer incited is a serving member of the NCIS. There is no defence of reasonable excuse to a charge of incitement to disaffection.[2]

1 *R v Fuller* (1797) 2 Leach 790; cf *R v Bowman* (1912) 76 JP 271.
2 *R v Arrowsmith* [1975] 1 All ER 463.

3 The National Crime Squad

INTRODUCTION

3.1 The amalgamation of the existing regional crime squads into a National Crime Squad (NCS) seems to have been welcomed by many as having been long overdue.[1] Unlike other parts of the 1997 Act, the proposal to create a national investigation unit did not encounter significant opposition during the passage of the Bill through Parliament. Jack Straw, MP, Shadow Home Secretary at the time, seemed to accept both the function of and the spirit behind the NCS—

> 'Our tradition of locally based policing, with independent chief police officers, is key to the success of the British police and the fact that they are far more sensitive to local communities than many of their counterparts in other countries. However, we undermine rather than strengthen that tradition if we pretend that all policing can be undertaken within the boundaries of a local force. Serious crime and terrorism are national and international. The overall organisation of the police must reflect that.'[2]

1 Baroness O'Cathain, HL 2R, 11 November 1996, col 814. 'In Part II the proposal to create a national crime squad seems eminently sensible and falls into the category of, 'Why didn't someone propose this when the regional crime squads . . . were set up in 1965?' In contrast see paras 1.3 and 1.4 for reference to the long political debate over the principle of national policing.

2 HC 2R, 12 February 1997, cols 363–364.

3.2 Unlike the NCIS the NCS did not exist as a separate organisation before the Police Act 1997. There have been initiatives in the past that have involved several police forces. In the 1990s 'Operation Bumblebee' has used forces from all over Southern England to co-ordinate an offensive against organised burglary. Nationwide law enforcement offensives have, however, remained the subject of controversy. This was never greater than when police forces from around the country were used to combat the National Union of Mineworkers during the miners' strike in 1984–1985.[1] As a half-way house between a national squad and local police forces the regional crime squads (RCSs) were introduced in 1965.[2] The squads had a national co-ordinator, but the co-ordinator did not have the power to direct and control operations in the way that the Director General of the NCS is empowered to do under the 1997 Act, s 56. The NCS is thus intended to provide a national framework for the type of work which until now has been carried out by the RCSs.

1 M Kettle, 'The National Reporting Centre' in B Fine and R Millar (eds) *Policing the Miners' Strike* (1985).

2 Just as civil liberties commentators were concerned that the NCIS did not exist within a statutory framework (see para 2.3), there was also concern that the NCIS was collaborating with the RCSs in a way that could not be subject to control and supervision: 'NCIS 'Secret' Agreements', 8 Statewatch, November–December 1995.

3.3 The work of the NCS is likely to have a more immediate impact on operational policing than the more policy-orientated work of the NCIS. The function of the NCS is defined as being 'to prevent and detect serious crime which is of relevance to more than one police area in England and Wales' (s 48(2)). The principal function of the NCIS, on the other hand, is to 'gather, store and analyse information in order to provide criminal intelligence' (s 2(2)(a)). Whereas the NCIS has 536 staff, the RCSs had approximately 1,200. During 1995–96 the squads made 3,180 arrests, seized drugs with a total street value of £252m and recovered property worth £33m.[1]

1 Timothy Kirkhope, HC SC F, 4 March 1997, col 120.

3.4 The NCS has a narrower geographical jurisdiction than the NCIS. Under s 48(2) the NCS will operate only in England and Wales, whereas the NCIS will operate over the whole of the United Kingdom. The NCIS is also not limited to focusing on 'serious' crime. It will act as an apex to the police intelligence hierarchy and will be capable of supporting and influencing all other policing. Nevertheless, the 1997 Act does provide for extensive operational collaboration between the two organisations. Responsibility for putting the national strategies of the NCIS into practice will fall primarily on the NCS.[1] Unlike the NCIS, the NCS will have the power to institute proceedings (s 48(3)(b)). Furthermore, it is likely that the NCS will make the most frequent use of the new statutory powers to interfere with and bug properties.[2]

1 Home Office Affairs Committee into Organised Crime, para 37. 'The principal users as well as suppliers of intelligence to the NCIS are the seven Regional Crime Squads.'
2 See the Police Act 1997, Pt III.

3.5 Despite these different functions, Part II of the Act creates an organisation which is broadly similar to the NCIS in structure and procedure. The NCS will be maintained by a Service Authority, with a Director General responsible for direction and control of the organisation. The higher rank membership of the squad will be drawn from the Association of Chief Police Officers (ACPO) ranks and will be employed on a permanent basis, whilst other police members will be seconded from forces on a temporary basis. The Service Authority and Home Secretary will draw up annual objectives after a process of consultation. The Home Secretary will have the power to choose the chairman of the police authority, to draw up the short list of persons from whom the authority chooses the Director General, to order general and specific reports, and to order inquiries by the Inspectorate of the Constabulary.

THE SERVICE AUTHORITY

3.6 A body corporate to be known as the NCS Service Authority is created by the 1997 Act, s 47. The core functions of the Authority are—

- (a) to maintain the NCS (s 48(1));
- (b) to secure that it is efficient and effective (s 49(1));
- (c) to publish service plans (s 50(1));
- (d) to publish an annual report (s 51(1)).

Like its NCIS counterpart, the Authority is to have no concern with operational matters, although it will be staffed in part by senior police officers and will have responsibility for drawing up objectives and ensuring efficiency and effectiveness (see para 3.7). The Authority will consist of 17 members, as opposed to 19 members on the NCIS Authority. After a process of consultation with the existing Authority and with the police authorities and the chief constables of the police forces of England and Wales, the Secretary of State may order that the number of members be a specified odd number greater than 17.

Functions

3.7 The function of the Service Authority is to ensure that the NCS is efficient and effective (s 49(1)). In order to achieve this the Authority shall, before the beginning of each financial year, determine the objectives of the NCS for the coming year. These objectives must be framed so as to be consistent with the objectives determined for the NCS by the Secretary of State under the 1997 Act, s 71, although the Authority has the power to set objectives with regard to 'other matters' (s 49(3)). Before framing any objectives the authority must consult the Director General of the NCS, the NCIS Service Authority and persons whom it considers to represent the police authorities of England and Wales. The duty to consult is designed to ensure that objectives and services are not duplicated or undermined by different police organisations in different parts of the country.

3.8 The Authority is required to publish a service plan before the beginning of each financial year (s 50(1)). The service plan should set out the arrangements enabling the NCS to carry out its functions throughout the year. As with the annual objectives, the plan must not contradict any objectives or performance targets framed for the NCS by the Secretary of State under ss 71 and 72. The Authority will also need to consult a draft service plan prepared by the Director General of the NCS before preparing the final draft (s 50(3)). In the event that the Authority's service plan is likely to conflict with the draft service plan submitted by the Director General the Authority must consult the Director General (s 50(4)). As soon as possible after the end of the financial year the Authority is required to publish an annual report, including an assessment of the extent to which the service plan for the previous year has been carried out.

Links with the NCIS Service Authority

3.9 Although the NCIS Service Authority and the NCS Service Authority are being introduced as separate organisations, the legislation provides for important links between them. The Service Authority of the NCS will share the same 10 core members as the NCIS Service Authority. The authorities will have the same chairman, who is to be appointed by the Secretary of State (Sch 1, Pt I, paras 1, 2).[1] There is nothing to prevent a member of the NCIS Authority who is not a core member from also being a member of the NCS Authority (Sch 1, para 11).

[1] See also para 2.7 above. Sir John Wheeler, the former Conservative chairman of the Commons Home Affairs Committee, was chosen to be the first chairman (Guardian 14 August 1997).

Core, additional and co-opted members

3.10 Any expansion of the authority must ensure that the prescribed ratio between representatives of the police authorities, the chief constables, the

Metropolitan police and the Home Office remains the same (see para 2.7). The Authority itself has the power to co-opt additional members as it thinks fit (s 47(6)). That power does not however permit the co-option of those who would be disqualified to serve as members of the Authority under Sch 2, paras 1–4. The Authority is also prevented from co-opting a customs officer by Sch 2, para 18(3). In keeping with the statutory requirements for the composition of Police Authorities under the Police Act 1996, all police authority appointments to the Service Authority should, as far as is practicable, reflect the balance of political parties for the time being prevailing among local authority members of police authorities nationally (Sch 1, para 12). As with the NCIS, the non-police authority members will be appointed directly by the Secretary of State. For the rules governing membership qualification of both the NCIS and NCS Service Authority, see para 2.11.

Voting rights

3.11 The independence of local police authorities is to some extent maintained by denying any police officers who serve on the Authority the right to vote on a motion of censure of the Director General or any other members of the NCIS, including any other motion on disciplinary action to be taken (Sch 2, para 18(3)). In addition, Crown servants appointed by the Secretary of State are not entitled to vote on any issue (Sch 2, para 14).

Jurisdiction of the Service Authority

3.12 The jurisdiction of the Service Authority is confined to England and Wales. There will be no direct involvement or consultation with Chief Officers from the RUC and Scotland, or the Commissioners of Customs and Excise (s 49(4)). It remains to be seen what actual powers the Authority will have over the NCS. Although the Service Authority is obliged to issue objectives and a service plan, it is not permitted to frame any policy which would contravene the objectives set by the Secretary of State (see para 3.8). It may require the Director General to submit to it a report on such matters connected with the activities of the NCS as may be specified in the requirement (s 57(3)). However, if it appears to the Director General that a report in compliance with the requirement would contain information which in the public interest ought not to be disclosed, or indeed is not needed for the discharge of the functions of the Service Authority, he or she may ask the Service Authority to refer the requirement to the Secretary of State, and the requirement shall have no effect unless it is confirmed by the Secretary of State (s 57(5)). Functions (and indeed powers) are distributed between the Service Authority and the Director General so that the Director General retains overall responsibility for the direction and control of the NCS.

Codes of Practice

3.13 Under s 73, the Secretary of State may issue codes of practice relating to the discharge by the NCS Service Authority of its functions. The codes will be issued by the Secretary of State without the requirement of a statutory instrument. This provision is identical to the Police Act 1996, s 39, which deals with ordinary police authorities. During the passage of the Bill the Government resisted attempts by the

Opposition to give greater weight to the codes, emphasising that the practices of the Authority were to be purely administrative matters and would have nothing to do with police operations (see paras 2.23, 2.24).

AIMS AND OBJECTIVES OF THE NCS

Functions

3.14 The function of the NCS as defined in s 48(2) is confined to the prevention and detection of 'serious crime' (see para 3.3). No statutory definition of the word 'serious' is given in this Part of the Act. However, a definition is provided in Pt III with regard to authorising entry or interference with property or wireless telegraphy which states that—

> '. . . conduct shall be regarded as serious crime if, and only if,—
> (a) it involves the use of violence, results in substantial financial gain or is conduct by large number of persons in pursuit of a common purpose, or
> (b) the offence or one of the offences is an offence for which a person who has attained the age of twenty-one and has no previous convictions could reasonably be expected to be sentenced to imprisonment for a term of three years or more.' (s 93(4))

In the absence of a definition of 'serious crime' in Pt II it seems likely that the NCS will define the ambit of its work on the basis of this definition. However, it should be noted that the definition of 'serious' in s 93(4) is potentially extremely wide and has been the subject of significant opposition (see paras 4.51–4.54).

Jurisdiction of the squad

3.15 The fact that jurisdiction of the NCS relates to England and Wales does not necessarily mean that the ambit of the squad's activity will be confined to offences occurring in this jurisdiction. Section 48(3) and (4) give the NCS power to work with the NCIS, any other police forces in the United Kingdom and any law enforcement agency anywhere in the world (regardless of whether the agency concerned exists on a statutory footing).[1] When the NCS acts in support of police forces of England and Wales, or co-operates with other police forces in the United Kingdom and law enforcement agencies around the world, it may do so for the purposes of preventing and detecting 'serious crime'. However, when the NCS acts in support of the NCIS it may do so with regard to 'the activities of the NCIS' whether or not these are concerned with serious crime.[2]

1 The definition for law enforcement agency is provided in s 52(2).

2 An amendment to alter the function of the NCIS to deal with the prevention and detection of serious crime in line with the function of the NCS was resisted by Government during the parliamentary debates.

3.16 Under the 1997 Act, s 23, there is also provision for potentially extensive aid by and for the NCIS when the situation requires. In particular, the NCS may also provide constables and other assistance to the NCIS, on application by the Director General of the NCIS, 'for the purposes of enabling the NCIS to meet any special demand on its resources' (s 23(1), (2)). Further, if 'satisfactory arrangements cannot be made, or cannot be made in time', then the Secretary of State can order the NCS to provide constables and assistance to enable the NCIS to meet any special demand or objective, where it appears (to him or her) to be 'expedient in the interests of public safety or order' (s 23(3)(a), (b)).

3.17 Bearing in mind that the function of the NCIS is to 'gather, store and analyse information in order to provide criminal intelligence' the legislation provides for the NCS to do work beyond its primary function of 'preventing and detecting serious crime'. Furthermore, despite Government denials that the 1997 Act paves the way for a national police force, it would appear from the above provisions (coupled with the links between the two Service Authorities) that the current arrangements are appropriately poised to act as a stepping stone towards a national force.[1]

1 Consider the comments of Jack Straw during the Second Reading in the House of Commons: 'I believe that we have to keep an open mind on whether at some stage, and in the light of experience, a single national body would be the more effective arrangement.' (HC 2R, 12 February 1997, col 364).

POWER TO INSTITUTE PROCEEDINGS

3.18 Under s 48(3)(c) the NCS is given the power to institute proceedings. There is a practical legislative agenda behind the provision. Police officers who were attached to the RCSs used to remain members of their police forces and therefore were able to instigate proceedings under the Prosecution of Offences Act 1985 in the same way as any other officer. Police officers attached to the NCS are on a period of seconded service under the Police Act 1996, s 97, and will generally cease to be members of their respective police forces. As a result, proceedings initiated by the NCS officers would not constitute proceedings 'instituted on behalf of a police force' under the Prosecution of Offences Act 1985, s 3(2)(a). Thus the Government chose to bring in a new power for the NCS officers to instigate proceedings.[1] Although it might appear to be more sensible to have simply amended the 1985 Act, s 3(2)(a), to include officers of the NCS, such a course would have conflicted with the notion, albeit a somewhat artificial one, that the NCS is not a police force.

1 Timothy Kirkhope, HC SC F, 4 March 1997, col 122.

3.19 While some RCSs were often praised in parliamentary debates, it is also the case that some had acquired a reputation for advancing improper prosecutions. This occurred to such an extent that the Court of Appeal has taken judicial notice of the fact that there are certain officers in RCSs upon whom the 'requisite confidence cannot be placed' in convictions which are dependent upon uncorroborated convictions.[1] Whether miscarriages of justices were able to occur because the RCSs were permitted too great a degree of autonomy, may never been known. But it is to be hoped that the creation of the NCS will bring with it a greater degree of supervision and accountability.

1 *R v Williams and Smith* [1995] 1 Cr App R 74 at 80.

DIRECTOR GENERAL OF THE NCS

Functions

3.20 The NCS will have a Director General appointed by the Service Authority (s 52(1)). Like his or her counterpart at the NCIS, the general function of the Director General will be the 'direction and control' of the NCS. In this respect, the Director will have a far more extensive influence on the operational policy of the NCS than was the case with the national co-ordinator of the RCSs.

3.21 The Director General will, at the end of each financial year submit a report to the Service Authority on the activities of the squad during that year. The report is to be published in such manner as appears to the Authority to be appropriate (s 57(1), (2)). In carrying out his functions the Director General is to have regard to the Service Plan issued by the Authority (s 56(2)). If required by the Authority, the Director General can be asked to submit a report on a particular issue, but he has a right to have such a requirement referred to the Secretary of State if he believes that complying with the request would be contrary to the public interest or would involve an improper discharge of the Authority's functions (s 57(3), (5)) (see paras 2.11, 2.12). In addition, the Secretary of State may require the Director General to submit a report at any time on any specified matter connected with the activities of the NCS. The Director General is put under an obligation by s 78 to provide criminal statistics to the Secretary of State when requested to so, which are then laid before Parliament in the form of a 'consolidated and classified abstract'.

Appointment

3.22 The Director General will be appointed by a panel of members from the Service Authority who will have the opportunity to choose from a short list supplied by the Secretary of State (s 52(2)). The panel can only consist of members of the Authority appointed by the Secretary of State (other than a Crown servant) or by local authority members of the police authorities (s 52(4)). There is no requirement in the 1997 Act as to any ratio between the police authority members and the Home Office appointees on the panel. Neither is there any requirement that the members of the panel should necessarily be core members.

3.23 A person is eligible for appointment as Director General if he holds—

(a) the rank of chief constable of any police force in Great Britain or the RUC;

(b) the rank of Commissioner, Assistant Commissioner or Deputy Assistant Commissioner in the Metropolitan Police;

(c) the rank of Commissioner in the City of London Police (s 52(3)).

When the posts of the Director Generals were advertised there was a notable lack of senior officers who were willing to put their names forward to be short listed.[1]

1 Guardian, 14 August 1997.

3.24 The Authority, acting with the approval of the Secretary of State, may call upon the Director General to retire 'in the interests of efficiency and effectiveness' (s 53(1)). The Secretary of State may request the Authority to exercise its power of removal under this section (s 74), and may also request the Authority to remove any other member of the squad. In considering the removal of a Director General or another member, the Secretary of State will be required to give the relevant person an opportunity to make representations and shall consider the representations. The same criteria 'of the interests of efficiency and effectiveness' apply when the Secretary of State considers whether or not to approve a removal. These provisions determine the nature of the relationship between the Director General on the one hand and the Authority and the Executive on the other. The Director General is responsible for the policy behind the NCS operations, but he can be called to account both by the Authority and by the Secretary of State if the results are unsatisfactory.

3.25 By s 54 the Director General is obliged to appoint a Deputy who will assume all the powers of the Director General—

(a) during any absence, incapacity or suspension from duty of the Director General, or

(b) during any vacancy in the office of the Director General.

Before making such an appointment the Director General must consult the Service Authority. A person can only be appointed as a Deputy if he holds the rank of chief constable in a police force in Great Britain or in the RUC.

3.26 There are restrictions on designating powers to the Deputy. First, no more than one person can be designated to exercise the powers of the Director General at any one time. Secondly, a person who is authorised to exercise the powers of the Director General shall not do so for a continuous period exceeding three months without the consent of the Secretary of State. These restrictions are important, because in the absence of the Director General, the Deputy appointed under s 54 will assume the role of an authorising officer with regard to authorising police interferences with property under s 93 of the Act (s 94(4)(c)).

3.27 The Director General will assume the rank of a chief constable and will have all the powers and privileges of that rank (s 52(6)). The legal paradox of being a chief constable of an organisation that is not legally recognised as a police force, is necessary in order for mutual aid agreements to be made with other chief constables[1] and for the purposes of employers' liability. The Director General will be liable for torts committed by the NCS in the performance or purported performance of their functions, in the same way as an employer is liable for torts committed by his employees in the course of their employment (s 86(1)). The Director General is to be indemnified from the NCS service fund against damages or costs incurred as a result of the wrongful acts of his officers (s 86(2)). Any civil proceedings in respect of a claim made by virtue of the Director General's vicarious liability are to be brought against the occupant of the post of Director General at the time the proceedings are initiated (s 42(3)). The same provisions apply to the Director General of the NCIS (see para 2.29) and are based on the rules that apply to ordinary chief constables under the Police Act 1996, s 88.

1 As to the position where mutual aid arrangements come into being see ss 23, 24 and para 3.39.

THE NCS STAFF

3.28 The staffing system of the NCS will operate on the same statutory lines as the NCIS. Although under s 58(2), all positions will be appointed by the Service Authority on such terms and conditions as it sees fit, s 55(8) obliges the Authority to delegate its powers of appointment to the Director General. There will be a distinction between 'police members' and civilian 'employees' (s 55(1)(b), (c)).

Permanent police members

3.29 The 'police members' will be split into two categories. The first will be the permanent police members who will take on the rank of assistant chief constable in the NCS (s 55(2)(a)). A person will be eligible for this position if—

(a) he holds the rank of assistant chief constable or a higher rank in a police force of Great Britain or the RUC;

(b) he holds the rank of commander in chief or a higher rank in the metropolitan police force or the City of London police force; or

(c) he is a constable who would be eligible for appointment to the above ranks (s 55(3)).

Temporary police members

3.30 The second category of police membership will cover all subordinate officers who are to be engaged with the NCS on a period of temporary service (s 55(2)(b)). This category will embody the mainstay of the squad's manpower. This provision allows for a period of secondment from one force to another under the Police Act 1996, s 97. During the secondment the officer will cease to be a member of his or her original force.[1] The temporary placement will take place without prejudice to any existing pension rights. Under the 1997 Act, s 66(1), the Authority will simply adopt the pension payments for the period of the secondment. The 1997 Act does not specify a maximum or minimum period of secondment, but provides that all police officers (other than those appointed as the permanent assistant chief constables) cease to be members of the NCS at the end of their period of temporary service unless they are reappointed under s 55(7). The appointment of both the assistant chief constables and the temporary officers is to be delegated by the Service Authority to the Director General (s 55(9)).

1 This was not the case with the members of the RCSs who continued to be members of their original forces See para 3.18 for the implications regarding the institution of proceedings.

Employees

3.31 The category of 'employees' encompasses all staff that are not police officers, and will therefore include not only civilian staff in the strict sense but also customs officers and members of the security services. Again, the Service Authority will generally delegate the function of appointment to the Director General under s 55(8). However, s 59 creates a separate power specifically to be exercised by the Authority, to appoint a person to be a clerk to the Authority.

FINANCES

3.32 When the RCSs were in existence, the funding for their work came from the budgets of the respective police authorities which made up each region. This approach to funding was inappropriate for the NCS since each authority might try to minimise its share of the overall financial liability. Such 'lowest common denominator budgeting' also suffered from the reluctance of police authorities to invest in national strategies.[1] Under the 1997 Act, s 62(1) the level of each police authority's contribution is to be determined by the Service Authority.

1 Steve Uglow and Venous Telford, *The Police Act 1997* (1997), para 2.17.

3.33 The Service Authority is required by s 61 to establish and maintain a central fund known as the 'service fund' (s 61(1)). All funding received by the Authority, with the exception of funding with regard to pensions under s 66, is to be paid into the service fund. All expenditure is to be met out of the fund (s 61(2)). The Service Authority is to keep accounts of payments made into and out of the fund (s 61(3)). These provisions mirror those under the Police Act 1996, s 14, which require individual police authorities to establish and maintain a 'police fund'.

3.34 The Act provides for four sources of funding—

- (a) the issuing of levies to the police authorities in England and Wales;
- (b) direct funding from the Home Office;
- (c) the payment of fees or charges for the provision of services; and
- (d) the receipt of gifts or loans including commercial sponsorship.

3.35 The principal funding for the NCS will come from levies which are issued by the Service Authority to police authorities in England and Wales and the Receiver for the Metropolitan Police District (s 62). Whereas the funding of the RCSs was decided by the police authorities themselves, the Service Authority will now judge what contribution each police authority is to make to the maintenance of the national squad. The Secretary of State will make orders under s 62(3) ratifying the levies which the Service Authority decides upon and conferring a right to interest on sums unpaid. A levy cannot be issued by the Service Authority unless it is approved by the Secretary of State (Sch 5, para 2(1)). Where the approval of the Secretary of State is refused, he has the power to intervene directly and to require the Authority to set such levies as he considers appropriate (Sch 5, para 3(2)).

3.36 Schedule 5 of the 1997 Act deals with the procedure which the Service Authority will follow in order to decide on the issuing of levies. While the creation of the NCS will mean that the local police authorities will lose the financial controls which they had over the RCSs, they will retain a certain amount of influence through their representatives on the Service Authority.[1] Police members of the Authority are excluded from taking part in the decision as to the amount of a levy, which is to be determined by the independent members and police authority members only (Sch 5, para 1(1)). Moreover the determination of the amount of a levy must involve a majority of the police authority members making the decision (Sch 5, para 1(2)). A decision on levies can only be approved if at least half of both the independent members and the police authority members making the decision are in agreement (Sch 5, para 1(3)).

[1] There is a similar procedure with regard to the levies which will be issued by the NCIS Service Authority; see para 2.38.

3.37 The Secretary of State will supply the initial funding of the NCS in respect of all expenditure incurred at any time before the financial year in which the revenue is first received as a result of levies on the police authorities (s 63).

3.38 As with the NCIS Service Authority, s 64 allows the Authority to make charges in respect of services provided (see s 19) and s 65 allows the Authority to accept gifts or loans of other property, on such terms as appears appropriate (see s 20). Although these provisions have been the subject of controversy they are based on provisions that already exist with regard to ordinary police forces. Police forces may make charges for services provided under the Police Act 1996, s 25 and gifts and loans can be accepted as is appropriate under s 93 of the 1996 Act (see paras 2.40, 2.41).

MUTUAL AID AND RELATED ARRANGEMENTS

3.39 Sections 22 and 23 provide for a range of opportunities for the NCS to work with other law enforcement agencies (see para 2.42(a), (b)). Section 69 allows for the Director General of the NCS to provide services to any person at any premises or any locality in England and Wales, provided such services are consistent with the functions of, and do not prejudice the efficiency and effectiveness of, the squad.[1] These provisions reflect the intention behind Pts I and II of the 1997 Act, namely to facilitate efficient and effective co-operation between police and other law enforcement agencies on a national basis. In fulfilling this intention Parliament has also made it likely that the NCS could become involved in investigations beyond England and Wales and could focus on activity which is not strictly confined to the prevention and detection of serious crime (see paras 3.15–3.17). There is no requirement that the Director General should consult either the Service Authority or the Home Office before providing such special services.

[1] For a discussion of the similar section relating to the provision of special services by the Director General of the NCIS (s 24) see para 2.42.

CONTROL BY THE SECRETARY OF STATE

3.40 The Secretary of Sate is required under s 70 to exercise his powers 'in such a manner and to such an extent to be best calculated to promote the efficiency and effectiveness of the NCS'. The Secretary of State will have the same powers with regard to the Service Authority and the NCS as he has with the NCIS and its Service Authority. With regard to the Service Authority the Secretary of State will have powers—

(a) to appoint the chairman (Sch 1, para 2(3));
(b) to appoint three core members (including the chairman) (Sch 1, para 2(1));
(c) to appoint a core member in his capacity as the police authority for the metropolitan police district (Sch 1, para 5);
(d) to appoint a core member who will be a Crown servant (Sch 1, para 6);
(e) to approve the decision on police authority levies by the Authority or make his own orders (Sch 5, paras 2 and 3);

(f) to issue codes relating to the discharge of the Authority's function (s 73(1));
(g) to request reports from the Authority on such matters connected with the discharge of its function, or otherwise with the activities of the NCS (s 76(1));
(f) to provide the short list from which the Service Authority chooses the Director General (s 52(2)).

In addition, the power of the Secretary of State to determine objectives and set performance targets will take priority over the objectives and service plans that are issued by the Service Authority (see paras 3.8, 3.9).

3.41 The Secretary of State will have control over the short list of eligible candidates for the post of Director General (s 52(2)). The powers of the Director General and Home Office are separated so that the former is concerned with 'direction and control' of the NCS, whereas the latter is limited to securing 'efficiency and effectiveness'. Under s 76 the Secretary of State can order the Director General to submit a report on any aspect of the NCS. Although the power to remove the Director General lies with the Service Authority, the Secretary of State can call upon the Service Authority to exercise the power (s 74).

3.42 Whilst the direction and control of operations is supposed to be the domain of the Director General, the Secretary of State has the power to determine annual objectives and performance targets (ss 71 and 72). While the statutory concepts of 'objectives' and 'performance targets' are derived from modern concepts of managerial efficiency, they are not necessarily confined by the legislation to measures which promote the efficiency of the organisation as a whole.[1] There is little to stop the prioritising of certain objectives, and the pitching of performance in order to suit the broader policy objectives of the Home Office.

1 These provisions were first introduced with regard to ordinary police forces by the Police and Magistrates' Courts Act 1994 (now the Police Act 1996, ss 37, 38). See S Baker and J English, *The Police and Magistrates' Courts Act 1994* (1994), Ch 6.

3.43 Other powers of the Secretary of State include powers to—

(a) require the relevant inspectors of the constabulary to carry out an inspection of the NCS (s 75(1));
(b) direct the Authority to take remedial action in the event of an adverse report (s 75(2));
(c) establish a public or private inquiry into any matter connected with the NCIS (s 79(1));
(d) make regulations concerning the standard of equipment to be used by the NCS (s 80);
(e) require the NCS to use specified facilities or services in conjunction with the NCIS, if he considers that it would be in the interest of efficiency or effectiveness for them to do so (s 36);
(f) intervene if he considers that the general consultation arrangements established by the Authority and the Director General under s 85 are inadequate (s 85(4), (5));

These provisions mirror those in Pt I which relate to the NCIS. The Home Office has been given significant powers to offset the dangers of the NCS enjoying excessive autonomy. However, such an investment of powers in the Secretary of State will also have the effect of undermining the traditional authority of local government which the 1997 Act purports to maintain.

Duty to consult

3.44 The Secretary of State has a duty to exercise his powers with regard to promoting the efficiency and effectiveness of the NCS. Questions can therefore be asked in Parliament and in certain instances a failure by the Secretary of State to exercise his statutory powers could be amenable to judicial review proceedings. Moreover, before making an order to determine the objectives of the NCS under s 71, the Secretary of State is obliged to consult—

(a) the NCS Service Authority;
(b) the Director General of the NCS;
(c) persons whom he considers to represent the interests of the police authorities of England and Wales;
(d) persons whom he considers to represent the interests of the chief officers of police forces in England and Wales;
(e) the NCIS Service Authority;
(f) the Director General of the NCIS (s 71(2)).

A duty to consult involves both carrying out consultations and considering the results of those consultations.[1]

1 *R v Secretary of State for Social Services, ex p Association of Metropolitan Authorities* [1986] 1 All ER 164.

INQUIRIES

3.45 As with the NCIS, the Secretary of State can cause an inquiry to be held by a person appointed by him into any matter connected with the NCS (s 79). Whether such an inquiry is public or private is a matter within the discretion of the Secretary of State. There is a power to call witnesses and order documents to be produced. It is a summary criminal offence for a person either to refuse to testify or to destroy relevant documents. Once an inquiry reports its findings and conclusions, a summary of the report shall be made known by the Secretary of State 'so far as appears to him consistent with the public interest' (s 79(4)).

DISCIPLINE AND COMPLAINTS

3.46 Section 81 empowers the Secretary of State to issue regulations relating to the conduct of members of the NCS and the maintenance of discipline. A right of appeal against dismissal is provided by s 82. Complaints from the public are to be handled in a manner which corresponds with a complaint made against a member of an ordinary police force (s 83(1), (2)),[1] and the 1997 Act envisages that regulations made by the Secretary of State for this purpose may confer additional functions on the Police Complaints Authority (s 83(2)). The complaints system will therefore be limited to questioning the conduct of individual officers. There will be no remedy by which members of the public can question the policy of the Director General with regard to fulfilling his function of controlling and directing the NCS.[2] The complaints system will apply in the same manner to non-police employees as it does to police members of the NCS.

1 Police Act 1996, Pt I.

2 A decision by a Director General with regard to operations is unlikely to be amenable to judicial review unless it can be shown to be 'Wednesbury unreasonable': *R v Chief Constable of Sussex, ex p International Trader's Ferry Ltd* [1997] 2 All ER 65.

INCITEMENT AND DISAFFECTION

3.47 Section 87 creates an offence of incitement to disaffection. Any person who causes, or attempts to cause, or does any act calculated to cause, disaffection among police members of the NCS (whether permanent or temporary) or induces or attempts to induce any such member to withhold his services is guilty of an offence punishable on indictment with up to two years' imprisonment or a fine or both. The maximum penalty on summary conviction is six months' imprisonment or a fine or both. This section replicates s 43 of the 1997 Act which applies to the NCIS; for details see para 2.50.

4 Intrusive surveillance

INTRODUCTION

4.1 In *Malone v United Kingdom*[1] the European Court of Human Rights held that the system whereby telephone and mail interception were conducted under a warrant from the Secretary of State, with no statutory framework, afforded insufficient legal protection to satisfy the requirements of Article 8 of the European Convention on Human Rights. Article 8 provides—

> '1. Everyone has a right to respect for his private and family life, his home and his correspondence.
>
> 2. There shall be no interference by a public authority with the exercise of this right except such as is in accordance with the law and is necessary in a democratic society in the interests of national security, public safety or the economic well-being of the country, for the prevention of disorder or crime, for the protection of health or morals, or for the protection of the rights and freedoms of others.'

1 (1984) 7 EHRR 14.

4.2 In the *Malone* case the Court established the following important principle on the application of Article 8—

> 'The law must be sufficiently clear in its terms to give citizens an adequate indication as to circumstances in which and the conditions on which public authorities are empowered to resort to this secret and potentially dangerous interference with the right to respect for private life and correspondence.'[1]

Following this decision, the Government introduced the Interception of Communications Act 1985. The 1985 Act established a statutory framework with the requirement of the prior issue of a warrant by the Secretary of State, and subsequent review by a Commissioner acting as an appropriate independent tribunal.

1 (1984) 7 EHRR 14, para 67.

4.3 In passing the 1985 Act the Government endeavoured to limit the use to which telephone interceptions would be put, and thus by extension, to protect rights of privacy. The Home Office White Paper 'The Interception of Communications in the United Kingdom'[1] that accompanied the 1985 Act, stated at para 12(f)—

> 'The Bill will provide for controls over the use of intercepted material. By making such material generally inadmissible in legal proceedings it will ensure that interception can be used only as an aspect of investigation, not prosecution'.[2]

This restriction has not been applied to subsequent intrusive surveillance legislation, and is not part of the regime established by the 1997 Act.

1 Cmnd 9438.
2 Affirmed in *R v Preston (Stephen)* [1994] 2 AC 130, per Lord Mustill at 147.

THE CURRENT POSITION

4.4 Secret surveillance of private property through the use of bugging devices is as much an intrusion of privacy as a telephone interception. Indeed, it frequently involves a greater intrusion since access is often gained to private property in order to 'plant' a device. Yet such surveillance remained entirely unregulated by statute until the Security Service Act 1989 (see now the Intelligence Services Act 1994, as amended by the Security Service Act 1996). The 1989 Act placed MI5 onto a statutory footing, and provided a system of prior authorisations for intrusive surveillance, which was subsequently found to satisfy the requirements of Article 8 of the Convention.[1] Under the 1989 Act an application for a warrant to enable the Security Services (MI5) to interfere with property or wireless telegraphy was to be made to the Secretary of State, and was subject to scrutiny by a Tribunal and Commissioner. This procedure was extended to encompass the Intelligence Services (MI6) and GCHQ by the Intelligence Services Act 1994.[2]

1 See *Esbester v United Kingdom*, Commission's Report, 2 April 1993 18601/91. See para 4.21.
2 Section 5(3) of the 1994 Act originally prohibited the grant of a warrant in respect of criminal investigations which did not involve an element of national security where the action to be taken related to property in the British Isles. This prohibition was lifted so far as the Security Services were concerned by the Security Service Act 1996, s 2.

4.5 However, intrusive surveillance other than telephone and mail interception conducted by the *police* was not covered by either the 1985 Act or the 1989 Act. Although such surveillance has been carried out routinely in major police investigations for many years, it has until now been subject only to non-statutory Guidelines issued by the Home Office.[1] The key provisions of the Home Office Guidelines were contained in paragraphs 4 and 5 which provided—

> '4. In each case in which the covert use of a listening device is requested the authorising officer should satisfy himself that the following criteria are met—
>
> (a) the investigation concerns serious crime;[2]
> (b) normal methods of investigation must have been tried and failed, or must, from the nature of things, be unlikely to succeed if tried;
> (c) there must be good reason to think that use of the equipment would be likely to lead to an arrest and a conviction, or where appropriate, to the prevention of acts of terrorism;
> (d) use of equipment must be operationally feasible.
>
> 5. In judging how far the seriousness of the crime under investigation justifies the use of particular surveillance techniques, authorising officers should satisfy themselves that the degree of intrusion into the privacy of those affected by the surveillance is commensurate with the seriousness of the offence. Where the targets of the surveillance might reasonably assume a high degree of privacy, for instance in their homes, listening devices should be used only for the investigation of major organised conspiracies and of other particularly serious offences, especially crimes of violence.'

1 The Guidelines on the Use of Equipment in Police Surveillance Operations, (19 December 1984, Dep NS 1579).
2 Note however that para 7 of the Guidelines recognised that the requirement that the investigation must 'concern serious crime' could be dispensed with in cases where one of the parties consents to the recording of a telephone conversation, eg, the investigation of malicious or obscene telephone calls.

4.6 The procedural rules were contained in paragraphs 6 to 11 of the Guidelines. Paragraph 6 provided that in normal circumstances, covert operations with surveillance devices required the authorisation of a Chief Constable or the equivalent. Under para 7, the power to authorise could be delegated to an Assistant Chief Constable where the relevant equipment was to be—

> '(a) knowingly carried by a person other than a police officer who is party to a conversation which is to be recorded or transmitted;
> (b) carried by a police officer whose identity is known to at least one other non-police party to a conversation which is to be recorded or transmitted;
> (c) installed in premises, with the consent of the lawful occupier, to record or transmit a conversation in circumstances where at least one of the parties to the conversation will know of the surveillance;
> (d) used, with the consent of one of the parties concerned, to record a telephone conversation . . . ;
> (e) used, with the consent, in the case of a vehicle, of the owner (though not necessarily the driver) to track a vehicle, package or person.'

Under paras 8, 9 and 11 there were provisions with regard to keeping a record of both the information obtained, and the circumstances in which an authorisation for the surveillance was given (para 11). The maximum period for which an authorisation was to last was one month, after which, if the operation was to continue, a fresh application had to be made to the authorising officer (para 8).

4.7 Paragraph 10 of the Guidelines expressly recognised the potential use of material obtained from intrusive surveillance as part of the evidence in a criminal prosecution—

> 'It is accepted that there may be circumstances in which material obtained through the use of equipment by the police for surveillance as a necessary part of a criminal investigation could appropriately be used in evidence at subsequent court proceedings . . .'

The position with regard to aural and visual surveillance devices under the Home Office Guidelines therefore contrasted directly with the provisions governing telephone tapping and the interception of postal communications.[1]

1 See para 4.3.

4.8 According to Home Office statistics, in 1995 there were approximately 2,100 authorisations by chief officers of intrusive surveillance operations in the UK undertaken by police and customs.[1] This figure includes 1,300 authorisations by police officers in England and Wales. The use of such devices has risen sharply since 1977 when there were between 500 and 600 authorisations granted.[2] Despite the prevalence of the practice, during the Parliamentary Debates on the 1997 Act one former Home Secretary disclaimed all knowledge of the scale of intrusive surveillance by the police during his period of office.[3]

1 HC Debs, 21 January 1997, col 512W.
2 Baroness Blatch, HL Report, 20 January 1997, col 401.
3 Lord Callaghan, HL Report, 20 January 1997, col 401.

R v Khan

4.9 The inadequacy of the Home Office Guidelines as a system of supervising secret surveillance was finally exposed by the House of Lords' decision in *R v Khan*.[1] The defendant in that case was charged with importation of heroin. Acting on the authority of a Chief Constable, police officers placed a listening device in a house in which he was staying and recorded a series of highly incriminating conversations. At his trial the defendant argued that the tapes were inadmissible since they had been obtained in consequence of an act of criminal damage and/or a trespass. He submitted in the alternative that the evidence ought to be excluded in the exercise of the trial judge's discretion under the Police and Criminal Evidence Act 1984 (PACE), s 78. The trial judge accepted that the absence of legislation governing such surveillance was unsatisfactory—

> 'In the absence of statutory authority and clear parameters of the extent of police powers in these matters, the whole situation is riddled with uncertainties.'[2]

He also accepted for the purposes of the argument, that the surveillance was unlawful. Nevertheless he went on to hold that the evidence was admissible, and that it would not have such an adverse effect on the fairness of proceedings as to require its discretionary exclusion under s 78. Following the ruling the defendant pleaded guilty and appealed.

1 [1997] AC 558.
2 Transcript of the first instance decision.

4.10 The Court of Appeal upheld the trial judge's decision to admit the evidence, but noted that—

> 'There are, in the United Kingdom, no statutory provisions which govern the use by the police of secret listening devices on private property. This is to be contrasted with the position in relation to the interception of public telephone calls or postal communications . . . It is also to be contrasted with the controls on the use of surveillance devices by the security service, laid down in the Security Service Act 1989.'[1]

The Court of Appeal was therefore moved to comment that the use of bugging devices should be more strictly regulated and the criteria more generally promulgated—

> 'The Home Office guidelines, and other documents to which we have referred, certainly prescribe criteria and procedures limiting such use. However, although not a legal rule, "An Englishman's home is his castle" is a tenet jealously held and widely respected. It is, in our view, at least worthy of consideration as to whether the circumstances in which bugging a private home by the police can be justified should be the subject of statutory control. It may be thought that such control is, by analogy with the 1985 Act, just as desirable for bugging devices as for telephone tapping.'[2]

1 *R v Khan (Sultan)* [1994] 3 WLR 899 at 902.
2 Ibid.

4.11 The House of Lords agreed.[1] Although they dismissed the appeal, their Lordships held that in exercising the discretion under PACE, s 78, a trial judge was entitled to have regard to breaches of Article 8 of the European Convention on Human Rights. Moreover, the discretionary powers of the trial judge to exclude evidence were characterised as marching hand in hand with Article 6(1) of the Convention (right to a fair trial).[2] Lord Slynn therefore concluded—

> '. . . I consider that fairness both to accused persons and to those who have to exercise this discretion make it highly desirable that such interceptions should be governed by legislation.'[4]

1 *R v Khan (Sultan)* [1997] AC 558.
2 Per Lord Slynn of Hadley, at p 165, 166 and per Lord Nicholls of Birkenhead at p 176, relying on *Schenk v Switzerland* (1988) 13 EHRR 242.
3 Per Lord Slynn at p 166.

4.12 In delivering the leading judgment in *Khan*, Lord Nolan expressed his relief that a man who had admitted his involvement in a large importation of heroin should not have his conviction set aside because his privacy had been invaded. However, his Lordship concluded his speech with the following remarks—

> 'The sole cause of this case coming to your Lordships' House is the lack of a statutory system regulating the use of surveillance devices by the police. The absence of such a system seems astonishing, the more so in view of the statutory framework which has governed the use of such devices by the Security Service since 1989, and the interception of communications by the police as well as by other agencies since 1985. I would refrain, however, from further comment, because counsel for the Crown was able to inform us, on instructions, that the Government proposes to introduce legislation covering the matter in the next session of Parliament.'[1]

1 *R v Khan (Sultan)* [1997] AC 558 at 1785H.

4.13 The journey of *Khan's* case through the Appellate courts was thus the immediate catalyst for Pt III of the 1997 Act. As the Parliamentary debates make clear,[1] intrusive surveillance carried out under the existing arrangements was undoubtedly both unlawful under domestic law, and in breach of the requirements of Article 8 of the Convention.[2] The Home Office Guidelines did not have the force of law, and were not properly published. For that reason alone they were incapable of satisfying the requirements of Article 8.[3] Moreover, there was no requirement for the obtaining of a warrant prior to the use of a covert listening device by the police.[4] The authorisation of the Chief Constable did not provide the requisite element of independence for the purposes of Article 8,[5] and stood in contrast to provisions in the Security Service Act 1989, and the Intelligence Services Act 1994, where a warrant is required before any action is taken in relation to the secret surveillance of property.

1 Lord Lloyd, HL Report, 20 January 1997, col 415. See also *Entick v Carrington* State Trials 1065.
2 As to the Convention see paras 4.14–4.22.
3 *Hewitt and Harman v United Kingdom* (1989)14 EHRR 657.
4 Home Office Guidelines op cit, paras 6, 7.
5 See eg *Klass v Germany* (1978) 2 EHRR 214.

THE EUROPEAN CONVENTION ON HUMAN RIGHTS

4.14 The decisions of the European Court and Commission of Human Rights establish a number of important principles governing the use of secret surveillance. Such powers constitute an 'interference' with the right guaranteed by Article 8.[1] Powers of secret surveillance of private life are tolerable in a democratic society only in so far as strictly necessary for safeguarding democratic institutions. But in order to counter threats of espionage and terrorism secret surveillance can in principle be justified.[2] Subject to the 'necessity principle', the same is also true of the other aims prescribed in Article 8(2), including the prevention of crime.

1 *Klass v Germany* (1978) 2 EHRR 214; *Malone v United Kingdom* (1984) 7 EHRR 14; *Huvig v France* (1990) 12 EHRR 528).
2 *Klass v Germany* ibid.

4.15 Although States enjoy a certain latitude in deciding the conditions under which a system of surveillance can be operated, they do not enjoy an unlimited discretion to subject citizens to secret surveillance. Since such surveillance 'can undermine or even destroy democracy on the ground of defending it', there must be adequate and effective safeguards against abuse.[1] Although it is desirable that the machinery of supervision should be in the hands of a judge, this is not a requirement either of Article 8 or of Article 13. Supervisory bodies will be capable of providing an adequate and effective safeguard against abuse providing they enjoy sufficient independence to give an objective ruling.[2]

1 *Klass v Germany* (1978) 2 EHRR 214.
2 Ibid.

4.16 Prior to the Security Service Act 1989, the system for authorising MI5 surveillance or telecommunications interception lacked the requisite element of independence.[1] However, the machinery established by the 1989 Act,[2] whereby an application for a warrant is made to the Secretary of State, subject to scrutiny by the Tribunal and Commissioner, is sufficient to provide the necessary measure of independent scrutiny. In *Esbester v United Kingdom,*[3] the Commission's report stated that—

> 'In the absence of any evidence or indication that the system is not functioning as required by domestic law, the Commission finds that the framework of safeguards achieves a compromise between the requirements of defending a democratic society and the rights of the individual, which is compatible with the provisions of the Convention.'

The 1989 Act is indistinguishable for this purpose from the Interception of Communications Act 1985 and the Intelligence Services Act 1994.

1 *Hewitt and Harman v United Kingdom* (1989) 14 EHRR 657.
2 Now set out in the Intelligence Services Act 1994, ss 5–10.
3 2 April 1993 18601/91.

4.17 The term 'in accordance with the law'[1] is not limited to an examination of whether a particular measure is permitted or prohibited under domestic law. The law governing the use of the technique must itself be 'accessible and precise'.[2] The term 'in accordance with the law' has a special meaning when applied to secret surveillance or telecommunications interception; it does not entitle citizens to know in advance when the authorities are likely to observe them or intercept their communications and thereby enable them to adapt their conduct. Nevertheless, the law must give an adequate indication of the circumstances in which, and the conditions under which, authorities are empowered to resort to 'this secret and potentially dangerous interference with the right to respect for private life and correspondence'.[3]

1 Article 8(2).
2 *Malone v United Kingdom* (1984) 7 EHRR 14.
3 Ibid.

4.18 An unpublished non-statutory directive from a Department of State which is not legally binding is incapable of satisfying the requirements of accessibility and precision.[1] It is not necessary that the framework of safeguards should be provided entirely by statute. If, however, the common law is relied upon then it must be sufficiently clear and unambiguous to enable a citizen to know the precise extent of his/her legal entitlements without the necessity for extrapolation.[2] The rules must define with clarity the categories of citizens liable to be the subject of such techniques, the offences which might give rise to such an order, the permitted duration of the tapping, and the circumstances in which recordings are to be destroyed.[3]

1 *Hewitt and Harman v United Kingdom* (1989) 14 EHRR 657.
2 *Huvig v France* (1990) 12 EHRR 528.
3 Ibid; *Kruslin v France* (1990) 12 EHRR 547.

4.19 It is not necessary for the law to provide exhaustive definitions of the circumstances in which secret surveillance will be permitted. It is sufficient for the law to identify the types of activity which may fall within the scope of the power. Thus, the requirement for precision is satisfied by the system of safeguards introduced under the Security Service Act 1989. In *Hewitt and Harman v United Kingdom (No 2)*,[1] the Commission dismissed as manifestly ill-founded a complaint that the legislation provided powers so wide that the law lacked the requisite element of certainty, on the grounds that—

> 'The principles [in Article 8(2)] do not necessarily require a comprehensive definition of the notion "the interests of national security". . . the Commission considers that in the present case the law is formulated with sufficient precision to enable the applicants to anticipate the role of the Security Service.'

1 1 September 1993 20317/92.

4.20 Where an invasion of privacy through secret surveillance infringes Article 8 it is immaterial that the person who has been the primary victim of the invasion is not the person who complains of the violation, providing the complainant has also been affected.[1] For the purposes of Article 8 therefore, it is irrelevant that the telephone or premises which are subject to surveillance did not belong to the alleged victim.

1 *Kruslin v France* (1990) 12 EHRR 547.

4.21 Where surveillance has occurred unlawfully, domestic law must provide an effective remedy before a national authority, whether or not the surveillance has resulted in a criminal prosecution.[1] Such an authority need not necessarily be judicial, and the nature of the remedy may be determined by the sensitivity of the information.[2] The redress has to be as effective as it can be having regard to the restricted scope for recourse inherent in any system of secret surveillance.[3] The system of Commissioners and Tribunals established under the Security Service Act 1989 and the Intelligence Services Act 1994 are sufficient to discharge the United Kingdom's responsibilities.[4]

1 See the Convention, Article 13.
2 *Klass v Germany* (1978) 2 EHRR 214 at para 67.
3 Ibid, at para 69.
4 *Esbester v United Kingdom* (2 April 1993 18601/91); *Hewitt and Harman v United Kingdom (No 2)* (1 September 1993 20317/92.

4.22 There seems to be little doubt that the existing position regarding police surveillance is in violation of Article 8.[1] Equally there is little doubt that the Bill as originally proposed by the Government failed to afford adequate protection of the right to privacy for the purposes of the Convention.[2] The question remains whether the prior authorisation provisions which were eventually introduced into the 1997 Act offer a sufficient guarantee of independence to survive challenge before the European Court of Human Rights. There are a number of situations in which prior authorisation is not required. For example, a chief officer may give authorisation to carry out intrusive surveillance on a person's home in cases of urgency. Furthermore, at the time of writing there is no requirement in the Act or in the draft Code of Practice for prior authority if the police have the consent of the owner of premises, such as an hotel, even though it is not the privacy of the owner that is being intruded upon. It is also open to question whether the definition of serious crime is narrow enough to satisfy the Strasbourg test of proportionality.[3]

1 At the time of writing the Commission has declared admissible an application alleging a violation of Article 8 arising out of the use of a listening device by the police in accordance with the Home Office Guidelines: *Govell v United Kingdom* 2737/95, (1996) 23 EHRR CD 101.
2 For the Parliamentary history, see para 4.23 et seq.
3 See para 4.51 et seq.

PARLIAMENTARY HISTORY

4.23 The Government's original proposals[1] were plainly incompatible with the principles established under Convention law. In particular, the initial decision to take action in respect of property or in respect of wireless telegraphy, was to reside with the police authorising officer alone (clause 89). The criteria for authorising intrusive surveillance were whether the authorising officer thought it was 'likely to be of substantial value in the prevention or detection of serious crime' and whether he or she was 'satisfied that what the action seeks to achieve cannot reasonably be achieved by other means' (clause 89(3)).

1 HL Bill 10 of 1996–1997. Note that the amended Bill that went to the House of Commons was HL Bill 88 of 1996–1997.

4.24 The proposals would have given the Chief Constable far more extensive powers than the 1984 Guidelines.[1] In particular, the Guidelines had narrower criteria for 'authorisation'; normal methods had to have been 'tried and failed'; the use of intrusive surveillance had to be 'likely to lead to an arrest and conviction'; devices involving substantial intrusion could only be used for 'major organised conspiracies, especially crimes of violence'; and the 1984 Guidelines only allowed the delegation of 'authorisation' from the Chief Constable where there was a 'degree of consent' by a member of the public. Moreover, the 1984 Guidelines set the limit for authorised surveillance at one month, whereas the initial proposed limit in the Police Bill was six months.

1 See para 4.5 et seq. See also Statewatch, Vol 6 No 6, November–December 1996, 'Police Bill: new powers to bug and burgle', pp 1, 21–23.

4.25 Human rights commentators, such as Liberty and Statewatch, focused particularly on the failure of the Bill to provide for prior independent authorisation. They noted that the absence of such a system would breach the requirements for independent scrutiny laid down by the Convention.[1] Liberty commissioned and published an influential Opinion by Michael Beloff QC, Peter Duffy QC and Murray Hunt which formed the basis of its Parliamentary briefings. The authors concluded that the Bill was fundamentally at odds with the requirements of Article 8 and the principles of common law—

> 'In our view, the proposals in Part III of the Police Bill go . . . against the constitutional grain, by providing for what are essentially administrative warrants to enter on and interfere with private property, with no independent previous scrutiny at all. Not only is there to be no prior judicial assessment of the necessity for such interference, there is not even to be an assessment at the ministerial level. The decision as to whether or not to interfere with one of the most cherished of the common law's presumptively protected values, the right to privacy in one's home, is to be taken at the administrative level, within the very enforcement agency which will be entitled to carry out the interference.'[2]

1 See para 4.15 and *Klass v Germany* (1978) 2 EHHR 214. See also 'The Police Bill–Liberty Briefing', November 1996, para 3.21.
2 Liberty 'Legal Opinion and Amendment to the Police Bill 1996'.

4.26 Statewatch characterised self-regulation as 'a recipe for abuse'—

> 'The idea that the police are more 'accountable' than the judiciary (in great need of reform though it is) is ill-judged. A judge, before granting

> a warrant, would have to take into account the circumstances of the case and any legal rulings or precedents interpreting and defining the use of such warrants. It is not the job of police officers to make such judgments. It is also an argument that confuses the constitutional roles of the enforcement of the law by the police and the interpretation of the law by the judiciary as set out in statutes passed by Parliament.'[1]

1 Statewatch, op cit, p 1.

4.27 The proposals thus sought to depart from the principle of prior authorisation, which is integral to all other legislation conferring powers to contravene privacy and enter private property. Powers of entry and search given under PACE, demand the prior approval of a magistrate or a circuit judge. The interception of telecommunications,[1] and entry and bugging of premises undertaken by the security services[2] requires a prior warrant from the Secretary of State, and is subject to the scrutiny of a Tribunal and a Commissioner, who is a senior judge.[3]

1 Interception of Communications Act 1985, s 2.
2 See the Intelligence Services Act 1994, ss 5–10.
3 Security Service Act 1989, s 4.

4.28 The Parliamentary opposition to the Bill saw a concerted attack by Liberal and cross-bench peers as well as a number of leading Law Lords. In particular, Lord Browne-Wilkinson delivered a series of speeches which indicated his grave reservations about this aspect of the Bill—

> 'Until the passing of the Security Service Act earlier this year—a Bill about which at the time I was not enthusiastic—there was only one exception to immunity from police invasion of our privacy; that is, a search warrant granted by an independent court and not by the executive . . . But now, following from the Security Service Act, we are sanctioning the entry onto our premises for police purposes not under warrant of the court or under any independent warrant, but under administrative action.'[1]

1 HL 2R, 11 November 1996, col 810.

4.29 The Government's original position was that it was not right to involve judges in early intelligence gathering procedures, because there was a danger that such involvement would compromise the independence of the judiciary.[1] Initially, it was not the policy of the Labour front bench to support the amendments to the Bill in the House of Lords. However, after the second reading debate, Jack Straw announced that the Labour party had reconsidered its position and was opposed to the lack of requirement for prior authorisation.[2] This change of policy came at a time when a substantial media campaign was being waged against the Bill.[3]

1 Baroness Blatch, HL 2R, 11 November 1996, col 837.
2 Guardian, 17 January 1997, 'Straw in 'spy bill' U-Turn'.
3 See Daily Telegraph, 3 January 1997 'Will bugging be warranted?'; Daily Mail 14 January 1997 'Bugging should be by judicial warrant'; The Times, 14 January 1997, 'A Bill too far'; Guardian, 13 January 1997 'Bugging is too important to be left to the police'; The London Review of Books, 6 February 1997, 'History of a Dog's Dinner'.

4.30 Subsequently the Labour front bench agreed to support amendments to the Bill in the House of Lords. Lord McIntosh successfully put forward an amendment which required prior authorisation from a Commissioner in order to bug properties without the owner's consent. Retrospective authorisation was to be maintained when it was 'not reasonably practicable' to apply to the commissioner in advance (clause 91). However, a Liberal Democrat amendment which was also passed, removed the power of Chief Constables to authorise bugging in any way, passing the responsibility to a circuit judge. Under the Liberal Democrat proposal there was no provision for urgent cases (clause 92(4)). The Government was not only defeated on a vital principle in Pt III, but it was defeated by inconsistent amendments which produced contradictory systems of authorisation. There followed a period of intense negotiation between the Conservative Government and the Labour front bench with the object of avoiding a Government defeat in the House of Commons.

4.31 The Bill that the Government finally proposed in the Commons, essentially adopted the Labour Party amendment on authorisation. Other amendments, aimed at narrowing both the definition of 'serious crime' and the circumstances in which surveillance could be carried out, were defeated. In bowing to the Opposition over prior authorisation, Michael Howard stressed that 'the Government is determined to strike the balance between the operational effectiveness of these crucial techniques and ensuring that a careful watch is kept on their use.'[1]

1 Parliamentary Research Paper 97/22, p 41.

THE STATUTORY SCHEME

4.32 The 1997 Act thus creates a statutory scheme for 'Authorisation of Action in Respect of Property'.[1] Although the primary purpose of Part III is to regulate the bugging of private property, there is no reference to the use of listening devices in the provisions. In that respect, the possible 'actions' that could take place have no statutory limitation. Because of the way in which the Act is worded, police officers will in principle be able to use the provisions to search premises and seize documents without the requirement of a warrant under PACE.[2] Although a measure of prior approval by an independent Commissioner has been introduced, s 94 provides for circumstances where action can be taken in the absence of an authorising officer, and without a Commissioner's approval where it is not 'reasonably practicable'.

1 This is the title of Pt III of the 1997 Act.
2 HL Report, 20 January 1997, col 416.

4.33 Perhaps the most striking omission from the statutory scheme is that it fails to regulate other types of intrusive surveillance that do not require interference with property, such as the use of long distance sensitive microphones, and laser beam technology using window reflections and vibrations. The setting up of a Police Information Technology Organisation under Pt IV of the 1997 Act signals the importance of new technology in crime prevention. In years to come the surveillance capability of the police is likely to develop to such an extent that the current provisions will become pedestrian and obsolete.

THE AUTHORISING OFFICER

4.34 The cornerstone of the statutory scheme is the authorising officer, who must be a police officer of the rank of Chief Constable or equivalent (s 93(5)). Subject to the prior approval of a Commissioner for applications requiring such approval,[1] authorisation may be given by—

(a) the Chief Constable of any force in England and Wales;
(b) the Commissioner or an Assistant Commissioner of the Metropolitan Police;
(c) the Commissioner of Police for the City of London;
(d) the Chief Constable of a Scottish force;
(e) the Chief Constable or a Deputy Chief Constable of the RUC;
(f) the Director General of the NCIS;
(g) the Director General of the NCS;
(h) the customs officer designated by the Commissioners of Customs and Excise for the purpose of s 93(5) of the 1997 Act.

In the case of the Metropolitan Police and the Royal Ulster Constabulary, the functions of the authorising officer may be performed by an Assistant Commissioner and by the Deputy Chief Constable respectively (s 93(5)(b), (e)), without resort to the delegation provisions[2] of the 1997 Act. For the purposes of this Part of the 1997 Act (ss 91–108) the designated deputies in these two forces are treated as if they were in the same position as the Commissioner and Chief Constable.

1 See paras 4.62–4.64.
2 See paras 4.36–4.42.

4.35 Authorisations given by an authorising officer should normally be in writing (s 95(1)), unless the case is urgent in which case authorisation may be given orally, with effect for up to 72 hours (s 95(2)(a)).

4.36 If it is not reasonably practicable to obtain the authority of the appropriate authorising officer, then the power to authorise intrusive surveillance may be delegated to a designated deputy of any force. Section 94(4) defines a designated deputy, in the case of an ordinary police force, as an officer of at least the rank of assistant chief constable who is designated to act in the absence of the chief constable, under the Police Act 1996, s 12(4), or the Police (Scotland) Act 1967, s 5(4). In the case of the NCIS or NCS, the designated deputy will be the Deputy Director General appointed under the 1997 Act, ss 8, 54 (s 94(4)(c)).

4.37 The 1997 Act permits a second tier of delegation in cases where it is not reasonably practicable to obtain the authority of any of the above. Section 94(2) provides that in such circumstances, providing the case is urgent, authorisation may be given by—

(a) an Assistant Chief Constable of any force in the UK;
(b) a Commander in the Metropolitan Police or the City of London Police;
(c) a person designated for this purpose by the Director General of the NCIS or the NCS;
(d) a customs officer designated for this purpose by the Commissioners of Customs and Excise.

4.38 Where authorisation is granted by a designated deputy under s 94, it must always be given in writing (s 95(1)), and is limited in duration to 72 hours (s 95(2)(a)).

Geographical limitations

4.39 Where an authorisation is to be given by the Chief Constable of an ordinary police force, or his designated deputy, the powers conferred in Pt III of the 1997 Act are confined to the geographical police area covered by the relevant force.

4.40 Thus, the power to authorise interference with property may only be exercised in relation to action to be taken 'in the relevant area' (s 93(1)). For ordinary police forces, this means the police area for which the authorising officer is responsible (s 93(6)(a)–(c)).

4.41 Similarly, s 93(3) provides that the authorising officer may only authorise intrusive surveillance if the application was made by an officer from within his force.[1]

1 This restriction applies to the NCIS, the NCS or HM Customs and Excise, but see para 4.42.

4.42 These restrictions confine the scope of the power to 'bug and burgle', but are of limited practical significance in relation to interference with wireless telegraphy, since this will generally cut across police boundaries. Moreover, the geographical limits will not restrict the activities of the three law enforcement agencies with national jurisdiction: namely the NCIS, the NCS and HM Customs and Excise. For the NCS, the relevant area is defined as being England and Wales (s 93(6)(e)), while for the NCIS and HM Customs and Excise, it is the UK as a whole (s 93(6)(d), (f)).

AUTHORISATIONS TO INTERFERE WITH PROPERTY: THE CRITERIA

4.43 Section 93(2) provides that authorisation may be given where the authorising officer believes—

- (a) it is necessary for the action specified to be taken on the ground that it is likely to be of substantial value in the prevention or detection of serious crime (s 93(2)(a)), and
- (b) what the action seeks to achieve cannot reasonably be achieved by other means (s 93(2)(b)).

An objective test

4.44 The use of the term 'believes' (in s 93(2)) suggests that a subjective judgment is called for, and that it is not necessary for the authorising officer to have reasonable grounds for his belief. But it is clear both from the other provisions of the 1997 Act and from the Parliamentary debates, that this was not the Government's intention. Where an authorisation requires the approval of a Commissioner, the authorising officer will have to be able to demonstrate that his belief was held 'on reasonable grounds' (s 97(5)).[1] The apparent conflict between these two formulations was explained by Lord Mackay, the Lord Chancellor, during the Committee Stage of the Bill, when he gave an assurance that the test to be applied by the authorising officer was intended to be the same as that applied by the Commissioner—

> 'While some mention is made by the noble Lord of an objective test, what the clause requires is that the authorising officer be satisfied. If that

judgment is to be scrutinised by the Commissioner, it is difficult to see how any less information would require to be available for the officer to be satisfied than for him to reasonably believe a certain view. Indeed, the whole structure of the clause requires authorising officers to proceed on a reasonable basis. If they fail to do so and complaints are made, the Commissioner will undoubtedly intervene; equally, in the absence of any complaint, he will deal with such a matter in the reports he is required to make.'[2]

1 See para 4.63.
2 HL Committee, 26 November 1996, col 232.

Alternative methods of surveillance

4.45 Authorisation is not to be given unless the action is 'necessary' (s 93(2)(a)), and unless the specified objective 'cannot reasonably be achieved by other means' (s 93(2)(b)). Clearly, if the relevant information can be obtained through ordinary policing methods, then this test will not be satisfied. However, advances in police technology have produced a range of technical devices which are nowadays capable of eavesdropping without the necessity for an officer to enter a premises or a vehicle physically.[1] None of these methods are regulated by the 1997 Act, for the simple reason that they do not involve an 'interference' with property. Thus, in principle at least, it is only if none of these methods can produce the necessary level of intrusion that officers will need to resort to the authorisation procedure. But what happens if a particular force has insufficient resources to purchase the necessary technology? It would appear that the wording of s 93(2)(b) ('*reasonably* be achieved by other means') is wide enough to permit authorisation of an entry onto property on the grounds that more costly methods of surveillance are not immediately available.

1 See para 4.33.

Substantial value

4.46 The authorising officer must believe that the information will be 'of substantial value' (s 93(2)(a)) in the prevention or detection or serious crime. This obviously begs the question of how important the information must be to an investigation before an authorisation to enter private property should be granted. During the Committee Stage of the Bill, a Labour amendment was tabled which sought to restrict the circumstances in which authorisations would be granted, by replacing these words 'of substantial value' with the word 'necessary'. Replying for the Government, the Lord Chancellor pointed out that—

> 'these are primarily intelligence-gathering operations against sometimes elusive and certainly very difficult criminals to track down and to get evidence against. It would be very difficult for an authorising officer to be sure that the action he is authorising will ultimately lead to the prevention or detection of serious crime. What he can be satisfied of, however—and again this will be subject to scrutiny—is that the action is likely to be of substantial value in the investigation process in which he is engaged.'[1]

1 HL Committee, 26 November 1996, col 233.

4.47 The amendment was withdrawn following an assurance that the requirement for proportionality of response would be addressed in the Code of Practice issued under s 101.[1] Clause 2.2 of the draft Code provides—

> 'A person giving an authorisation should satisfy themselves that the degree of intrusion into the privacy of those affected by the surveillance is commensurate with the seriousness of the offence. This is especially the case where the subject of the surveillance might reasonably assume a high degree of privacy, for instance in their houses.'

1 See paras 4.115–4.116.

Prevention or detection

4.48 In focusing attention on the 'prevention or detection' of crime, rather than the prosecution of crime, s 93(2)(a) follows the wording of the Interception of Communications Act 1985, s 2(2). In *R v Preston*[1] the House of Lords held that the product of a telephone intercept obtained under the 1985 Act is inadmissible in evidence in criminal proceedings. It was thus unnecessary for the 1985 Act to cater for the use of such material in the course of a prosecution, or for its disclosure as unused material to the defence. Indeed, s 6 of the 1985 Act makes specific provision for the destruction of the product of an intercept when it is no longer necessary for the prevention or detection of crime.

1 [1994] 2 AC 130, [1993] 4 All ER 638, HL.

4.49 The 1997 Act, by contrast, contains no statutory prohibition on the use of such material in evidence. On the contrary, it is clear that intrusive surveillance evidence obtained under the Act is intended to be admissible in criminal proceedings.[1] During the Committee Stage of the Bill, the Lord Chancellor was at pains to point out that evidence obtained from intrusive surveillance *might* never see the light of day in a criminal trial—

> 'In some instances that one can imagine, the authorisation having been used and some information obtained, evidence will then be recovered from other sources, the accused or defendant will stand trial, and he may be prosecuted or convicted in court without anyone being aware of the existence of the authorisation.'[2]

1 As to the position under the Home Office Guidelines, see para 4.7.
2 HL Committee, 26 November 1996, col 225.

4.50 Later in the debates however, the Lord Chancellor acknowledged that the product of an authorisation under the 1997 Act might well be introduced into evidence, and was for that reason prima facie discloseable to the defence in criminal proceedings, subject of course to a public interest immunity application to the judge—

> 'There is a fundamental difference between the provisions of this Bill and the provisions of the Interception of Communications Act 1985. Unlike the provisions of the latter Act, there is no statutory bar in this Bill on the evidential use of surveillance material in court proceedings,

nor is there any prohibition on its disclosure in accordance with the provisions of the recently enacted Criminal Procedure and Investigations Act 1996. This is an important factor to be borne in mind. It means that if material obtained by the police may be relevant to a criminal investigation it must be retained and made available to the prosecutor who will consider it for disclosure to the accused. That means that it would be wrong to place in the hands of an authorising officer a decision which may give rise to an argument on the part of an accused or a defendant that his rights at trial have been prejudiced.'[1]

1 HL Committee, 26 November 1996, col 251.

Serious crime

4.51 The definition of 'serious crime' is set out in s 93(4) of the 1997 Act—

'conduct which constitutes one or more offences shall be regarded as serious crime if, and only if,—

(a) it involves the use of violence, results in substantial financial gain, or is conduct by a large number of persons in pursuit of a common purpose, or

(b) the offence or one of the offences is an offence for which a person who has attained the age of twenty-one and has no previous convictions could reasonably be expected to be sentenced to imprisonment for a term of three years or more'.

4.52 The wording of this section follows that of the Interception of Communications Act 1985, s 10(3) and the Intelligence Services Act 1994, s 5(3B).[1] Significantly, the three year sentence qualification is shorter than the period required for an offence to qualify as an arrestable offence under PACE, s 24. Despite its long pedigree, this statutory definition of 'serious crime' was the subject of intense opposition during the passage of the Bill on the ground that it permitted intrusive surveillance in connection with offences which would not be regarded as serious by the general public. Lord Browne-Wilkinson in particular pointed to the fact that it was wide enough to encompass most organised protest groups—

'Suppose Mr A is one of a large number of protesters against making a new road; for example, the Newbury bypass. The form of the protest, as in all these cases, is likely to involve the commission of a crime; for example criminal damage to property or obstruction of the police. Such crime will, to some eyes—surprisingly—constitute a serious crime within the meaning of the Bill, because it is a large number of persons acting together.'[2]

1 As amended by the Security Service Act 1996, s 2.
2 HL 2R, 11 November 1996, cols 811, 812.

4.53 In order to meet this concern the Labour Peer Lord McIntosh of Haringey tabled an amendment which would have required the two limbs of the definition to be read conjunctively, so that an offence would only qualify as serious crime if it attracted a sentence of three years or more *and* involved violence, substantial financial gain, or the pursuit of a common purpose by a large number of persons—

> 'Those two parts of the definition, joined, as they are, by the word 'or' result in a definition of serious crime which defies common language . . . Unless [the common purpose criterion] is linked with a definition of serious crime which includes the provision of a reasonable expectation of a sentence of imprisonment of three years or more, it clearly extends the definition of serious crime beyond common language and beyond common sense.'[1]

[1] HL Committee, 26 November 1996, col 236.

4.54 The amendment was resisted by the Government on the ground that the wording of s 93(4) had the advantage of consistency with the previous legislation, the object of which was to combat organised crime that is 'notoriously difficult to define'. In support of this position, the Lord Chancellor pointed to an example of an offence which is plainly serious, but which would fall within only one limb of the statutory definition—

> 'Perhaps one may imagine a disgruntled employee who threatens to contaminate a product of his former employer. The motivation of such an employee need not involve any use of violence, need not result in any substantial financial gain, and need not be conducted in association with anybody else. The intention might be to give ample warning that the product had been contaminated with a view to all the potential products affected being destroyed. On any view, that would be regarded as serious crime.'[1]

This example is undoubtedly a persuasive argument in favour of permitting intrusive surveillance in connection with offences that fall within the second part of the statutory definition, but do not fall within the first. But it is no answer to the complaint that intrusive surveillance should not be permissible in relation to a series of minor offences, whether or not they are committed pursuant to a common purpose. As Lord Browne-Wilkinson pointed out,[2] the obvious example is that of organised protest, where the offences involved, taken individually, are usually of a comparatively trivial nature. The answer may simply be that the Government intended Chief Constables to have the power to conduct intrusive surveillance against organised political protesters and militant trade unionists, whose activities involve the incitement or commission of a large number of offences by different individuals which, though not serious in themselves, when taken together would pose a threat to public order. If that is so, then it may have been helpful if the Government had acknowledged this in the debates, so that the statutory intention was made clear. As matters stand it is difficult to predict whether the Commissioners will give their approval to authorisations aimed at subversive political activity involving only minor offences. On the one hand the wording of the 1997 Act is wide enough to encompass this, but on the other hand paragraph 2.2 of the Draft Code of Practice makes it clear that the degree of intrusion must be 'commensurate with the seriousness of the offence'.[3]

[1] HL Committee, 26 November 1996, col 237.
[2] See para 4.52.
[3] See para 4.47.

PROCEDURE AND DURATION

4.55 An application for authorisation may be made by an officer of any rank, providing he is a member of the relevant police force or agency. If the authorising officer approves the application, then the approval must be given in writing (s 95(1)). The only exception to this requirement is that an authorising officer may, in an urgent case, give authorisation orally for up to 72 hours. Authorisations given by a designated deputy under the delegation provisions in s 94[1] must always be given in writing (s 95(1)).

1 See paras 4.36–4.38.

4.56 An authorisation will ordinarily remain in force for a period of up to three months (s 95(2)(b)).[1] However, a maximum period of 72 hours is permitted where the authorisation has been given orally by an authorising officer, and where any authorisation has been given by a designated deputy within the meaning of s 94(4) or by a senior officer under s 94(2) (s 95(2)(a)).

1 This compares to a period of one month in the Netherlands (Art 125 Penal Code) and in the United States (18 US 2518).

4.57 At any time before an authorisation would otherwise cease to have effect, the authorising officer may extend the period of the authorisation for three months, beginning with the day on which it would cease to have effect (s 95(3)). Thus, the authorising officer may extend a 72 hour authorisation to three months, providing this is done within the 72 hour period. Similarly, he may extend a three month authorisation up to six months. In either case, the extension is only to be given if the authorising officer considers it necessary for the authorisation to continue to have effect for the purpose for which it was issued. The authorising officer is under a statutory obligation to cancel any authorisation or extension if he is satisfied that it is no longer necessary (s 95(4)).

4.58 In the Metropolitan Police district, the powers of extension and cancellation may be exercised by the Assistant Commissioner and in the Royal Ulster Constabulary they may be exercised by the Deputy Chief Constable (s 95(6)). In other forces and agencies covered by the Act they may be exercised by a designated deputy in the absence of the authorising officer (s 95(7)). Otherwise, both powers must be exercised by the authorising officer personally. In particular, they may not be delegated to a senior officer in accordance with s 94(2).

4.59 Any approval, renewal or cancellation given under Pt III of the 1997 Act, whether by an authorising officer, a designated deputy, or another senior officer, must be notified in writing to a Commissioner, as soon as is reasonably practicable (s 96). The contents of such a notice must specify the following information—

(a) whether the authorisation is one which requires the prior approval of a Commissioner under s 97[1] (s 96(3)(a)); and

(b) where the prior approval has not been obtained for an authorisation falling within s 97, the grounds upon which the case is believed to be one of urgency (s 96(3)(b)).

1 See paras 4.62–4.64.

THE FUNCTIONS OF THE COMMISSIONERS

4.60 Section 91 provides for the appointment by the Prime Minister of a Chief Commissioner, and such other number of Commissioners as the Prime Minister thinks fit. Commissioners must hold, or have held, high judicial office within the meaning of the Appellate Jurisdiction Act 1876, s 25.[1] They are to hold office for a period of three years (s 91(4)), but may be reappointed (s 91(5)). Removal from office generally requires a resolution of both Houses of Parliament (s 91(6)). However, a Commissioner may be removed by the Prime Minister if he has been adjudged bankrupt, has been disqualified from being a company director, or has been convicted of a criminal offence and sentenced to imprisonment (s 91(7)).

1 Ie, they must be, or have been, appointed to the High Court, the Court of Appeal or the House of Lords.

4.61 Allowances are to be paid to Commissioners at such rate as the Secretary of State considers appropriate (s 91(8)). The Secretary of State is also under a duty to provide the Commissioners with sufficient staff to enable them to discharge their functions (s 91(9)).

Authorisations requiring the prior approval of a Commissioner

4.62 Section 96 requires that notification must be given in writing to a Commissioner as soon as is reasonably practicable after an authorising officer, a designated deputy or another senior officer has given, renewed or cancelled an authorisation under Pt III of the 1997 Act. Certain authorisations generally require the prior approval of a Commissioner under s 97, namely—

- (a) where the property specified in the authorisation is used wholly or mainly as a dwelling, or as a bedroom in a hotel (s 97(2)(a)(i));[1]
- (b) where the property specified in the authorisation constitutes office premises (s 97(2)(a)(ii));[2]
- (c) where the action authorised is likely to result in any person acquiring knowledge of matters subject to legal professional privilege (s 97(2)(b)(i));
- (d) where the action authorised is likely to result in any person acquiring knowledge of confidential personal information (s 97(2)(b)(ii));
- (e) where the action authorised is likely to result in any person acquiring knowledge of confidential journalistic material (s 97(2)(b)(iii)).

1 A hotel is defined as 'a premises used for the reception of guests who desire to sleep on the premises' (s 97(8)).

2 The term 'office premises' has the meaning given in the Offices, Shops and Railway Premises Act 1963, s 1(2) (s 97(8)).

4.63 If the authorising officer *believes* that the authorisation falls within one of the categories specified above, the notice under s 96 must state that s 97 applies. When a Commissioner receives such a notice, he is under a duty to decide whether to give or withhold approval as soon as is reasonably practicable (s 97(4)). This applies to renewals as well as initial authorisations. The Commissioner must determine whether there are reasonable grounds for believing[1] the matters specified in s 93(2).[2] If, but only if, the Commissioner considers that reasonable grounds exist, he may approve the authorisation or renewal (s 97(5)). The requirement for reasonable grounds implies that a Commissioner should only approve an authorisation or renewal if there is some objective evidence on which the authorising officer has based his belief.[3]

1 As to the apparent conflict between this test and the test laid down in s 93(2) for the granting of an authorisation by an authorising officer ('where the authorising officer believes') see para 4.44.
2 See para 4.43.
3 See para 4.44.

4.64 Having decided whether to give or withhold approval, the Commissioner must give written notice of the decision to the authorising officer as soon as is reasonably practicable (s 97(4)(b)). If the Commissioner has refused approval then he must make a report of his findings to the authorising officer (s 97(6)). The authorising officer then has a right of appeal to the Chief Commissioner under s 104.[1]

1 See para 4.106.

Protected material

4.65 Section 97 of the 1997 Act follows PACE, ss 9–14, in providing a special regime of protection for legally privileged information, confidential information and journalistic material. Under the 1997 Act all three categories of information are treated in the same way. Where it is likely that intrusive surveillance will result in any person acquiring knowledge of such information then the prior approval of a Commissioner is necessary before an authorisation can take effect.

4.66 The categories of protected material (privileged, confidential and journalistic material) mirror the categories which are subject to the special procedure for obtaining search warrants under PACE, ss 9–14, Sch 9. Under the 1984 Act an application which affects material of this kind must be made to a circuit judge on notice to the person affected. The judge then has the opportunity to balance the competing arguments in favour of, and against, disclosure. In the event that there are disputed questions of fact at stake, he may hear evidence on oath. Under the 1997 Act, by contrast, the Commissioner deciding the question will only have the benefit of one side of the argument. There is no provision for the hearing of evidence on oath. The question of whether to give or refuse approval is to be resolved by representations alone. If an authorising officer asserts that the material which he seeks does not attract the protection of s 97, or that the protection should be overridden in the particular circumstances, then it may be very difficult for the Commissioner to test the factual basis for that assertion.[1]

1 But see para 4.91.

Matters subject to legal professional privilege

4.67 Section 98 defines legal professional privilege by reference to four categories of information—

(a) communications between a lawyer and his client, or any person representing his client, which are made in connection with the giving of legal advice to the client (s 98(2));

(b) communications between a lawyer and his client which are made for the purpose of existing or contemplated legal proceedings (s 98(3)(a));
(c) communications between a lawyer (or his client) and any third party which are made for the purpose of existing or contemplated legal proceedings (s 98(3)(b));
(d) any item enclosed with, or referred to, in communications which fall within any of the previous categories (s 98(4)).

4.68 This definition follows the statutory definition of legal professional privilege in PACE, s 10.[1] The absolute nature of legal professional privilege was recently re-emphasised in *R v Derby Magistrates' Court, ex p B*,[2] where the House of Lords held that the courts had no power to order disclosure of a privileged document in any circumstances, in the absence of a waiver of privilege by the client. In his speech in *ex p B*, Lord Taylor CJ pointed out that the UK was, in any event, obliged to protect the confidentiality of the lawyer/client relationship under the European Convention on Human Rights.[3] The European Court of Human Rights has held that Article 6 of the Convention (the right to a fair trial) and Article 8 (the right to privacy) require strict rules protecting the confidentiality of communications between an accused person and his lawyer.[4]

1 The definition in s 10 of PACE has been said by the House of Lords to be consistent with the position at common law: *R v Central Criminal Court, ex p Francis & Francis (a firm)* [1989] AC 346, [1988] 3 All ER 775, per Lord Goff.
2 [1996] 1 AC 487, [1995] 4 All ER, 526.
3 Ibid at 507H.
4 *Golder v United Kingdom* (1975) 1 EHRR 524; *McCallum v United Kingdom* (1990) 13 EHRR 597; *Schoenberger and Durmaz v Switzerland* (1988) 11 EHRR 202; *S v Switzerland* (1991) 14 EHRR 670; *Campbell v United Kingdom* (1992) 15 EHRR 137.

4.69 At common law, legal professional privilege does not extend to material in the possession of a person who is not entitled to it. Neither does it extend to communications or items held by a lawyer for the purpose of furthering a criminal purpose.[1] These two common law exceptions are preserved by s 98(5). Thus, in a case where apparently privileged information is believed by the authorising officer to be held by a solicitor for the purpose of furthering a client's criminal activities, the authorising officer need not seek the prior approval of a Commissioner before carrying out intrusive surveillance of the solicitor's office. It is perfectly logical for the 1997 Act to follow the common law definition of privilege. However, the inclusion of s 98(5) creates a gap in the statutory protection and is open to potential abuse. Commissioners would be unlikely to give approval for eavesdropping on a solicitor's office simply in order to gain access to privileged information on the legitimate preparation of a criminal defence. The possibility of conducting intrusive surveillance of a solicitor's office will tend to arise only when the authorising officer suspects that the lawyer/client relationship is being abused for a criminal purpose. So the effect of s 98(5) is that it is precisely when surveillance of a solicitor's office is most likely to occur that the prior approval of a Commissioner becomes unnecessary.

1 *R v Cox and Railton* (1884) 14 QBD 153.

4.70 There is obvious potential for abuse of this exception and care will have to be taken to ensure that it is restrictively applied. In order for communications to lose the protection of privilege there must be *prima facie* evidence of an intention for legal advice to be obtained (or given) in furtherance of a criminal purpose.[1] The exception applies if the legal adviser is aware of, or is a party to, the criminal purpose, but not if he merely volunteers a warning to his client that certain conduct could result in a prosecution.[2] If neither the legal adviser nor the client are aware of the improper purpose, but there is a third party who is manipulating the lawyer-client relationship for criminal purposes, then the exception *may* apply. In *R v Central Criminal Court, ex p Francis & Francis (a firm)*,[3] the majority of the House of Lords held that no privilege attached to documents relating to the purchase of a property while innocently held by a solicitor, because a third party (a relative of the client) intended them to be used to further his criminal purpose in laundering the proceeds of illegal drug trafficking.

1 *O'Rourke v Darbishire* [1920] AC 581.
2 *Butler v Board of Trade* [1971] Ch 680.
3 [1988] QB 532.

4.71 In deciding whether given communications fall outside the protection of legal professional privilege, close attention should be paid by the Commissioners to the actual communications themselves.[1] This principle would not necessarily prevent an initial surveillance of a solicitor's office, although clearly an authorising officer would need some other form of *prima facie* evidence before any authorisation could be justified.[2] However, when a Commissioner is asked to give or renew approval of an authorisation, he should examine the relevant communications and decide whether they constitute an abuse of privilege. In order to discharge this function, a commissioner should, at the very least, be given the gist of all the surveillance material previously collected, and should read or listen to the specific parts of a surveillance recording which the authorising officer seeks to rely upon in order to continue the covert operation. A simple summary of the allegedly incriminating extracts of a covert recording would not suffice, because a commissioner would be denied the opportunity to consider the context in which such communications were being made.

1 *R v Governor of Pentonville Prison, ex p Osman* [1990] 1 WLR 277.
2 *O'Rourke v Darbishire* [1920] AC 581.

Confidential personal information

4.72 The inclusion of confidential personal information, as a category for which prior approval is needed for surveillance to be carried out, reflects the increasing importance which the law attaches to the right to personal privacy. The categories of information regarded as confidential under the 1997 Act are, however, significantly narrower than the common law categories.

4.73 At common law the tort of breach of confidence protects any information which is obtained or held subject to a duty of confidentiality. The disclosure of such information may be restrained by injunction. For an action in breach of confidence to lie, three conditions must be satisfied—[1]

(a) the information must have the necessary quality of confidence about it and must not have been published previously;
(b) the information must have been acquired in circumstances which impose an obligation of confidence;[2] and
(c) there must be an unauthorised use of the information to the detriment of the plaintiff.

1 *Malone v Metropolitan Police Comr (No 2)* [1979] Ch 344,[1979] 2 All ER 620.
2 For a prima facie duty of confidentiality to be imposed it is not necessary for the information to have been intentionally communicated, or for it to have been acquired subject to an express or implied promise to keep it confidential. Accidental disclosure of obviously confidential information imposes a duty of confidentiality on the recipient: *A-G v Guardian Newspapers (No 2)* [1990] 1 AC 109, [1988] 3 All ER 545, HL.

4.74 The duty to preserve confidentiality, even in civil proceedings, is not absolute. Unlike legal professional privilege, which cannot be set aside without the consent of the client,[1] confidential information will lose the protection of the law if there is a strong public interest in favour of its disclosure.[2] Thus, doctors and priests can be compelled to disclose information imparted in the surgery or the confessional.

1 *R v Derby Magistrates' Court ex p B* [1996] AC 487, [1995] 4 All ER, 526.
2 *A-G v Guardian Newspapers (No 2)* [1990] AC 109.

4.75 The common law rules are flexible and judges have been willing to extend the categories of confidential information to include material in the possession of law enforcement agencies such as the police. In *Hellewell v Chief Constable of Derbyshire*[1] Laws J held that a duty of confidence arose where the police photographed a suspect without his consent at a police station, such that any subsequent disclosure had to be justified as being in the public interest. In that case the limited circulation to local shopkeepers of a 'mugshot' of a persistent offender was held to be justified by reference to the public interest in the prevention of crime. But in the course of his judgment Laws J suggested *obiter* that the law of confidence would also protect confidential personal information obtained by means of long distance surveillance—

> 'If someone with a telephoto lens were to take from a distance and with no authority a picture of another engaged in some private act, his subsequent disclosure of the photograph would, in my judgment, as surely amount to a breach of confidence as if he had found or stolen a letter or diary in which the act was recounted and proceeded to publish it. In such a case, the law would protect what might reasonably be called a right of privacy, although the name accorded to the cause of action would be breach of confidence. It is, of course, elementary that, in all such cases, a defence based on the public interest would be available.'[2]

1 [1995] 4 All ER 473, [1995] 1 WLR 804.
2 Ibid at 476.

4.76 By contrast, the categories of information which are classified as confidential for the purposes of the prior approval requirement in s 97 are strictly limited and closely defined. Three conditions must be satisfied—[1]

(a) the information must have been acquired in the course of a trade, business, profession, or other occupation, or for the purpose of a paid or unpaid office (s 99(1)(a));
(b) it must relate to the physical or mental health of an identifiable individual, or to spiritual counselling or assistance given to him or her (s 99(2)); and
(c) it must have been acquired subject to an express or implied undertaking to hold it in confidence, or subject to a statutory restriction on disclosure (s 99(3)).

1 Cf, PACE, s 12.

4.77 The 1997 Act consequently requires the prior approval of a Commissioner before intrusive surveillance is carried out on the premises of a doctor, a counsellor or a priest. But it does not require prior approval in relation to any of the other categories of confidential information which are protected by the general law of confidence, such as credit status, financial information or personal diaries. The 1997 Act certainly does not require prior approval in relation to the taking of photographs of a person 'engaged in some private act'[1] or the recording of information relating to personal and sexual relationships.

1 Per Laws J in *Hellewell v Chief Constable of Derbyshire* [1995] 4 All ER 473, [1975] 1 WLR 804; see para 4.75.

Confidential journalistic material

4.78 The need to preserve the confidentiality of a journalist's sources has long been recognised as an important element in the protection of a free press in a democratic society.[1] Nevertheless, the Courts in this country retain the power to compel journalists to reveal their sources under the Contempt of Court Act 1981, s 10. Before examining the limited protection afforded under the 1997 Act, it is helpful to set out the background to the existing statutory protection of journalistic sources. This again is an area which depends heavily on the provisions of the European Convention on Human Rights.

1 See *British Steel Corpn v Granada Television* [1981] AC 1096, [1981] 1 All ER 417, HL.

4.79 Article 10 of the Convention provides—

> '1. Everyone has the right to freedom of expression. This right shall include the freedom to hold opinions and to receive and impart information and ideas without interference by public authority . . .
>
> 2. The exercise of these freedoms, since it carries with it duties and responsibilities, may be subject to such formalities, conditions, restrictions or penalties as are prescribed by law and are necessary in a democratic society, in the interests of national security, territorial integrity or public safety, for the prevention of disorder or crime, for the protection of health or morals, for the protection of the reputation or rights of others, for preventing the disclosure of information received in confidence, or for maintaining the authority and impartiality of the judiciary.'

4.80 In *Sunday Times v United Kingdom*[1] the European Court of Human Rights held that the English law of contempt of court, as it then stood, was too wide to satisfy the requirements of Article 10. As a result of this ruling, the Government enacted the Contempt of Court Act 1981, s 10, which provides—

> 'No court may require a person to disclose, nor is any person guilty of contempt of court for refusing to disclose, the source of information contained in a publication for which he is responsible, unless it be established to the satisfaction of the court that disclosure is necessary in the interests of justice or national security or for the prevention of disorder or crime.'

1 (1979) 2 EHRR 245.

4.81 The protection afforded by s 10 of the 1981 Act has not always been found sufficient to satisfy the requirements of Article 10 of the Convention.[1] In general however, the section creates a strong presumption in favour of protecting journalistic sources and places a heavy burden on a party seeking disclosure to displace that presumption. In *Secretary of State for Defence v Guardian Newspapers*[2] a copy of a classified document concerning the arrival of cruise missiles at Greenham Common was leaked to The Guardian, which published it. The Ministry of Defence sought an order for recovery of the photocopy in order to determine the identity of the informant. The House of Lords ruled that the protection afforded by s 10 applied, so as to place a burden on the party seeking disclosure to show that this was *necessary* for one of the statutory purposes, and not merely expedient.

1 See for example *Goodwin v United Kingdom* (1996) 22 EHRR 123.
2 [1985] 1 AC 339, [1984] 3 All ER 601, HL.

4.82 There is no doubt that the powers of intrusive surveillance provided by the 1997 Act pose a considerable threat to the confidentiality of journalistic sources. In its original form the Bill made no special provision for this category of material, leaving it to the discretion of the authorising officer. During the early Parliamentary debates it was repeatedly pointed out that the bugging of newspaper's offices would enable the authorities to circumvent the protection of journalistic sources which is provided by s 10, and would in all probability, lead to violations of Article 10 of the Convention. In *Goodwin v United Kingdom*[1] the European Court of Human Rights laid down the following principle on the application of Article 10—

> 'The Court recalls that freedom of expression constitutes one of the essential foundations of a democratic society and that the safeguards to be afforded to the press are of particular importance. Protection of journalistic sources is one of the basic conditions for press freedom . . . without such protection, sources may be deterred from assisting the press in informing the public on matters of public interest. As a result the vital public watchdog role of the press may be undermined and the ability of the press to provide accurate and reliable information may be adversely affected. Having regard to the importance of the protection of journalistic sources for press freedom in a democratic society, and the potentially chilling effect an order of source disclosure has on the exercise of that freedom, such a measure cannot be compatible with Article 10 of the Convention, unless it is justified by an overriding requirement in the public interest.'

1 (1996) 22 EHRR 123, at para 39.

4.83 As a result of concerns expressed during the debates, s 97(2)(b)(iii) was introduced, which includes confidential journalistic material in the list of categories requiring prior judicial approval before an authorisation takes effect. Section 100 defines such material as 'material acquired or created for the purposes of journalism' which—

(a) is being held for the purposes of journalism (s 100(1)(a)(i));
(b) is held subject to an express or implied undertaking to hold it in confidence, or is subject to a statutory restriction on disclosure (s 100(1)(a)(ii)); and
(c) which has been continuously held subject to such an undertaking, restriction or obligation since it was created or acquired (s 100(1)(a)(iii)).

4.84 The wording of s 100 of the 1997 Act can be compared with s 13 of PACE. The 1984 Act also affords special protection to this type of material which provides considerably greater protection than the 1997 Act. Section 14 of PACE provides that ordinary searching procedures are not to have effect in relation to journalistic material (other than material excluded under s 11 of that Act) and creates a special procedure for obtaining a warrant from a circuit judge. Where the journalistic material qualifies as 'confidential', it is immune from an ordinary search warrant and the interested party has a right to be heard before an order is made.[1] The 1997 Act thus provides a means by which the police can gain access to confidential journalistic materials which is not available to them under the 1984 Act. This aspect of the 1997 Act undoubtedly has the potential to give rise to violations of Article 10 of the European Convention on Human Rights.[2]

1 See PACE, s 9, Sch 1, para 7.
2 See paras 4.79–4.82.

4.85 There is no statutory definition of the term 'journalism' in either the 1984 Act or the 1997 Act. It clearly encompasses material intended for publication in a periodical of any kind. Does the definition also apply to books, pamphlets or internet communications? There is no clear answer to this question, but it is submitted that the decisive criterion should be an intention to publish the material. It would be wholly illogical if a journalist collecting material for an exposè of Government misconduct were to be protected by s 97 if the material was intended for publication in a series of newspaper articles, but not if it were intended for publication in a book. At the time the material is being collected, the journalist may not even know where or in what form it is to be published.

Cases of urgency

4.86 Section 97(3) creates another major loophole in the statutory scheme. The requirement to seek prior approval from a Commissioner before conducting intrusive surveillance on a person's home, a hotel or a business premises, or in relation to privileged, confidential or journalistic material, does not apply if the person giving the authorisation believes that the case is one of urgency. In such a case, surveillance may be carried out on the authority of the authorising officer alone.

4.87 Where this course has been followed there remains a limited measure of independent scrutiny provided by the Commissioners. The notice required under s 96[1] must state whether or not s 97 applies to the authorisation (s 96(3)(a)). If prior approval was not obtained, the notice must also state why the case was believed to be one of urgency (s 96(3)(b)). On receiving the notice, the Commissioner may quash the authorisation if he is satisfied that there were no reasonable grounds for believing that the case was one of urgency which did not require prior approval (s 103(2)).[2]

1 See para 4.59 and 4.63.
2 By then of course the damage may already have been done: see para 4.92.

Quashing or cancellation of an authorisation

4.88 Where a notification under s 96 has been received by a Commissioner, he has the power to quash or cancel the authorisation or renewal under s 103. This power applies even if a Commissioner has given prior approval for an authorisation under s 97 (s 103(8)). The Commissioner can act on any one of three grounds.

No reasonable grounds

4.89 Under s 103(1) the Commissioner may quash any authorisation or renewal if he is satisfied that at the time it was given there were no reasonable grounds for believing that—

(a) the action to be taken is necessary and is likely to be of substantial value in the prevention or detection of serious crime (s 93(2)(a)); and
(b) what the action seeks to achieve cannot reasonably be achieved by other means (s 93(2)(b)).

4.90 In order to reach a decision on this ground, the Commissioner ought to require some objective evidence on which the authorising officer could have based his belief. The section is, however, unfortunately worded. Read literally, it creates a presumption that the authorisation is legitimate, which is only displaced if the Commissioner is 'satisfied' that no reasonable grounds existed. This suggests that if the Commissioner were genuinely in doubt, the authorisation should be upheld. Such a construction would be a clear violation of Article 8 of the Convention. Under Article 8 the necessity[1] for using secret surveillance must be subject to independent review by a body which is 'vested with sufficient powers and competence to exercise an effective and continuous control'.[2] The burden always rests on the state to justify an infringement of personal privacy, particularly where it is conducted by secret state surveillance. As the European Court of Human Rights pointed out in *Klass v Germany*—

> 'Powers of secret surveillance of citizens, characterising as they do the police state, are tolerable under the Convention only insofar as strictly necessary for safeguarding democratic institutions'.[3]

1 Article 8 requires any interference with the right to privacy to be 'necessary in a democratic society.' The term 'necessary' in this context has been strictly interpreted: *Klass v Germany* (1978) 2 EHRR 214 at p 215, para 42.
2 *Klass v Germany* (1978) ibid at p 215, paras 55, 56.
3 Ibid.

4.91 Since the wording of s 103(1) raises an issue of construction, Article 8 must be taken as a guiding principle in its interpretation. If the evidence before the Commissioner is inadequate or inconclusive, then he must have an implied power to require further information or to direct that further inquiries are carried out, in order to be able to perform his statutory function. The wording of the section obviously vests a wide discretion in the Commissioners as to the level and reliability of the information they require. This is a judicial discretion and as such it must be exercised with regard to the UK's obligations under Article 8. There is no provision within the 1997 Act for the hearing of evidence on oath, although this does not relieve the Commissioners of their duty to conduct a searching and anxious scrutiny where human rights are involved.[1] The adequacy of the entire system of supervision established under the 1997 Act will depend upon the standard of scrutiny that Commissioners choose to adopt.

1 See *R v Ministry of Defence, ex p Smith* [1996] 1 All ER 257; *Bugdaycay v Secretary of State for the Home Department* [1987] AC 514; *Vilvarajah v UK* [1991] 14 EHRR 248.

Where prior authorisation should have been obtained

4.92 Section 103(2) governs the power of the Commissioners to quash any authorisation or renewal to which s 97 does not apply (because the authorising officer did not *believe* that the criteria for prior authorisation were met). The Commissioner may quash such an authorisation or renewal if he is satisfied that prior approval should have been sought because at the time it was given or renewed—

(a) there were reasonable grounds for believing that the authorisation permitted surveillance on a person's home, hotel room or business premises, or in relation to privileged, confidential or journalistic material (s 103(2)(a)); and
(b) there were no reasonable grounds for believing the case to be one of urgency (s 103(2)(b)).

4.93 The wording of s 103(2) again suggests that it creates a presumption that the authorisation was valid. Thus, the observations made in relation to s 103(1)[1] above apply equally to s 103(2). However, there is a further lacuna in this provision. If, at the time of issuing the authorisation, the authorising officer correctly concludes that there are no reasonable grounds for believing any of the matters specified in s 97(2), but it subsequently transpires that the surveillance does in fact intrude upon a person's home, hotel room or business premises, or involves privileged, confidential or journalistic material, then s 103(2) does not grant the Commissioner a power to quash.

1 See para 4.90–4.91.

Where the surveillance criteria are no longer applicable

4.94 Section 103(4) allows the Commissioner to cancel an authorisation at any time if it becomes apparent that the criteria in s 93(2) are no longer satisfied. This power applies only to a change of circumstance relating to surveillance criteria. It does not apply to a change of circumstance in relation to the requirement for prior approval. In the absence of a duty on the authorising officer to make regular reports on the progress of an investigation, it is not clear how the Commissioner is to be made aware of the matters which would enable him to exercise this power.

4.95 Where a Commissioner quashes or cancels an authorisation or renewal under any of the powers set out above, he may order that the authorisation continue for a sufficient period to enable the retrieval of any equipment which has been left on the property (s 103(6)).

Destruction of records

4.96 Where a Commissioner has quashed an authorisation or renewal he may order the destruction of any record relating to information obtained by virtue of the authorisation or renewal (s 103(3)). In the case of a decision to quash a renewal, this power is confined to records which relate to information acquired after the authorisation was renewed. Where an authorisation has ceased to have effect without being quashed, either because it has lapsed or because it has been cancelled by the authorising officer, or by a Commissioner under s 103(4), the Commissioner may order the destruction of records if he is satisfied that at any time during the period of the authorisation there were no reasonable grounds for believing the matters specified in s 93(2) (s 103(5)). The power under s 103(5) is confined to the destruction of records relating to information obtained after the time that reasonable grounds ceased to exist.[1]

1 Obviously, if there were no such grounds from the beginning then the Commissioner is likely to have quashed the authorisation under s 103(1), so that the destruction powers would be governed by s 103(3). But in the event that the authorisation has, for any reason, not been quashed under that subsection the power to order destruction would extend to all information obtained.

4.97 An order to destroy records is subject to an exception where the records are required for pending criminal or civil proceedings (s 103(3), (5)). An order for destruction is not to take effect until the period for appealing the decision[1] has expired or, if an appeal has been made, until the appeal has been determined by the Chief Commissioner under s 104[2] (s 103(8)).

1 See para 4.112.
2 See para 4.105 et seq.

REPORTS

4.98 When a Commissioner exercises any power to quash or cancel an authorisation, or orders the destruction of records, he must make a report of his findings, as soon as reasonably practicable, to the authorising officer and to the Chief Commissioner (s 103(7)).

COMPLAINTS

4.99 The 1997 Act provides a system for determining complaints from members of the public who believe that they have been the subject of intrusive surveillance. It is to be noted that the 1997 Act does not cater for complaints about the manner in which surveillance is conducted. The Commissioners are not permitted to have regard to breaches of the Code of Practice issued under s 101 in exercising their function of adjudicating complaints (s 101(8)). Similarly, the 1997 Act fails to cater for complaints concerning unauthorised surveillance. The mechanism is confined to complaints concerning action taken in pursuance of an authorisation under s 93. The criteria for upholding such a complaint are identical to those which apply to the quashing or cancellation of an authorisation. Under s 102(1) the Commissioners are under an obligation to investigate any complaint which relates to surveillance on the complainant's home or place of work (s 102(2)), providing the complaint is not frivolous or vexatious (s 102(3)).

4.100 Schedule 7 governs the procedure for the making and determination of complaints. The Commissioner's first task is to determine whether or not there was a relevant authorisation (Sch 7, para 1). If the Commissioner finds that there was a relevant authorisation, he must make a determination in favour of the complainant if he is satisfied that—

(a) at the time when the authorisation was given or renewed, there were no reasonable grounds for believing that the criteria under s 93(2) were satisfied, namely that the action was necessary and would be of substantial value in the prevention or detection of serious crime, and that the objectives of the action could not reasonably be achieved by other means (Sch 7, para 2(2)); or
(b) in cases where prior approval was not obtained, there were reasonable grounds for believing any of the matters specified in s 97(2) and there were no reasonable grounds for believing that the case was one of urgency (Sch 7, para 2(3)); or
(c) the criteria in s 93(2) were fulfilled when the authorisation was granted but have ceased to be so following a change in circumstance, and action has been taken in relation to the property at any time after the criteria were no longer satisfied (Sch 7, para 2(4)).

4.101 Once the complaint has been determined, the Commissioner must serve a notice on the complainant stating whether or not the complaint was upheld (Sch 7, para 3(1)(a), (2)). He must not, however, give any reasons for his decision either way (Sch 7, para 3(3)). If the complaint has been upheld the Commissioner may direct the authorising officer to pay a specified sum in compensation (Sch 7, para 5(1)). This power arises whether or not the Commissioner has also exercised his power to quash or cancel an authorisation under s 103. The award of compensation is not to take effect until any appeal by the authorising officer has been dismissed, or the time for appealing has elapsed (Sch 7, para 5(2)). The authorising officer is to be indemnified for any sum paid in compensation from the appropriate police fund, service fund, or in the case of the Commissioners of Customs and Excise, by the Commissioners (Sch 7, para 6).

4.102 During the Committee stage of the Bill, Lord Lester of Herne Hill enquired whether the power to award compensation (which is strictly limited to loss) was to replace the court's current powers to award exemplary damages for oppressive, arbitrary or unconstitutional acts by Government servants.[1] The Lord Chancellor replied—

> 'As I understand the draftsman's intention, while it is clear that the decisions of the Commissioner should not be subject to appeal, or liable to be questioned in any court, the fact that payment of compensation is ordered by the Commissioner does not exclude any other remedies which an affected proprietor may have.'[2]

It seems to follow that if unlawful surveillance amounting to trespass has occurred, then the courts would have the power to award exemplary damages in an ordinary civil action. More importantly, if the courts were to take the step which the House of Lords all but took in *Khan*[3] and recognise the existence of a common law tort of breach of privacy, then it would in principle be open to an affected complainant to sue in private law for exemplary damages for unlawful surveillance. In practical terms, however, it would be extremely difficult, if not impossible, for a complainant to be able to prove that unlawful action had occurred.

1 *Rookes v Barnard* [1964] AC 1129, [1964] 1 All ER 367.
2 HL Committee, 26 November 1996, Col 228.
3 *R v Khan (Sultan)* [1997] AC 558.

4.103 Where a complaint has been upheld the Commissioner also has a duty to make a report of his findings to the authorising officer, and to the Chief Commissioner (Sch 7, para 3(1)(b)). If the authorising officer has not appealed against the decision, then the Chief Commissioner is to make a report under s 107(2) to the Prime Minister (Sch 7, para 4).

THE FUNCTIONS OF THE CHIEF COMMISSIONER

4.104 The principal role of the Chief Commissioner is to oversee the functioning of Pt III of the 1997 Act, and to review the performance by the Commissioners and the authorising officers (and their designated deputies) of their statutory functions (s 107(1)). More specifically the Chief Commissioner's functions include—

(a) hearing appeals from authorising officers under s 104;[1]
(b) establishing the system for complaints under s 102;[2]
(c) hearing appeals from unsuccessful complainants;[3]
(d) making an annual report on the work of the Commissioners to the Prime Minister and reporting at any time to the Prime Minister on any matter involving the Commissioner's functions (s 107(2)).[4]

1 See paras 4.105–4.112.
2 See para 4.99.
3 See para 4.113.
4 The annual report should be laid before Parliament but may exclude any matters which might be prejudicial to the prevention or detection of serious crime, or otherwise hamper the functions of police authorities, the Service Authorities of the NCIS or the NCS, or the duties of the Commissioners of Customs and Excise (s 107(3), (4)).

Appeals to the Chief Commissioner

4.105 The Chief Commissioner has the function of hearing appeals from authorising officers against the following decisions.

A refusal of prior authorisation under s 97 (s 104(1)(a))[1]

4.106 In determining an appeal from a refusal of prior authorisation under s 97, the Chief Commissioner must allow the appeal and direct the Commissioner to give approval if he is satisfied that there are reasonable grounds for believing the matters specified in s 93(2)[2] (s 104(3)). It should be noted that the wording of s 104(3) creates a presumption that the Commissioner's refusal was correct, which is displaced only if the authorising officer can satisfy the Chief Commissioner of the matters set out. Unlike the reverse presumption which appears in the wording of s 103(1),[3] the imposition of a burden on the authorising officer to satisfy the Chief Commissioner of the justification for approval involves no breach of the Convention.

1 See paras 4.62–4.64.
2 See para 4.90.
3 See para 4.43.

A decision to quash an authorisation under s 103(1) (s 104(1)(b))[1]

4.107 As above, the Chief Commissioner must allow an appeal against a decision to quash an authorisation under s 103(1) unless he is satisfied that at the time the authorisation was given or renewed there were no reasonable grounds for believing the matters specified in s 93(2)[2] (s 104(4)). The presumption, however, *operates the other way.* Section 104(4) requires the Chief Commissioner to allow the appeal unless he is satisfied that there were no reasonable grounds on which the authorising officer could have acted. In so far as this creates a presumption in favour of intrusive surveillance, the comments made in relation to s 103[3] apply. In cases of doubt the Chief Commissioner should conduct further inquiries to enable him to discharge his statutory duty. Where a Commissioner who quashes the original authorisation has also made an order for the destruction of records pursuant to s 103(3), and the Chief Commissioner allows the authorising officer's appeal, he must also quash the order for destruction (s 104(8)(a)).

1 See para 4.89.
2 See para 4.43.
3 See para 4.90.

A decision to quash an authorisation under s 103(2) (s 104(1)(c))[1]

4.108 The Chief Commissioner must allow an appeal against a decision to quash an authorisation under s 103(2) unless he is satisfied that prior approval should have been sought, because at the time that the authorisation was given or renewed—

(a) there were reasonable grounds for believing that the authorisation permitted surveillance on a person's home, a hotel or business premises, or in relation to privileged, confidential or journalistic material (s 103(2)(a)); and
(b) there were no reasonable grounds for believing the case to be one of urgency (s 103(2)(b)).[2]

Again, the wording of s 104(5) appears to create a presumption in favour of intrusive surveillance, and the comments made in relation to s 103[3] apply. As with s 104(4), where a Commissioner quashes the authorisation and makes an order for the destruction of records, if the authorising officer's appeal is allowed, then the destruction order is to be quashed.

1 See para 4.92.
2 Section 104(5).
3 See para 4.90.

A decision to cancel an authorisation under s 103(4) (s 104(1)(d))[1] *or to order the destruction of records under s 103(5) (s 104(1)(e))*[2]

4.109 The Chief Commissioner must allow the appeal unless he is satisfied that at the time to which the decision relates, there were no reasonable grounds for believing the matters specified in s 93(2) (s 104(6)). Similarly, the wording of s 104(6) suggests that there must be positive grounds before the Chief Commissioner should interfere.[3]

1 See paras 4.94, 4.95.
2 See para 4.96.
3 See para 4.90.

A refusal to continue the authorisation to enable equipment to be removed under s 103(6) (s 104(1)(f))[1]

4.110 The Chief Commissioner must allow the appeal and order that the authorisation is to be effective for this purpose, for such period as he may specify, if he is satisfied that there are reasonable grounds for making such an order (s 104(7)). The authorising officer must satisfy the Chief Commissioner that there are reasonable grounds for a temporary continuation.

1 See para 4.95.

A determination in favour of a complainant under Sch 7 (s 104(1)(g))[1]

4.111 The criteria for allowing an authorising officer's appeal against a Commissioner's determination upholding a complaint are the same as those which apply to an appeal against a Commissioner's decision to quash an authorisation under s 103(1) or (2), to cancel an authorisation under s 103 (4) or to order the destruction of records under s 103(5) (s 104(4)(b), (5)(b), (6)(b)). Where the Commissioner who has determined a complaint in favour of the complainant has also made an award of compensation, then if the Chief Commissioner allows the authorising officer's appeal against the determination of the complaint he is also to quash any direction to pay compensation to the complainant (s 104(8)(b)).

1 See paras 4.99–4.103.

4.112 All such appeals must be brought by the authorising officer or his designated deputy (s 105(3)) within seven days of the day on which the decision appealed against is notified to the authorising officer (s 104(2)). Where the Chief Commissioner has determined an authorising officer's appeal he is to give notice of his decision to the authorising officer (s 105(1)(a)), to the Commissioner appealed against (s 105(1)(a)(ii)) and to the complainant in the case of an appeal against a determination of a complaint under s 102 (s 105(1)(a)(iii)). The notice is not to specify any reasons for the decision (s 105(2)), but if the Chief Commissioner has dismissed the appeal, he is to make a report of his findings to the authorising officer (s 105(1)(b)(i)), the Commissioner concerned (s 105(1)(b)(ii)) and the Prime Minister (s 105(1)(b)(iii)).

Appeals by complainant

4.113 The Chief Commissioner also has the function of determining appeals from complainants whose complaints have been determined unfavourably. Where a complainant is notified under Sch 7, para 3(2)[1] that his complaint has not been upheld, he may appeal to the Chief Commissioner within seven days of the day on which he receives notification of the decision (s 106(1)). On considering such a complaint the Chief Commissioner has all the powers and duties conferred by Sch 7[2] on a Commissioner who is required to investigate a complaint (s 106(2)(a)), and all the powers to quash or cancel an authorisation or renewal and to order the destruction of records which are conferred on a Commissioner by s 103 (s 106(2)(b)).[3]

1 See para 4.101.
2 See paras 4.99–4.103.
3 See paras 4.88–4.95.

No further right of appeal

4.114 By s 91(10) the decision of the Chief Commissioner or (subject to appeals under ss 104, 105) that of any other Commissioner, cannot be appealed or questioned in any court of law.[1] Although this position would at first glance appear to remove the right of an effective remedy for a breach of other rights under the European Convention, it has been held that a system of Tribunals and independent Commissioners is sufficient to discharge the United Kingdom's responsibilities.[2]

1 There is a similar provision in the Interception of Communications Act 1985, s 7(8).
2 *Esbester v United Kingdom* (2 April 1993 18601/91); *Hewitt and Harman v United Kingdom* (No 2) (1 September 1993 20317/92) See para 4.17 below.

CODE OF PRACTICE

4.115 Under s 101 the Secretary of State must issue a Code of Practice to regulate the work of authorising officers. Such a Code should lay down guidelines for the application of the 1997 Act so that authorising officers know what is expected of them. The Code is only to be issued after a draft has been published, and the Secretary of State has considered any representations made on the draft, and modified the Code accordingly (s 101(2)). The draft Code is to be made public and laid before Parliament (s 101(3)). Once approved by a resolution of both Houses of Parliament, the Code may be brought into operation by statutory instrument (s 101(4), (5)).

4.116 All persons concerned in the process of intrusive surveillance, other than the Commissioners, are to have regard to the provisions of the Code in the performance of their functions (s 101(8)). The exclusion of the Commissioners from this requirement ensures that authorisations may not be quashed or cancelled, and complaints may not be upheld or compensation ordered, on the ground that the police or other agencies have acted in breach of the Code. Section 101(9) expressly provides that a failure on the part of any person to comply with any provision of the Code of Practice is not of itself to render him liable to any criminal or civil proceedings. This section follows the wording of PACE, s 67(10). The implication appears to be that a failure to comply with the terms of the 1997 Act itself would expose the person concerned to criminal or civil liability. But the effect is not so straightforward. Criminal liability would only be imposed if the manner in which the surveillance was carried out involved the commission of an offence such as criminal damage.[1] It is not the intention of Pt III of the 1997 Act to create new criminal offences. As far as civil liability is concerned, an interference with property which was not authorised under the 1997 Act would amount to trespass, even in the absence of s 101(9). However, by implicitly providing that a breach of the 1997 Act (as distinct from the Code of Practice) may impose civil liability, s 101(9) raises the possibility of an action for breach of statutory duty. Such an action has been permitted to proceed under the equivalent provisions of the 1984 Act.[2]

1 In *R v Khan* the Court of Appeal and the House of Lords proceeded on the assumption that the planting of a bugging device on private premises would involve an offence of criminal damage, of however technical a nature.

2 *Roques v Metropolitan Police Comr* (9 September 1995, unreported), Central London County Court.

4.117 Section 101(10) provides that the Code of Practice is to be admissible in evidence in any criminal or civil proceedings. Any provision of the Code may be taken into consideration if it appears to the court or tribunal conducting the proceedings that it is relevant to any question arising. The most obvious application of this provision would be in the course of a submission to exclude evidence under PACE, s 78. The House of Lords in *R v Khan*[1] held that in a case involving intrusive surveillance, a breach of the Convention would also be a material consideration to the exercise of the discretion under s 78. On the facts however, it was held that even in the absence of a statutory framework to regulate intrusive surveillance by the police, the admission of the evidence did not have such an adverse effect on the fairness of the proceedings that the court ought to have excluded it.

1 See para 4.9 et seq.

5 The Police Information Technology Organisation

INTRODUCTION

5.1 Every aspect of the 1997 Act—gathering and providing nationwide intelligence (Pt I), preventing and detecting serious crime (Pt II), electronic surveillance (Pt III), and certificates of criminal convictions (Pt V)—depends on information technology. Part IV, therefore puts the existing Police Information and Technology Organisation (PITO) on a statutory footing. While other parts of the Bill were the subject of controversial debate in Parliament, there were few references to PITO and those who spoke on Pt V did so essentially to express approval for the creation of an Organisation that would ensure the modernisation of police information technology (IT).[1]

1 The only parliamentary speech that specifically focused on the importance of the section was that of Sir Michael Marshall, HL 2R, 12 February 1997, col 424—'I believe that the battle against crime in the 21st century will be fought over information technology.'

Relevance of PITO to other parts of the Act

5.2 The function of the NCIS in 'gathering, storing, and analysing information in order to provide criminal intelligence' (s 2(2)(a)), will be heavily dependent on the facilitation of information technology. Efficiency in inputting, cross-referencing and analysing data is obviously essential, as is the ability to disseminate intelligence information on a national scale and in a form that is easily accessible. The standardisation of IT communication networks and better access to the PNC (Police National Computer) and the HOLMES (Major Inquiry Programme) Systems have become a priority. Albert Pacey, the first Director General of the NCIS, commented on the benefits of the NCIS intelligence computer system ALERT—

> 'It offers a tremendous leap forward in our capacity to retrieve, analyse, store and disseminate intelligence. Additionally we have produced an information strategy for the future.'[1]

1 See further commentary in the 'National Criminal Intelligence Service, Annual Report 1994–95.'

5.3 Neither the NCIS nor the NCS can achieve their purpose of co-ordinating the prevention and detection of serious crime unless they have access to information about criminal activity around the country. This process will become particularly important in the event of a major inquiry. During the passage of the 1997 Bill it was emphasised on many occasions that organised criminals make use of modern technologies themselves and that it is therefore essential that the police are able to match their criminal counterparts in terms of resources.[1]

1 Michael Howard, Secretary of State for Home Department, HL 2R, 12 February 1997, col 345.

5.4 Statutory powers to interfere with property and wireless technology will potentially produce large amounts of information that has to be cross-referenced and analysed. Moreover, if Pt III of the Act is an indication of an even greater emphasis on the use of surveillance techniques, the development of technical devices capable of eavesdropping without an officer physically entering premises or vehicles is likely to be improved and advanced considerably in the future. Such methods of surveillance would not be regulated under Pt III of the Act given that they do not involve 'interference' with property.[1] They would however fall within the statutory responsibility now vested in PITO.

1 See para 4.45.

5.5 The provision of criminal conviction certificates under Pt V of the Act will be both functionally and legally dependent on the ability of a computer system to provide accurate and coherent information as quickly as possible. On several occasions during the debates on Pt V, concerns were raised over the tendency for unreliable information to be contained in PNC printouts and other sources of police IT. The Human Rights organisation Liberty used as an example the case of three Welsh football fans Alun, Gwilym and Rhys Boore. The Boore brothers had been mistakenly placed on an NCIS computer record in 1990, following an incorrect account by Belgian police of drunken and disorderly behaviour at a Wales match in Belgium. This subsequently led to Rhys Boore's 'administrative arrest' and deportation when he returned to Belgium in 1992. These events occurred because his name was on a list resupplied by the NCIS to the Belgian police. Liberty's complaint to the EC Commission[1] led to both the UK and Belgian authorities confirming that the Boore brothers would no longer appear on any computerised systems.[2]

1 EC Commission Complaint Nos 94/4998 and 94/4999.
2 '*The Police Act 1997—Liberty Briefing*'.

Organisation of police information technology prior to the 1997 Act

5.6 The development of information technology has become essential to modern policing for four reasons—

(a) all modern organisations are obliged to consider the development of IT in order to facilitate managerial processes;
(b) crime prevention and detection resources are wasted if there is insufficient communication and exchange of information between different police forces and law enforcement agencies around the country;
(c) a significant amount of crime now specifically utilises IT (for example computer fraud and hacking, credit card forgery, paedophile networks and production of pornographic and racially inflammatory material on the Internet).[1]
(d) ordinary administrative resources of the police could be saved by the development of IT resources.[2]

1 For further explanation see D Rowland and E Macdonald, '*Information Technology Law*' (1997), Ch 8 '*Policing Cyberspace*'.
2 Consider the example given by Sir Michael Marshall—Chairman of the All-Party parliamentary information technology group, that more than a quarter of all calls made by individuals on police stations are made in order to produce documents in connection with motoring offences. He pointed

out that a considerable amount of time and effort could be saved if kiosks were set up in public places that were capable of providing a document recognition facility: HL 2R, 12 February 1997, col 425.

5.7 The Home Office has been assisting the police in the development of its information technology services for over 20 years.[1] However, much local police information technology has been developed without co-ordination and is incompatible between forces.[2] As with the resourcing of RCSs, police authorities with limited funding have tended to concentrate on local needs rather than national initiatives.[3] Clearly there is a general need for the co-ordination of information technology resources and such a need extends as much to a local village police station as it does to the NCS.

1 Baroness Blatch, HL 2R, 11 November 1996, col 793.
2 Michael Howard, HC 2R (Police and Magistrates' Courts Bill 1994), 26 April, col 110.
3 S Uglow and V Telford (1997), '*The Police Act 1997*', para 5.1.

5.8 It was against this background that PITO was set up on a non-statutory basis in April 1996. Section 57 of the Police Act 1996 (formerly the Police Act 1964, s 41) confers on the Secretary of State the power to provide and maintain such organisations, facilities and services as he considers necessary or expedient for promoting the efficiency and effectiveness of the police. Since its development PITO has worked on a number of IT projects. These include the following—

(a) redeveloping the PNC;
(b) installing the Phoenix Programme which gives police stations direct access to data concerning records of arrests, bail decisions and convictions;
(c) developing a computer programme so that cautions can be recorded on a national basis for the first time;
(d) installing GRASP (Global retrieval access and information system for property items) which enables victims to trace stolen property around the world;
(e) developing a DNA database and a national automated fingerprint identification system (NAFIS) in line with the introduction of these forensic tools by the Criminal Justice and Public Order Act 1994; and
(f) the development of standard software which will focus on providing uniform computer facilities with regard to custody in a police station, assisting the CPS in case preparation, crime reports, crime reporting, redeveloping HOLMES (major inquiry), and vehicle procedure applications for issuing and enforcing fixed penalty notices.[1]

1 See Uglow and Telford, ibid.

THE ORGANISATION

5.9 Section 109(1) of the 1997 Act creates a body corporate to be known as the Police Information Technology Organisation. Detailed provisions as to the organisation's constitution, members, staff, committees, proceedings, evidence, money and annual reports are set out in Schedule 8. Particular regard should be had to Sch 8, para 18 which characterises the status of the Organisation as follows—

> 'The Organisation shall not be regarded as the servant or agent of the Crown or as enjoying any status, immunity or privilege of the Crown; and the property of the Organisation shall not be regarded as property of, or property held on behalf of, the Crown.'

Although PITO is to be funded directly by the Home Office and its members are to be appointed by the Home Secretary, the status of the Organisation will be that of an executive non-departmental public body (NDPB). Several organisations, including the PCA and the Gaming Board, hold a similar status.[1]

[1] Guidance on the creation of, and the framework of control for, NDPBs is set out in the Treasury/ Cabinet office publication 'Non-Departmental Public Bodies: A Guide for Departments'.

5.10 According to the Home Office note on 'Accountability and Funding Arrangements for the Police Information Technology Organisation'[1] the NDPB model was adopted after a process of consultation with the chief officers and police authority associations concluded that—

> 'The model allows these outside interests to be directly involved in the strategic management of national police information technology services. At the same time, the NDPB status removes decisions about IT priorities for the police services away from the government framework and into the hands of the users, while at the same time continuing to recognise Ministers' own strategic interests in the provision of police IT.'

The semi-autonomous position of an NDPB may to some extent offset suspicions about excessive Executive control. There are various measures by which PITO is made accountable to Parliament and the Secretary of State.[2] However, given the enormous influence that PITO's activity may have, there may be accountability risks in allowing the Organisation to be an NDPB. While the Gaming Board and the PCA have the same constitutional stature as PITO these organisations function as independent governing and disciplinary bodies, whereas PITO will be directly supporting police activities. The 1997 Act vests considerable responsibility in the Secretary of State for supervising the activities of PITO. This may not be the best solution for ensuring accountability, because it may result in PITO's independence being compromised by Executive control.[3]

[1] HDEP 96/92, quoted in Parliamentary Research Paper 97/21, 11 February 1997, page 46.
[2] See paras 5.28 to 5.31.
[3] See paras 5.26 to 5.27.

5.11 Unlike the NCIS or the NCS, PITO does not have a Service Authority. According to the Home Office—

> 'The service authority model is not appropriate to PITO's circumstances. This model has been designed to meet the needs of NCIS and the National Crime Squad in view of their operational policing responsibilities. PITO, in contrast, is a provider of non-operational support services to forces. The NDPB model allows the Organisation to benefit from the hands of an executive board on which all tripartite partners (Home Office, chief constables and police authorities) are represented.'[1]

PITO is thus characterised as an operationally neutral organisation. But this position will be difficult to maintain as IT capabilities continue to develop. In future the direction and control of police operations will almost certainly become indistinguishable from the IT facilities on which they rely.

1 Parliamentary Research Paper 97/21 op cit, page 47.

FUNCTIONS

5.12 PITO's primary function is to 'carry out activities (including the commissioning of research) relating to information technology equipment and systems' (s 109(3)). Such activities may be carried out for the use of—

(a) police authorities and police forces (s 109(3)(a)) and
(b) such other bodies as the Secretary of State may determine by order made by statutory instrument (s 109(3)(b)).

As a secondary function s 109(4) provides that PITO may also procure or assist in procuring other (non-IT) equipment, systems and services for any body falling within s 109(3)(a) or (b).

Clients

5.13 Section 111(1) states that for the purposes of this Part of the Act 'police authority' means all the police authorities in Great Britain and Northern Ireland and the Service Authorities of the NCIS and the NCS. 'Police force' means any police force in Great Britain and the RUC as well as the NCIS and the NCS (s 111(3)). Given the provisions for the jurisdiction of the NCIS and the NCS, as outlined in Pts I and II of the Act, it is possible that PITO could be collaborating directly or indirectly with any government department or any organisation investigating crime anywhere in the world.[1] There are, of course, no jurisdictional boundaries in cyberspace.

1 See the definition of 'law enforcement agency' in ss 2(3), 48(4). Consider also the powers of both the Directors General to provide 'special' services to any person at any premises or in any locality provided such services are consistent with the functions of their organisations (ss 24 and 69).

5.14 Under s 109(3)(b), PITO can carry out activities on behalf of 'other bodies' (non-police organisations). There is no definition as to what organisations could or could not be included as civilian clients of PITO. However, the provision of such services cannot take place without a statutory instrument being laid before Parliament by the Secretary of State. There is no requirement that Parliament should positively affirm such an order, but s 109(5) does give either House of Parliament the power to annul the order on a specific resolution. As with the NCIS and the NCS there is a facility for PITO to impose commercial charges for the provision of goods and services, equipment and systems (Sch 8, para 14).

Definition of information technology

5.15 For the purposes of Pt IV of the Act, 'information technology' includes—

> 'any computer or other technology by means of which information or other matter may be recorded or communicated without being reduced to documentary form.' (s 109(6)).

5.16 During the course of the debates, Baroness Blatch, on behalf of the Government, said that, 'PITO is concerned with the provision of computer and communications systems to police forces.'[1] This however underestimates the role of the organisation. Under s 109(3)(b) PITO can provide its services to local authorities. Moreover it is certainly not confined to computer technology. The connection between PITO and the power of local authorities to set up CCTV systems was raised in debate. In reply the Government suggested that the making of such a connection was 'ingenious'.[2] But on the wording of the Act it is quite clear that CCTV systems would fall within s 109(6), because they are a form of technology by which 'information or other matter may be recorded or communicated without being reduced to documentary form.' The question therefore arises whether PITO's work may involve technologies that are more controversial than computers.

1 HL Committee, 26 November 1996, cols 254-255.
2 Baroness Blatch, ibid.

5.17 There are many forms of new technology available which record information in non-documentary form and which extend well beyond the rubric of providing computer and communications systems to police forces. Such technologies include: satellite surveillance, long distance sensitive microphones, laser beam technology using window reflections and vibrations, the monitoring of electro-magnetic rays from computer screens and devices that use either infra-red light or microwave technology. Again all these techniques would fall within the definition of IT in s 109(6).

CONSTITUTION OF THE ORGANISATION

5.18 PITO will consist of a Chairman and other members who are appointed by the Secretary of State (Sch 8, para 1(1)). In making the appointments the Secretary of State will have a duty to consult persons whom he considers to represent the interests of the police authorities and the chief officers of the police forces. As with the Service Authorities for the NCIS and the NCS, the appointment system has to reflect a set ratio between police authorities, police officers and the government. According to the Home Office—

> 'The appointment of members by Ministers is in keeping with the arrangements in place for the generality of NDPBs and was reported by the first report of the Committee on Standards in Public Life (the Nolan Committee) which recommended that ultimate responsibility for appointments should remain with Ministers. The appointment procedures for the chairman and additional members will be in accordance with Nolan principles. While the chief officer and police authority members will be formally appointed by ministers the members will be nominated by the relevant organisations.'[1]

1 Parliamentary Research Paper 97/21 op cit, page 48.

5.19 Apart from the Chairman, the members shall include—

(a) at least three members nominated by persons whom the Secretary of State considers represent—

(i) the police authorities for areas in England and Wales;
(ii) the chief officers of police forces of England and Wales;

(b) and at least one member nominated by persons whom the Secretary of State considers represent—
(i) the police authorities for areas in Scotland;
(ii) the interests of the chief constables of police forces in Scotland;
(iii) the Police Authority of Northern Ireland;
(iv) the Chief Constable of the RUC;
(v) and at least one other member.[1]

1 Sch 8, para 1(3).

Members and staff

5.20 Members of the Organisation will be given employment contracts (Sch 8, paras 2, 3). A member shall not be appointed for more than five years at a time. The Organisation will pay its members' salaries and make contributions to their pensions on the basis of determinations made by the Secretary of State. A person can resign as a member or as Chairman by notice in writing to the Secretary of State. Provided the Secretary of State consults with all the relevant organisations as referred to in Sch 8, para 1(3)(a)–(f), he or she can remove a member or the Chairman if satisfied that the member—

(a) has without reasonable excuse failed to discharge his function for a continuous period of three months;
(b) has without reasonable excuse been absent from three consecutive meetings of the Organisation;
(c) has been convicted of a criminal offence;
(d) has become bankrupt, his estate has been sequestrated or he has made an arrangement with or granted a trust deed for his creditors;
(e) has failed to comply with the terms of his appointment; or
(f) is otherwise unable or unfit to discharge his functions.

5.21 PITO has the power to employ staff to carry out its functions. However, both the terms and conditions of the appointment and the appointment itself must first be approved by the Secretary of State (Sch 8, para 4). Likewise, the Secretary of State will approve the provision of salaries and pensions. Many of the staff will be police officers who are seconded from their forces for a temporary period under the 1996 Act, s 97. Given that such officers would cease to be members of their original force during the period of secondment, arrangements have been made to ensure a continuity of their pension rights (Sch 8, para 5).

Day-to-day management of PITO

5.22 For its day-to-day management PITO will rely on a committee and a number of sub-committees. No person who is not a permanent member of PITO may be a member of the committee or a sub-committee unless they have first been approved by the Secretary of State (Sch 8, para 8). PITO will appoint a chief executive to co-ordinate its different services. This post is not an equivalent position to that of the Directors General of the NCIS and the NCS. As PITO is 'a provider of support services to police forces', it was decided by the Government not to give the Chief Executive the type of 'operational independence' that is enjoyed by chief constables and the Directors General.[1]

1 Parliamentary Research Paper, 97/21 op cit, page 48.

5.23 The characterisation of PITO as merely 'a provider of support services to the police', prompted the Government not to duplicate the service authority principle used for the NCIS and the NCS and not to issue PITO with a code of practice.[1] Similarly, PITO will not have formal duties to consult the relevant organisations. [2]

1 See para 5.11.
2 See para 5.31.

FINANCES

Funding

5.24 PITO's principal source of funding will be payments made by the Secretary of State from money provided by Parliament (Sch 8, para 13). The initial funding will be a grant-in-aid paid by the Home Office, with contributions from the Scottish and Northern Ireland Offices. The majority of NDPBs are funded in this way. According to the Home Office—

> 'This form of financing is appropriate where the Government has decided, subject to Parliamentary and essential department controls, that the recipient should operate at arm's length.'[1]

PITO will have the power to charge for its services, although in the first instance the Secretary of State will be entitled to any payments that are made to the Organisation (Sch 8, para 14(1), (2)). Any sums that the Secretary of State is to be paid will be deposited in the Consolidated Fund. However, with the consent of the Home Office and the Treasury, PITO may be allowed to keep such payments. In due course, the Organisation will be expected to cover most of its costs by charging its customers. There are no equivalent provisions for PITO to accept gifts and sponsorship as is enjoyed by police forces, the NCIS and the NCS.

1 Parliamentary Research Paper 97/21, p 51.

Accounting

5.25 The Organisation has an obligation to keep proper accounts and also proper records in relation to its accounts (Sch 8, para 16). It has to prepare an annual statement of its accounts and copies must be sent to the Secretary of State in such a form and containing such information as the Secretary of State, with the consent of the Treasury, directs. Copies of the statement must also be sent to the Comptroller and the Auditor General.

ROLE OF THE HOME SECRETARY

5.26 In exercising its function PITO is obliged to comply with any general or specific directions given in writing by Secretary of State (s 110(1)). In giving such directions the

Secretary of State has a duty to consult the Organisation—but no one else (s 110(2)). PITO must also provide the Secretary of State with such information about its activities as he may request. Clearly these provisions ensure that the Organisation remains accountable to the Government and in turn to Parliament. Yet, if one looks at the other powers that the Secretary of State has with regard to PITO, it is questionable whether the Organisation will necessarily 'operate at arm's length' from the Government.[1]

[1] See para 5.24.

5.27 The other powers of the Secretary of State will include the power to—

(a) determine such other bodies for whom PITO may carry out its statutory function (s 109(3)(b));
(b) appoint and remove the chairman and members of the Organisation (Sch 8, paras 1, 2);
(c) determine members' salaries, pensions and levels of compensation (if any) for a person who ceases to be a member or chairman (Sch 8, para 3);
(d) approve the numbers and terms and conditions of service of employees (Sch 8, paras 4(1), 5);
(e) consent to the appointment of the chief executive (Sch 8, para 4(2));
(f) consent to the appointment of persons who are not members of the Organisation to a committee or a subcommittee (Sch 8, para 8(1));
(g) make payments to the Organisation out of money provided by Parliament (Sch 8, para 13);
(h) direct, with the consent of the Treasury, that the Organisation need not pay receipts from charges back to the consolidated fund (Sch 8, para 14);
(i) direct, with the consent of the Treasury, the form and content of the Organisation's statement of accounts (Sch 8, para 16(3)).

ACCOUNTABILITY

5.28 The accountability of PITO will be based on the existing arrangements for other NDPBs. PITO will be responsible for carrying out its statutory functions, but the Home Secretary will bear the overall responsibility for PITO to Parliament.

5.29 As a government body PITO will be subject to wide-ranging executive powers, including directions to carry out activities and requests to disclose information.[1] In addition, PITO will still be subject to scrutiny from the National Audit Office, the Public Accounts Committee, the Home Affairs Committee of the House of Commons and the Parliamentary Commissioner for Administration (the Ombudsman). PITO's Chief Executive can be called to appear before any of these bodies.

[1] See paras 5.26 and 5.27.

5.30 PITO will be obliged to prepare an annual report which is to be sent to the Secretary of State and laid before both Houses of Parliament (Sch 8, para 17). This direct publication of an annual report can be contrasted with the annual reports of the respective Service Authorities and Director Generals of the NCIS and the NCS.[1] All these reports are to be published 'in such manner as the Secretary of State considers to be appropriate.'

1 See ss 5(3), 11(2), 51(3) and 57(2).

5.31 There is no specific duty for PITO to consult the relevant police forces, police authorities or Customs and Excise. Given that PITO is designed to facilitate a centralised approach to IT, the omission of a statutory duty to consult would appear to be an oversight. However, during the Parliamentary passage of the Bill, assurances were given that the tripartite system of consultation will be intrinsic to day-to-day management—

> ' . . . I can assure the committee that PITO will have arrangements in place to consult both chief officers and police authorities. Indeed, our whole purpose in reforming the way police information technology services are provided is to place the strategic management of these services into a proper tripartite footing.' [1]

1 Baroness Blatch, HL Committee, 26 November 1996, col 253.

5.32 PITO will be liable in respect of torts committed by its police members in the same way that employers are ordinarily liable for the wrongful actions of their employees during the performance or purported performance of their duties (Sch 8, para 7). This paragraph specifically emphasises that it is to be PITO, as a corporate body, that will be liable for wrongful acts, as opposed to the Secretary of State. Section 97(9) of the 1996 Act which states that the Secretary of State is liable for the torts of seconded police officers, will not apply to PITO officers. Presumably PITO will also be liable for its non-police employees. It thus appears that although the Executive appoints, pays and draws up the terms of employment of all PITO's members and employees (police and non-police), it will be the Organisation rather than the Secretary of State who will be vicariously liable for their wrongful acts. Again, these provisions are reflective of the semi-autonomous relationship to the Government which is enjoyed by an NDPB.

6 Access to criminal records and personal information

INTRODUCTION

6.1 Part V of the 1997 Act creates a statutory framework regulating access to criminal records and criminal intelligence for employment purposes, as well as for voluntary sector appointments. At present, police forces conduct criminal record checks free of charge on behalf of a large number of employers and organisations. Local authorities, licensing offices and charities, as well as other voluntary organisations such as the Scouts Association between them account for several hundred thousand such requests each year. The former Government's White Paper 'On the Record'[1] identified a number of serious deficiencies in the existing arrangements. In short, they were found to be inconsistent, time consuming and costly. Certain employers who are unable to approach the police directly were found to have adopted a practice of requiring potential employees to make an application under the Data Protection Act 1984, known as 'enforced subject access'. Such an application circumvents the requirements of the Rehabilitation of Offenders Act 1974 since the information provided often contains both spent and unspent convictions. In addition, the ad hoc nature of the existing arrangements has left them open to abuse, with corrupt police officers reportedly selling criminal records information to private detectives and others.[2]

1 'On the Record. The Government's proposals for access to criminal records for Employment and related purposes in England and Wales.' (1996) Cm 3308; see also the Green Paper 'Disclosure from Criminal Records for Employment Vetting Purposes' (1993) Cm 2319.
2 See eg 'Corrupt police sell secrets in Yard scandal' Sunday Times, 24 August 1997.

6.2 There was thus a strong case for reform. The primary aim of the 1997 Act was to improve the speed and quality of police checks on people seeking jobs with direct access to children. In practice however, the provisions of Part V go considerably beyond this, and create a wide-ranging system for certification which can be used by any employer. While many of the provisions of Part V will improve the present unsatisfactory situation, there are legitimate concerns about the extent to which the 1997 Act infringes rights of personal privacy, and damages the employment prospects of ex-offenders, thereby putting rehabilitation at risk.[1]

1 See eg Cooper 'Police Bill—Millions Presumed Guilty' The Lawyer, 4 February 1997; Gillies 'A certificate please—just for the record' Observer, 5 January 1997.

THE STATUTORY FRAMEWORK

An overview

6.3 The 1997 Act enables the Secretary of State to issue certificates relating to a criminal records check. The onus is placed upon the subject of the information to apply for a certificate, though certain requests require counter-signature by a 'registered person'[1] and limited categories of non-conviction 'intelligence' may be passed to the employer but withheld from the applicant employee.[2] Individuals are required to meet the cost of providing the certificate, though it is expected that employers and voluntary organisations requiring a certificate will in effect be obliged to adopt a policy of reimbursing applicants. As enacted, Part V provides that the system will be operated by a new Criminal Records Agency (CRA)[3] operating as part of the Home Office, and answerable to the Home Secretary. In Scotland, the work will be undertaken by the Scottish Criminal Records Office (SCRO), answerable to the Secretary of State for Scotland. Estimates suggest that about 8 million people are expected to apply to the CRA for certificates each year.[4]

1 See para 6.33.
2 See para 6.47.
3 The Labour Government is currently reconsidering whether the CRA is the most appropriate mechanism for providing such certificates.
4 Observer, 5 January 1997.

Types of certificate

6.4 Three types of certificate will be obtainable—

(a) The first, the basic 'criminal conviction certificate', will be available only to individual applicants, and will state whether or not they have convictions recorded in central police records which are not spent under the Rehabilitation of Offenders Act 1974 (1974 Act). These certificates are expected to cost about £6;

(b) The second, a 'criminal record certificate' will be available for occupations that are exempted from the provisions of the 1974 Act (such as nurses, lawyers, police officers and traffic wardens). A joint application will be made by an individual and the organisation that is seeking the check. The certificate will provide information about both spent and unspent convictions and, more controversially, about police cautions. Again, the cost of a certificate will be about £6.

(c) The third category, an 'enhanced criminal record certificate' will be restricted to those working on a regular, unsupervised basis with children or vulnerable adults, those holding certain statutory licensing posts carrying a serious risk of fraud and, prior to appointment, judges and magistrates. Again, a joint application will be made by an individual and the organisation that is seeking the check. In addition to the information contained in the criminal records certificate, an enhanced certificate may contain criminal intelligence information, including records of acquittals and the results of inconclusive police investigations, as well as uncorroborated allegations from informants. In certain circumstances, this additional information may be communicated to the employer, but withheld from the individual applicant. An enhanced criminal record certificate is expected to cost about £10.

Assessment

6.5 The creation of a consistent and reliable system for disclosing relevant criminal intelligence to prospective employers is undoubtedly welcome, and the system of requiring 'enhanced criminal records certificates' for certain categories of work will improve the protection that is currently available for vulnerable groups, especially children. But these improvements come at a cost. A number of potential problems were identified during the debates on the Bill, which do not appear to have been satisfactorily resolved.

6.6 The first area of concern relates to the potential impact of the provisions on the employment prospects of ex-offenders. Once the system is fully operational, it is inevitable that many employers will require the production of at least a basic 'criminal conviction certificate' as a prerequisite to an offer of employment. The Institute of Personnel and Development (IPD) has predicted that 'it will become second nature for employers to ask for a certificate. [The 1997 Act] sensitises people to the availability of the information'.[1] The latest available figures indicate that 34 per cent of men and eight per cent of women have a criminal conviction by the age of 35.[2] Indeed, according to the Government's own figures, 12% of all people born in 1973 have unspent convictions.[3] Based on these figures, the National Association for the Care and Resettlement of Offenders (NACRO) has suggested that the 1997 Act will 'increase the pool of people who are, in effect, unemployable'.[4] This appears to be confirmed by a recruitment survey published by the IPD in 1996, which quotes one recruitment consultant as saying—

> 'Of all the things to put off a client, a criminal record is the worst. It doesn't matter if it is a spent conviction for shoplifting or a five year stretch for GBH—clients run a mile.'[5]

1 Observer, 5 January 1997.
2 HL 2R, 11 November 1996, col 819.
3 The Lawyer, 4 February 1997.
4 Observer, 5 January 1997.
5 Ibid.

6.7 According to the Apex Trust, which exists to help former offenders find employment, few employers use any form of risk evaluation, and most do not consider how long ago the conviction occurred, whether it is relevant, or whether it shows a pattern of offending.[1] The Code of Practice to be issued under s 122[2] will require registered persons[3] countersigning an application for a criminal record certificate under s 113, or an enhanced criminal record certificate under s 115, to take such matters into consideration, and not to treat a past conviction as an automatic bar to employment. But the majority of employers will not be 'registered persons' and will be able to require only a basic criminal conviction certificate as a condition of employment. Employers in this category will not be required to apply the provisions of the Code.

1 Observer, 5 January 1997.
2 See para 6.52.
3 For the meaning of registered person, see para 6.33.

6.8 Even those organisations that are prepared to employ ex-offenders often find it difficult to do so because of the restrictions that insurance companies place on fidelity insurance. Fidelity insurance covers employers against theft and fraud by employees, but is usually invalidated if an employee has a criminal conviction. The anticipated increase in pre-employment criminal record checks will almost certainly be encouraged by pressure from the insurance companies. In an effort to meet this difficulty, the Apex Trust has worked with a well-known insurance broker to pioneer an individual bond for ex-offenders. But this initiative is unlikely to offset the employment disincentives created by the legislation.

6.9 It was the risk of reinforcing discriminatory practices, more than any other aspect of these provisions that attracted criticism during Parliamentary debates.[1] The basis for the concern was that such discrimination would act as an obstacle to rehabilitation. Figures provided by the Apex Trust suggested that ex-offenders who are unable to find work are three times more likely to re-offend than those in employment.[2]

1 Lord Rogers of Quarry Bank HL Committee, 2 December 1996, col 514; HC Standing Committee F, 13 March 1997, col 241.
2 HL 2R, 11 November 1996, col 819; see also 'Protecting the Public: The Government's Strategy on Crime in England and Wales', HMSO (1989).

6.10 The second area of concern relates to the potential costs implications for voluntary organisations that rely on large numbers of part time volunteers. The statutory scheme assumes that the costs to individual applicants of having to obtain a certificate will be met by potential employers. In addition to the cost of registering (approximately £15 to £20), employers and voluntary organisations will have to reimburse applicants for the certificate costs if they do not wish to see the number of volunteers falling sharply. For large voluntary organisations the aggregate costs may be prohibitive. The Scouts Association, for example, has 110,000 volunteers. The initial bill for carrying out certificate checks on all volunteers would be in the region of £500,000,[1] with a further substantial bill in relation to checks carried out on its three million or so regular helpers and supporters. However, s 112(1)(b) permits the Secretary of State to make regulations as to payment, and it would therefore be possible to exempt those employees or volunteers whose application is countersigned by certain organisations (or classes of organisation) from having to pay the prescribed fee.

1 These figures were quoted by Lord Dubs: HL 2R, 11 November 1996, col 818.

6.11 Thirdly, there is concern that the existence of the statutory scheme may expose voluntary organisations, employers and the police to additional civil liability in negligence, with corresponding increases in their insurance premiums. Employers who fail to require a statutory check before offering employment may be liable in negligence if an employee subsequently commits an offence in the course of his employment. Furthermore, a negligent error in the provision of relevant information by the police may also give rise to civil liability.[1]

1 It is impossible to predict whether the courts would uphold a claim to public policy immunity for the police in the event of a negligent error: *see Hill v Chief Constable of West Yorkshire* [1988] 2 All ER 238; *Alexandrou v Oxford* [1993] 4 All ER 328; *Osman v Ferguson* [1993] 4 All ER 344; *X v Bedfordshire County Council* [1995] 3 All ER 353; *Swinney v Chief Constable of Northumbria* [1996] 3 All ER 449.

EUROPEAN CONVENTION ON HUMAN RIGHTS

6.12 The new legislation has obvious implications for the right of privacy under Article 8 of the European Convention on Human Rights. Article 8 provides—

'1. Everyone has the right to respect for his private and family life, his home and his correspondence.
2. There shall be no interference by a public authority with the exercise of this right except such as is in accordance with the law and is necessary in a democratic society in the interests of national security, public safety or the economic well-being of the country, for the prevention of disorder or crime, for the protection of health or morals, or for the protection of the rights and freedoms of others.'

The primary purpose of Part V of the 1997 Act is to prevent potential offenders from gaining access to vulnerable individuals. This clearly constitutes a 'legitimate aim' for the purposes of Article 8(2) since it is directed at the prevention of crime, the protection of morals, and the protections of the rights of others. However, any measure which interferes with the right of privacy must be proportionate to the legitimate aim which it pursues. In *Leander v Sweden*[1] the European Court of Human Rights held that the disclosure of a police file to a prospective employer did not violate Article 8. The disclosure was aimed at the protection of national security. In concluding that the measure was proportionate to that aim the Court attached importance to the existence of a Parliamentary Committee and Commissioner to oversee the disclosure. Applying this principle of proportionality to Part V of the Act, care will have to be taken to ensure that any breach of privacy would be specifically relevant to the certificate application in question. A blanket policy of disclosure without due consideration of the particular facts may give rise to a complaint under Article 8.[2]

1 (1987) 9 EHRR 433.
2 See the judgment of Lord Bingham CJ in *R v Chief Constable of North Wales, ex p AB* [1997] 3 WLR 724.

6.13 Article 6 of the Convention protects the right to a fair trial. It arises whenever a person has been charged with an offence or has been made aware that consideration is being given to a charge.[1] The disclosure of a valid criminal conviction is unlikely to involve a violation of Article 6 since the subject will be taken to have been fairly convicted. However, non-conviction information is more problematic. Where the subject has been charged but acquitted he is entitled to the protection of Article 6(2) which safeguards the presumption of innocence. In *Minelli v Switzerland*[2] the European Court of Human Rights held that a refusal of defence costs to an acquitted defendant could violate Article 6(2) if the ground for the refusal contained an implication that the defendant was, in reality, guilty of the charge. The very fact of including an acquittal in an enhanced certificate furnished to a prospective employer arguably involves an implicit suggestion that the subject was guilty. Why else, it may be asked, is the information relevant to his suitability for employment? The disclosure of an acquittal may therefore violate the presumption of innocence in Article 6(2); and the same is true of criminal intelligence involving an allegation which has not been tested through a criminal prosecution.

1 *X v United Kingdom* (1979) 17 DR 122; *X v United Kingdom* (1978) 14 DR 26.
2 (1983) 5 EHRR 554.

6.14 Where this type of non-conviction information is to be included in an enhanced certificate the safest course is to ensure that special care is taken not to suggest that—or leaving the wording open to the inference that—the subject was in fact guilty of the offence. Expressions such as 'insufficient evidence to convict' should be avoided. This is obviously an imperfect solution since the very purpose of conveying such information to an employer is to enable it to be taken into account in determining whether or not to make an offer of employment. But it does at least have the virtue of ensuring accuracy, and thereby reducing the likelihood of a violation of Article 6(2).

6.15 Article 7 of the Convention prohibits retroactive criminal penalties. During the Parliamentary debates, Lord Lester of Herne Hill QC referred to the possibility that the inclusion of a caution in the Criminal Record Certificate and the Enhanced Criminal Record Certificate might constitute a retroactive penalty. On receiving a caution in the police station a person is told that it will not constitute a criminal record. The fact that cautions will now be included in certain certificates undoubtedly renders the initial disposal into a harsher measure. However it is doubtful whether the disclosure of a caution in the intended manner would constitute a 'penalty' within the autonomous definition which the European Court of Human Rights has given to that term for the purposes of Article 7. In *Welch v United Kingdom*[1] the Court listed a number of factors to be taken into account in determining whether a measure is a penalty for this purpose. The most important question is whether the measure was imposed following conviction for a criminal offence. This clearly does not apply to a caution which is an alternative to criminal prosecution. On the other hand, a caution does depend on an admission of guilt. Other factors which may be taken into account are 'the nature and purpose of the measure in question; its characterisation under national law, the procedures involved in the making and implementation of the measure; and its severity.'[2] Whether or not a caution is construed as a penalty for the purposes of Article 7, it will be important for the police to ensure that suspects who are offered a caution in the future are advised of the fact that the matter may be recorded in a job related certificate. This may of course deter suspects from accepting a caution and thus undermine the usefulness of this procedure as a method of diverting less serious offenders from the criminal courts.

1 (1995) 20 EHRR 247.
2 Ibid.

REHABILITATION OF OFFENDERS

The general principle

6.16 Part V of the Act distinguishes between spent and unspent convictions. Convictions which are spent within the meaning of the Rehabilitation of Offenders Act 1974 may not be included in a criminal conviction certificate, but only in a criminal record, *or* an enhanced criminal record certificate. The 1974 Act creates a statutory scheme governing the circumstances in which a person who has been convicted of a criminal offence in the past may nevertheless be treated as if the offence had not occurred. By virtue of the 1974 Act, s 4(1), a person who has become rehabilitated within the meaning of the Act—

> 'shall be treated for all purposes in law as a person who has not committed or been charged with or prosecuted for or convicted of or sentenced for the offence or offences which were the subject of that conviction'.

The effect of rehabilitation is generally to prevent questions being asked about spent convictions, whether in an employment context, in legal proceedings or in any other circumstances. Where a person who has a spent conviction is asked any question about his previous convictions or conduct, then unless the question is put in court proceedings, it is to be treated as relating solely to unspent convictions and the person questioned may not be prejudiced in law in any way by failing to refer to a spent conviction in his answer (s 4(2)).

Exceptions

6.17 However, there are a large number of exceptions to this general principle. These fall into four broad categories.

Exempted offences

6.18 Those who have been sentenced to imprisonment or detention for any term exceeding thirty months are excluded from rehabilitation under the 1974 Act, as are those who have been sentenced to preventative detention, or detention during Her Majesty's Pleasure (s 5(1)).

Exempted questions

6.19 Under the Rehabilitation of Offenders Act 1974 (Exceptions) Order 1975 (SI 1975/1023) (1975 Order) questions may be asked concerning spent convictions in a wide variety of situations—

(a) Any question may be asked in order to assess a person's suitability for admission to the medical profession, the profession of barrister, solicitor, chartered or certified accountant, dentist, vet, nurse or midwife, optician, chemist, osteopath or chiropractor (1975 Order, art 3(a)(i), Sch 1, Pt I). In Scotland, the professions of advocate and registered teacher are also included.

(b) Any question may be asked by a potential employer to assess a person's suitability for judicial office, employment with the Crown Prosecution Service (and its equivalent in Scotland), the office of court clerk, the office of police constable, any employment normally carried out within a prison or other custodial establishment, employment as a traffic warden, or as a probation officer (1975 Order, art 3(a)(ii), Sch 1, Pt II).

(c) Any question may be asked by a potential employer to assess a person's suitability for employment within a local authority social services department (or similar body) which would enable the employee to have access to persons over 65, persons suffering from serious illness or mental disorder of any description, persons addicted to alcohol or drugs, persons who are blind, deaf or dumb, or persons who are substantially or permanently handicapped by illness, injury or congenital deformity (1975 Order, art 3(a)(ii), Sch 1, Pt II, para 12).

(d) Any question may be asked by a potential employer to assess a person's suitability for employment concerned with the provision of health services that would bring the employee into contact with patients (1975 Order, art 3(a)(ii), Sch 1, Pt II, para 13).

(e) Any question may be asked by a potential employer to assess a person's suitability for any employment that is concerned with the provision, to persons under the age of 18, of accommodation, care, leisure and recreational facilities, schooling, social services, supervision or training, which would bring the employee into contact with persons under that age (1975 Order, art 3(a)(ii), Sch 1, Pt II, para 14).

(f) Any question may be asked by a potential employer to assess a person's suitability to pursue the occupation of firearms dealer; any occupation in respect of which a gaming licence is required from the Gaming Board; any appointment as director, controller or manager of an insurance company; any securities dealer, manager or trustee of a unit trust scheme; any occupation concerned with an establishment registered for the carrying out of abortions under the Abortion Act 1967, or any registered nursing home; and any occupation in connection with an establishment at which explosives are stored, and for which a certificate of fitness is required (1975 Order, art 3(a)(iii), Sch 1, Pt III).

Exempted certificate and licence applications

6.20 The 1974 Act does not apply to applicants for firearm and shotgun certificates under the Firearms Act 1968, or to applicants for licences under the Children and Young Persons Act 1933, s 25 (which relates to persons under the age of 18 being taken abroad for the purpose of performing or being exhibited for profit) (1975 Order, Sch 2).

Exempted proceedings

6.21 The 1974 Act does not prevent questions being asked during criminal proceedings,[1] service disciplinary proceedings, certain family proceedings including proceedings under the Children Act 1989, or proceedings relating to the termination or variation of a supervision order under the Children and Young Persons Act 1969 (1974 Act, s 7(2)).

1 As to the circumstances in which questions concerning spent convictions may be asked of a defendant or a witness in criminal proceedings, see *Practice Direction (Rehabilitation of Offenders Act 1974)* (1975) 61 Cr App Rep 260.

Rehabilitation periods

6.22 Where the 1974 Act does apply, the rehabilitation periods applicable to particular offences are prescribed by s 5(2), by reference to the sentence imposed (see Tables A and B). The rehabilitation periods applicable to sentences falling within Table A are subject to a one half reduction if the defendant was under 18 at the date of conviction. This does not apply to sentences falling within Table B which are, in any event, confined to young offenders. The rehabilitation period applicable to an absolute discharge is six months. For a conditional discharge or bindover, the period is one year or the date on which the order ceases to have effect, whichever is longer.

TABLE A

Rehabilitation periods subject to reduction by half for persons under 18

Sentence	*Rehabilitation period*
A sentence of imprisonment detention in a young offender institution or youth custody or corrective training for a term exceeding six months but not exceeding thirty months.	Ten years
A sentence of cashiering, discharge with ignominy or dismissal with disgrace from Her Majesty's service.	Ten years
A sentence of imprisonment detention in a young offender institution or youth custody for a term not exceeding six months.	Seven years
A sentence of dismissal from Her Majesty's service.	Seven years
Any sentence of detention in respect of a conviction in service disciplinary proceedings.	Five years
A fine or any other sentence subject to rehabilitation under this Act, not being a sentence to which Table B below or any of subsections (3), 4A to (8) below applies.	Five years

TABLE B

Rehabilitation periods for certain sentences confined to young offenders

Sentence	*Rehabilitation period*
A sentence of Borstal training.	Seven years
A custodial order under Schedule 5A to the Army Act 1955 or the Air Force Act 1955, or under Schedule 4A to the Naval Discipline Act 1957, where the maximum period of detention specified in the order is more than six months.	Seven years
A custodial order under section 71AA of the Army Act 1955 or the Air Force Act 1955, or under section 43AA of the Naval Discipline Act 1957, where the maximum period of detention specified in the order is more than six months.	Seven years
A sentence of detention for a term exceeding six months but not exceeding thirty months passed under section 53 of the said Act of 1933 or under section 206 of the Criminal Procedure (Scotland) Act 1975.	Five years
A sentence of detention for a term not exceeding six months passed under either of those provisions.	Three years
An order for detention in a detention centre made under section 4 of the Criminal Justice Act 1982, section 4 of the Criminal Justice Act 1961 . . .	Three years
A custodial order under any of the Schedules to the said Acts of 1955 and 1957 mentioned above, where the maximum period of detention specified in the order is six months or less.	Three years
A custodial order under section 71AA of the said Acts of 1955, or section 43AA of the said Act of 1957, where the maximum period of detention specified in the order is six months or less.	Three years

THE CRIMINAL RECORDS AGENCY[1]

6.23 At present there is no comprehensive national index recording all criminal records. Information relating to reportable offences (ie, offences which carry a sentence of imprisonment) is centrally held at New Scotland Yard by the National Identification Service (NIS). Information about non-reportable offences, cautions and low grade criminal intelligence is held locally. The creation of a new Criminal Records Agency (CRA) within the Home Office will bring all criminal record information under central control, though the Agency will continue to liaise with local police forces for other forms of criminal intelligence. The Agency will be non-statutory and self-financing (through fees paid for certificates). It will be responsible for criminal records for England, Wales and Northern Ireland and will be accountable to the Home Secretary. Criminal records in Scotland will be held by the Scottish Criminal Record Office, answerable to the Secretary of State for Scotland.

1 The Labour Government remains committed to introducing the three types of certificate that are provided for in Part V. However, at the time of writing the Home Office is reconsidering whether the proposed Criminal Records Agency is the most appropriate mechanism for providing such certificates.

6.24 In order to carry out its functions the Agency will have access to 'Phoenix', a new computerised national criminal justice record service. Phoenix has been in operation since May 1995 for new convictions and reportable offences. From November 1995 it began to store new police cautions for reportable offences. Once the Agency is fully operational all convictions, including those for non-reportable offences, and cautions will be held on the Phoenix system.

CRIMINAL CONVICTION CERTIFICATES

6.25 By s 112 of the 1997 Act any individual who makes an application in the prescribed form is entitled to receive a basic criminal conviction certificate on payment of the appropriate fee (s 112(1)). The application must be made by the subject of the certificate, in writing and by post. In order to prevent abuse, the applicant will be required to furnish two proofs of identity, and in cases of doubt he may be required to have his fingerprints taken, at his own cost (s 118(2)).

6.26 The certificate will give details of every conviction that is not spent within the meaning of the 1974 Act,[1] or will state that there are no such convictions recorded (s 112(2)). The combined effect of the 1997 Act, s 112(3) and the 1974 Act, s 1(4), is that certificates will include not only convictions before a Crown Court or a Magistrates Court, but any unspent conviction 'by or before a court outside the United Kingdom' (1974 Act, s 1(4)(a)); any conditional or absolute discharge; and 'any finding (other than a finding linked with a finding of insanity) in any criminal proceedings that a person has committed an offence or done the act or made the omission charged' (1974 Act, s 1(4)(b)). Thus, for example, a finding by a jury under the Criminal Procedure (Insanity) Act 1964, s 4A, that a defendant who is judged unfit to plead or stand trial did the act or made the omission charged against him, would constitute a criminal conviction for the purpose of a certificate under s 112.

1 See paras 6.16–6.22.

CRIMINAL RECORD CERTIFICATES

6.27 Section 113 creates a system of more comprehensive certification for sensitive areas of employment involving vulnerable groups, and those concerned with the administration of justice. This type of check is available only to employers and organisations who would be entitled to ask an exempted question under the 1975 Order.[1] A criminal record certificate will record all convictions within the meaning of the 1974 Act,[2] whether or not they are spent. To that extent it merely provides a means for exempted employers and organisations[3] to confirm the accuracy of information which they are already entitled to require. In addition however, the new criminal record certificate will record all police cautions, which would not previously have been discloseable, even to employers who are exempted by the 1975 Order.

1 See para 6.19.
2 As to the meaning of criminal conviction under the Rehabilitation of Offenders Act 1974, s 1(4), see para 6.26.
3 As to the meaning of exempted employment, see para 6.19.

Cautions

6.28 Whenever a custody officer considers that there is sufficient evidence to charge a person with a criminal offence, he has a discretion to issue a caution instead. It is an essential requirement of a caution that the offender admits his or her guilt. Records are kept of the administering of cautions which may influence the police in deciding whether to prosecute a person who re-offends, and cautions may be cited in any subsequent court proceedings. But they do not rank as a criminal conviction or sentence, and are not at present included in a person's criminal record.

6.29 In 1994 the Home Office issued a circular[1] establishing national standards governing the use of cautions as an alternative to a formal charge. According to the circular, the purposes of cautioning are threefold: to deal quickly and simply with less serious offenders; to divert them from unnecessary appearances in the criminal courts; and to reduce the chances of re-offending. In the case of juveniles there are strong policy reasons for delaying entry into the criminal justice system for as long as possible. The circular recognises that there is a presumption in favour of diverting juveniles away from the criminal courts, and refers to the general principle that a prosecution is unlikely to be justifiable in the case of a first time juvenile offender. For adults, there is no general presumption in favour of cautioning, but membership of certain vulnerable groups may point to sympathetic consideration. The groups mentioned in the circular are the elderly or infirm, young adults between the ages of 17 and 20, and those suffering from mental illness or impairment, or severe physical illness.

1 Home Office Circular 1994/18.

6.30 The inclusion of cautions in the category of information to be provided in a criminal record certificate and enhanced criminal record certificate was the subject of debate and proposed amendment in the Report Stage of the Bill.[1] Lord Lester of Herne Hill QC unsuccessfully moved an amendment to remove cautions from the scope of the certificates 'to avoid frustrating important objectives of the criminal justice system'.[2] He went on to say—

> '[B]y giving cautions wider circulation in criminal records certificates, it will become much more difficult to persuade minor juvenile and adult offenders, whether from vulnerable groups or otherwise, to admit their wrongdoing and accept the salutary warning given by a formal caution.
>
> Another concern . . . is about the lack of effective procedural safeguards if cautions are to become a form of quasi-conviction whose disclosure to a potential employer may severely prejudice the individual's chances of obtaining employment. At present there must be evidence of the offender's guilt, the offender must admit his guilt, and the offender must understand the significance of a caution and give informed consent to the caution. But there is no obligation at present on the police to offer someone a right to legal representation before deciding whether to admit his guilt and accept a caution. It is clear from the Home Office circular that there are also concerns in the Home Office itself about the accuracy and consistency of the recording of cautions . . .
>
> It is also unfair that existing cautions will be given wide currency in sensitive areas . . . even though they were administered at a time when those who admitted their guilt did so with no warning or expectation that such an admission of guilt would be permitted to be given wider currency and treated as relevant for employment purposes without any time limit or rehabilitation period . . .
>
> [The inclusion of cautions] will in that way impose a retrospective penalty on those who admitted their guilt under the old system without a fair warning.'[3]

1 HL Report, 20 January 1997, col 524.
2 Ibid col 524.
3 Ibid col 526. As to the implications of Article 7 of the European Convention on Human Rights, see para 6.15.

6.31 Despite these powerful objections, all existing and future cautions will be included in the category of information routinely supplied to employers and organisations who are entitled to ask exempted questions under the 1975 Order.

Procedure

6.32 As with the basic criminal conviction certificate, an application for a criminal record certificate is made by the individual subject, and must be accompanied by payment of the appropriate fee (s 113(1)(b)). However, the application must be countersigned by a registered person[1] (s 113(1)(a)), and must be accompanied by a statement by the registered person that the certificate is required for the purposes of an 'exempted question' (s 113(2)). An exempted question is a question to which the 1974 Act, s 4(2)(a), (b) has been excluded by an order of the Secretary of State under s 4(4) of that Act (s 113(5)). Thus, any question which is excluded by the 1975 Order will be an exempted question for the purposes of Part V of the 1997 Act. These include questions asked to assess a person's suitability for employment or appointment as a lawyer, judge, court clerk, accountant, police or prison officer, traffic warden; for employment in a senior position in a gaming organisation or insurance company, or in certain sectors of the financial services industry; for employment as a doctor, nurse or midwife, vet, optician, chemist, osteopath, chiropractor, or other health care worker; and for employment in connection with children, the elderly, and those with mental or physical disability.

1 As to the meaning of registered person, see para 6.33.

Registered persons

6.33 A registered person can be a body corporate or unincorporate, a person appointed to a statutory office, or an individual who employs others in the course of a business, providing that the body concerned has applied for, and been granted, registration by the Secretary of State in a register maintained for the purposes of the 1997 Act (s 120(1), (4)). In order to obtain registration the body must satisfy the Secretary of State that it is likely to ask exempted questions, or is likely to countersign applications on behalf of bodies or individuals asking exempted questions (s 120(5)). The Government envisages that registration will be restricted to bodies which are likely to make in excess of 200 applications each year.[1] Smaller organisations or employers are expected to seek access to criminal records checks through a larger umbrella organisation, which will countersign the application on behalf of its associated bodies. However, it should be noted that the direct employer must be entitled to ask exempted questions under the 1974 Act if an application under s 113 of the 1997 Act is to be lawfully countersigned.

1 See the draft Code of Practice contained in Annex C of the White Paper 'On the Record' (1996) Cm 3308; for a discussion on the Code of Practice, see para 6.52.

6.34 Under s 120(3) the Secretary of State may make regulations about the maintenance of the register, providing for the information which is to be included about registered persons, the removal from the register of persons who are, in his opinion, no longer likely to wish to countersign applications, and providing for the payment of fees.[1]

1 At the time of writing no regulations have been issued under this section.

6.35 Under s 122(3) the Secretary of State may refuse to issue a criminal record certificate under s 113 (or an enhanced criminal record certificate under s 115) if he is of the opinion that the registered person who countersigned the application, or the organisation or body on whose behalf the registered person countersigned the application, has failed to comply with the Code of Practice issued under s 122.

Crown employment

6.36 Where an application for a criminal record certificate is made by a person applying for Crown employment, there is no requirement for countersignature by a registered person. However, the application must be accompanied by a statement made by a Minister of the Crown that the certificate is required for the purposes of an exempted question to be asked in the course of considering the applicant's suitability for appointment by or under the Crown (s 114).

Disclosure to the registered person

6.37 Once the certificate is available it is to be issued to the applicant (s 113(1)). But the applicant has no right to withhold the certificate from his prospective employer, even if, on receipt of the certificate, he elects to withdraw his application for employment. Once an application under s 113 has been made with the appropriate countersignature, the Secretary of State is under a statutory duty to send a copy of the certificate to the registered person who countersigned the application (s 113(4)).

ENHANCED CRIMINAL RECORD CERTIFICATES

6.38 Sections 115 and 116 provide for the disclosure to potential employers, voluntary organisations and licensing authorities of criminal intelligence extending beyond convictions and cautions.[1] Such intelligence may include records of acquittals, the results of inconclusive or ongoing police investigations, and uncorroborated allegations from informants. Enhanced criminal record certificates are confined to those seeking appointment to positions of responsibility involving regular unsupervised access to children and vulnerable adults, the approval of a person's suitability to act as a child minder or foster parent, the most sensitive areas of licensing, and the appointment of judges and magistrates (s 115(3)–(5)). However, s 115(4)(a) gives the Secretary of State the power to make regulations including other categories of employment.

1 As to cautions, see paras 6.28–6.31.

Procedure

6.39 The formal requirements for enhanced criminal record certificates are the same as those that apply to a criminal record certificate issued under s 113. The application is to be made in writing by the individual subject, and must be accompanied by payment of the appropriate fee (s 115(1)). It must be countersigned by a registered person[1] (s 115(1)(a)), unless the application is made by a person applying for Crown employment.[2] It must also be accompanied by a statement by the registered person (or in the case of Crown employment, by a Minister) to the effect that the certificate is required for the purpose of an exempted question (ss 115(2), 116(2)).[3] However, unlike a simple criminal record certificate, an enhanced certificate will only be issued if the statement required by s 115(2) also confirms that the exempted question is to be asked in the course of considering the applicant's suitability for a position (whether paid or unpaid) which qualifies for an enhanced certificate under s 115(3) or (4) or s 116; or for a purpose relating to any of the matters listed in s 115(5) (approval of child minders and foster parents, and sensitive licensing applications) (s 115(2)(a), (b)).

1 'Registered person' is defined in s 120 and has the same meaning in s 115 as in s 113; see para 6.33.
2 As to Crown employment, see para 6.48.
3 'Exempted question' has the same meaning in s 115 as in s 113; see para 6.19.

Sensitive positions and appointments

6.40 Section 115(3) and (4) and s 116 define three categories of sensitive position that justify the issuing of an enhanced certificate. Firstly, positions involving regular caring for, training, supervising or being in sole charge of persons aged under 18 (s 115(3)). Secondly, positions involving regular caring for, training, supervising or being in sole charge of persons aged over 18 (s 115(4)(b)). Thirdly, judicial appointments (s 116(2)(a)).

6.41 The need, prior to appointment, for the fullest possible information about those working with children is self-evident. Public awareness of the systematic abuse of children in care has increased sharply in recent years, and there have been numerous reports of paedophiles gaining employment in positions of responsibility. Employment with vulnerable adults was not identified as requiring special attention in the White Paper 'On the Record'.[1] Its inclusion as a separate category in the 1997 Act was prompted in part by a number of well-publicised cases of abuse of physically and mentally disabled adults. As Lord Rix pointed out during the Second Reading debate—

> 'One of the sadder learning experiences of recent years has been that people who are clearly more vulnerable to abuse than their non-disabled peers actually suffer that abuse: that is, emotional, financial, physical and sexual.'[2]

1 (1996) Cm 3308.
2 HL 2R, 11 November 1996, col 824.

6.42 In addition to the specified categories, s 115(4)(a) enables the Secretary of State to issue a statutory instrument extending the enhanced certificate provisions to other categories of appointment.

Approval of child minders and foster parents

6.43 An enhanced certificate will also be granted if the statement by the registered person (or, in the case of Crown employment, a Minister) confirms that it is required for the purposes of an exempted question asked for the purpose of—

(a) the registration of child minders and day carers under the Children Act 1989, s 71, or the Children (Northern Ireland) Order 1995, art 118 (s 115(5)(e)); or
(b) the placing of children with foster parents (or the exercise of any other relevant duty) under the 1989 Act or the Northern Ireland Order (s 115(5)(f)); or
(c) the approval of any person as a foster carer under the Social Work (Scotland) Act 1968; the exercise by a local authority of their functions under the Foster Children (Scotland) Act 1984; or the placing of children with foster parents under the Children (Scotland) Act 1995 (s 115(5)(g)).

Sensitive licensing applications

6.44 A number of licensing and certification applications concerned with gambling and lotteries are deemed sufficiently sensitive to justify an enhanced certificate. These are—

(a) applications for certain certificates and licences under the Gaming Act 1968 (s 115(5)(a), (b));
(b) registration or certification under certain provisions of the Lotteries and Amusements Act 1976 (s 115(5)(c)); and
(c) a licence under the National Lottery etc Act 1993, ss 5 or 6 (s 115(5)(d)).

Disclosure of non-conviction information

6.45 An enhanced certificate will contain the prescribed details of every 'relevant matter' (ie, spent and unspent convictions and cautions)[1] together with any additional non-conviction information provided by the police to the CRA under s 115(7) (s 115(6)(a)). If however, the non-conviction information cannot be included in the certificate without risk to the prevention or detection of crime, then it may be provided to the registered person but withheld from the applicant (s 115(8), (9)).[2]

1 As to cautions, see paras 6.28–6.31.
2 See para 6.47.

6.46 There is no statutory restriction on the nature of the information which may be disclosed for these purposes, save that it must, in the opinion of the chief officer, be relevant to the purpose for which the certificate is sought (s 115(7)(a), (8)(a)). Thus, it may include records of acquittals, the results of inconclusive or ongoing police investigations, and uncorroborated allegations from informants. Concern was expressed during debates about the quality of information which may be provided under this section. Lord Dubs voiced the concern of some peers that the disclosure of potentially unreliable information may unfairly prevent a person from obtaining employment—

> 'At one level every employer wants the maximum information about a future employee. That is why employers take up references from previous employers about their experience of an individual. But I am worried that information that has not been tested, information which may be based more on rumour or hearsay . . . might debar a person from obtaining a job.'[1]

The disclosure of unconfirmed intelligence of this nature is undoubtedly controversial. However, on one view, it simply reflects the need, in the light of recent experience, to afford the maximum possible protection to vulnerable children or adults.[2]

1 HL 2R, 11 November 1996, col 820.
2 As to the implications of Articles 6 and 8 of the European Convention on Human Rights, see paras 6.12–6.14.

6.47 The statutory mechanism for obtaining non-conviction information requires local police forces to assess whether they are in possession of any information that may be relevant to the person's suitability for the appointment, approval or licence concerned. Furthermore, the police will need to assess whether the information can safely be disclosed to the applicant himself, or should be confined to the employer alone, or whether it is so sensitive it cannot be disclosed to either the applicant or to the employer. The procedure is as follows—

(a) On receipt of an application, the CRA is placed under a statutory duty to request the chief officer of every relevant police force to furnish any information which, in the opinion of the chief officer, might be relevant for the purpose of an exempted question directed towards one of the sensitive appointments listed above,[1] to a person's appointment as a child minder or foster parent, or to one of the specified licensing applications (s 115(7)(a), (8)(a)).

(b) Although the chief officer is under a statutory duty to provide records of convictions or cautions to the Agency for the purposes of an application under Part V of the 1997 Act (s 119(1)), he is not under a statutory duty to provide non-conviction intelligence. Instead, the 1997 Act vests a discretion in the chief officer to determine the relevance of the information, and the extent of its disclosure.

(c) If, in the opinion of the chief officer, the information can safely be disclosed to the applicant himself then it will be furnished to the Agency under s 115(7) and included in the certificate. The certificate will be supplied to the applicant (s 115(1)), and a copy will be furnished to the registered person who countersigned the application (s 115(9)(a)).

(d) If, in the opinion of the chief officer, the information should be withheld from the applicant in the interests of the prevention or detection of crime, but can, without harming those interests, be disclosed to the registered person, then it will be furnished to the Agency under s 115(8). In these circumstances, the information will not be included in the certificate furnished to the applicant, but it will be provided directly to the registered person together with a copy of the certificate which the applicant received (s 115(9)).

(e) If, in the opinion of the chief officer, the information is of such sensitivity that it cannot be disclosed either to the applicant, or to the registered person, without risk of damage to the prevention or detection of crime, then there is no statutory duty on the chief officer to provide the information to the Agency. He may, however, be answerable for his decision in private law, if a negligent failure to disclose information results in foreseeable harm to a potential victim.[2]

1 See para 6.40.

2 It is impossible to predict whether the courts would uphold a claim to public policy immunity for the police in the event of a negligent error: See *Hill v Chief Constable of West Yorkshire* [1988] 2 All ER 238; *Alexandrou v Oxford* [1993] 4 All ER 328; *Osman v Ferguson* [1993] 4 All ER 344; *X v Bedfordshire County Council* [1995] 3 All ER 353; *Swinney v Chief Constable of Northumbria* [1996] 3 All ER 449.

Crown employment

6.48 Where an application for an enhanced criminal record certificate is made by a person applying for a judicial appointment or for Crown employment in relation to children under s 115(3), or in relation to vulnerable adults under s 115(4), there is no requirement for countersignature by a registered person (s 116(1)). However, the application must be accompanied by a statement made by a Minister of the Crown that the certificate is required for the purposes of an exempted question to be asked in the course of considering the applicant's suitability for a judicial appointment, or for appointment by or under the Crown to a position to which s 115(3) or (4) applies (s 116(2)).

INACCURACIES IN A CERTIFICATE

6.49 Where an applicant considers that information contained in a certificate is inaccurate, he can apply in writing to the CRA under s 117 for a corrected certificate. The Agency is placed under a statutory duty to consider the application and, if it is of the opinion that the certificate is inaccurate, to issue a fresh certificate. The Agency may however refuse to consider such an application unless it is supported by such evidence of identity as the Agency requires, including, if appropriate, the fingerprints of the applicant (s 118(1), (2)). Where fingerprints are required, the cost of taking the fingerprints is to be paid by the applicant (s 118(2)(b)), but will be refunded if the original certificate is found to be inaccurate and a new certificate is issued (s 118(4)). Section 118(3) authorises the Secretary of State to make regulations requiring the destruction of fingerprints obtained for this purpose in specified circumstances.

6.50 The most obvious shortcoming in this system is that it does not provide any mechanism for correcting inaccurate non-conviction information provided to the registered person under s 115(8), but withheld from the individual applicant.[1] Section 118 applies only to information contained within the certificate. Additional information which is provided under s 115(8) is not included in the certificate, but is supplied separately to the registered person.

1 See para 6.47.

6.51 During the Report stage of the Bill a Labour amendment was tabled which would have created a Criminal Records Tribunal to examine the accuracy of disputed certificates.[1] The draft clause provided for a right of legal representation, a duty to give reasons, an appeal to the High Court, and a power to award compensation. The amendment was resisted by the Government on the ground that it would increase bureaucracy and therefore add to the costs of the new arrangements. The amendment was subsequently defeated.

1 HL Report, 20 January 1997, col 538.

CODE OF PRACTICE

6.52 Section 122 imposes an obligation on the Secretary of State to issue a statutory Code of Practice regulating the use of information provided to registered persons under Part V of the 1997 Act. Once published, the Code is to be laid before Parliament.[1] The White Paper 'On the Record'[2] set out the key requirements to be included in the Code of Practice—

(a) acceptance of the Code and an intention to abide by its mandatory provisions should be a prerequisite for registration under s 120;

(b) registration would be restricted to bodies likely to make in excess of 200 applications per year. Other groups for which the anticipated demand was less, would be expected to seek access to criminal record certificates through an umbrella organisation. Where such an arrangement is made, the umbrella organisation should ensure that all of its associate organisations have signified their acceptance of the Code in writing;

(c) failure to observe the provisions of the Code may lead to investigation by the CRA and the withdrawal of registered status.

1 At the time of writing no Code of Practice had been issued under s 122.
2 (1996) Cm 3308.

6.53 The Code of Practice will include provisions requiring that all registered organisations and associate bodies have a written policy on the employment of ex-offenders, and a written strategy for the implementation of the policy. The fact that a person has been convicted of an offence should not be an automatic bar to employment. The employer must consider whether the conviction is relevant to the job, the length of time that has elapsed, whether there was a pattern of convictions, and whether the offender's circumstances have since changed. Criminal records checks should only be carried out after a conditional offer of employment has been made unless time constraints necessitate the carrying-out of checks on all shortlisted applicants. Organisations must make every effort to ensure that the applicant's true identity has been established prior to the submission of the application. All job applicants should be informed when they first apply that a criminal records check will be carried out on the successful candidate(s), and a copy of the organisation's policy on the employment of ex-offenders should be supplied. Where there is a discrepancy between information supplied by the applicant and information supplied by the CRA, the discrepancy should be brought to the attention of the applicant and discussed with him before any decision is taken. Training and recruitment of staff should include a component relating to the employment of ex-offenders, including the effect of the Rehabilitation of Offenders Act 1974.[1] Criminal records information must be kept securely while the application is under consideration and destroyed thereafter. It must not be passed to any outside person or agency. Where an applicant is required to reveal previous criminal convictions in a job application, this should be the subject of a separate form and should be filed as confidential information. A statement of the organisation's willingness to employ ex-offenders, if appropriate, should be included on any form requesting conviction information.

1 See paras 6.16–6.22.

6.54 The Secretary of State may refuse to issue a criminal record certificate under s 113 (or an enhanced criminal record certificate under s 115) if he is of the opinion that the registered person who countersigned the application, or the organisation or body on whose behalf the registered person countersigned the application, has failed to comply with the Code of Practice (s 122(3)). The Secretary of State also has the power under s 120(3) to make regulations allowing for the removal from the register of bodies who have breached the Code. Persons who make an unauthorised disclosure of criminal record information commit an offence which carries a maximum of six months' imprisonment or a fine not exceeding level 3 on the standard scale, or both (s 124).[1]

1 See para 6.61.

6.55 The most obvious shortcoming of the Code of Practice is that it applies only to registered persons who countersign applications under ss 113 or 115. It does not regulate the practice of unregistered organisations and employers, who are able to require a basic criminal conviction certificate as a prerequisite for an offer of employment. This lacuna is significant since the majority of applications are expected to made under s 112. During the passage of the Bill it was argued that the provisions of the Code should be mandatory for any employer seeking access to criminal conviction information. The Government did not accept this proposal.

SCOTLAND

6.56 Criminal records checks in Scotland are currently carried out by the Scottish Criminal Records Office (SCRO), which holds the central database for criminal record information in Scotland. The SCRO is staffed by police officers on 'central service' for the Crown, within the meaning of the Police (Scotland) Act 1967, s 38. It is not part of the Home Office and could not, without specific legislation, carry out functions conferred on the Home Secretary by an Act of Parliament. The 1997 Act, s 121 gives the SCRO specific statutory powers to act on behalf of the Home Secretary and confers on the officers of the SCRO the same statutory immunity from civil liability that is conferred on the Home Secretary by s 119(5).[1] Pursuant to this section the SCRO may exercise any power conferred on the Home Secretary other than the power to make regulations, to issue or revise the Code of Practice, or to countersign applications in relation to Crown employment under s 114(2) or s 116(2).

1 See para 6.65.

CRIMINAL OFFENCES

Falsification of certificates

6.57 Section 123 creates four separate offences. Under s 123(1)(a) it is an offence if a person, with intent to deceive, makes a false certificate. First, the prosecution must prove the existence of a false certificate, ie a document purporting to be a certificate issued under the 1997 Act, issued or authorised by the CRA or the SCRO, which was not in fact issued, or authorised, by the agency concerned. The Forgery and Counterfeiting Act 1981, s 9(1) provides an exhaustive definition of the term 'false' for the purposes of s 1 of that Act, and the 1981 Act applies mutatis mutandis to the offence under the 1997 Act, s 123(1)(a). In *R v More*,[1] the House of Lords held that for an instrument to be false for the purposes of the 1981 Act, s 9, it must 'tell a lie about itself'. Thus, where the defendant has procured the CRA to include inaccurate information in a certificate, this is not a false certificate for the purposes of s 123(1)(a).[2] Secondly, the prosecution must prove that the defendant 'made' the document. The 1981 Act, s 9(2) defines the term 'make' for the purposes of that Act to include the alteration of a document so as to make it false. However, alteration of a certificate with intent to deceive is a specific offence under the 1997 Act, s 123(1)(b), and where there is evidence that the defendant has altered an otherwise valid certificate, this would be the appropriate charge. Thirdly, the prosecution must prove that the document was made with intent to deceive. For a discussion on the meaning of deception see Archbold *Criminal Pleading, Evidence and Practice (1998)*.[3] In general the term 'deceive' means—

> 'to induce a man to believe that a thing is true which is false, and which the person practising the deceit knows or believes to be false.'[4]

For the purposes of an offence under s 123(1)(a), it is submitted that the operative intention must be to mislead another as to the genuineness of the certificate, or as to the truth of its contents. Note however, that the use of a genuine certificate that relates to another person is not an offence under this paragraph since it is a requirement of the paragraph that the certificate itself must be false.[5] The offence under s 123(1)(a) is triable summarily, and carries a maximum penalty of six months' imprisonment or a fine not exceeding level 5 on the standard scale, or both.

1 (1986) 86 Cr App Rep 234.
2 See by analogy, *R v Hopkins* (1957) 41 Cr App Rep 231.
3 See paras 21–181.
4 *Re London and Globe Finance Corpn Ltd* [1903] 1 Ch 728.
5 Such conduct would however be an offence under s 123(1)(c).

6.58 Under s 123(1)(b) it is an offence if a person, with intent to deceive, alters a certificate issued under the 1997 Act. The prosecution must prove that a certificate has been issued by the CRA or the SCRO, that the defendant has altered it in a material particular, and that at the time the alteration was made it was the defendant's intention to use the altered certificate to deceive another person. It is submitted that on the wording of the paragraph the deception contemplated must relate to the particulars that have been altered. Again, the offence is triable summarily, and carries a maximum penalty of six months imprisonment or a fine not exceeding level 5 on the standard scale, or both.

6.59 Under s 123(1)(c) it is an offence if a person, with intent to deceive, uses a certificate which relates to another person in a way which suggests that it relates to himself. The prosecution must prove that the defendant has made use of a certificate issued by the CRA or the SCRO, that the certificate was intentionally used by the defendant in such a way as to suggest that it related to him when it did not, and that he has done so with intent to deceive another. It is submitted that the use of a certificate which has been obtained in the name of a fictitious person would not fall within s 123(1)(c) since the certificate would not then relate to another person. Again, the offence is triable summarily, and carries a maximum penalty of six months imprisonment or a fine not exceeding level 5 on the standard scale, or both.

6.60 Section 123(1)(d) creates a corresponding offence where a person allows a certificate issued under the 1997 Act in relation to himself, to be used by another person in a way which suggests that it relates to that other person. Again, the offence is triable summarily, and carries a penalty of six months imprisonment or a fine not exceeding level 5 on the standard scale, or both.

Unauthorised disclosure

6.61 Section 124 creates an offence of unauthorised disclosure of information provided for the purpose of a criminal record certificate (under s 113) or an enhanced criminal record certificate (under s 115). It is somewhat tortuously drafted. The offence is committed where—

(a) a member, officer or employee of a registered body[1] discloses such information, other than in the course of his duties, to another member, officer or employee of the same organisation, or of an associated organisation, or an individual on whose behalf the registered body countersigned the application pursuant to s 120(5) (s 124(1));
(b) a member, officer or employee of an associated body on whose behalf a registered person (or body) has countersigned an application discloses such information, other than in the course of his duties, to another member, officer or employee of the same associated body (s 124(2));
(c) an individual on whose behalf a registered person (or body) has countersigned an application discloses such information, other than to an employee of his for the purpose of the employee's duties (s 124(3)(a));
(d) an employee of an individual on whose behalf a registered person (or body) has countersigned an application discloses such information, other than in the course of his duties, to another employee of the same individual (s 124(3)(b));
(e) a person to whom such information has been disclosed in circumstances giving rise to an offence under s 124 discloses it to any other person (s 124(4)(a)).

1 See para 6.33.

6.62 It is not an offence under s 124 to disclose information if the disclosure is made with the consent of a person authorised by s 124(5) or (6) to give such consent, or if it is made pursuant to statutory authorisation under s 124(6)(b)–(f). The relevant conditions are as follows—

(a) information supplied to a registered person, but withheld from the applicant under s 115(8), may only be disclosed with the written consent of the chief officer supplying the information (s 124(5)).
(b) information contained in a certificate issued under s 113 or s 115 may be disclosed—
    (i) to any person, with the written consent of the applicant for the certificate (s 124(6)(a)),
    (ii) to a government department (s 124(6)(b)),
    (iii) to a person appointed to an office by virtue of any enactment (s 124(6)(c)),
    (iv) in accordance with a statutory obligation to provide information (s 124(6)(d)),
    (v) for the purposes of answering an exempted question of a kind specified in regulations issued by the Secretary of State (s 124(6)(e)), or
    (vi) for any other purpose specified in regulations issued by the Secretary of State (s 124(6)(f)).

6.63 Where the disclosure of information provided under s 115(8) is permitted with the consent of the chief officer (s 124(5)), it will nevertheless be an offence for the person in possession of such information to disclose it to any person who does not fall within the terms of the consent given (s 124(4)(b)). Similarly, where disclosure of the contents of a certificate issued under s 113 or s 115 is permitted with the consent of the applicant (s 124(6)(a)), or in accordance with a statutory obligation (s 124(6)(d)), or for any purpose specified in regulations (s 124(6)(e), (f)), it will nevertheless be an offence to disclose it to any person who does not fall within the terms of the consent or authorisation, unless the disclosure is otherwise authorised by s 124(6)(b) (disclosure to a government department) or s 124(6)(c) (disclosure to a person appointed to a statutory office).

6.64 Each of the offences created by s 124 is triable summarily, and carries a maximum penalty of six months' imprisonment or a fine not exceeding level 3 on the standard scale, or both.

IMMUNITY OF THE SECRETARY OF STATE

6.65 Section 119(5) provides that no proceedings shall lie against the Secretary of State by reason of any inaccuracy in the information provided in the certificates. Liability for inaccuracies in the information would therefore lie primarily with the CRA itself, the SCRO or with the police who provided the information.[1]

1 As to the question of public policy immunity for the police see para 6.47, footnote 2.

Appendix 1

Police Act 1997

Police Act 1997

(1997 c 50)

ARRANGEMENT OF SECTIONS

PART I
THE NATIONAL CRIMINAL INTELLIGENCE SERVICE

An Act to make provision for the National Criminal Intelligence Service and the National Crime Squad; to make provision about entry on and interference with property and with wireless telegraphy in the course of the prevention or detection of serious crime; to make provision for the Police Information Technology Organisation; to provide for the issue of certificates about criminal records; to make provision about the administration and organisation of the police; to repeal certain enactments about rehabilitation of offenders; and for connected purposes.

[21 March 1997]

Parliamentary debates.

House of Lords.

2nd Reading 11 November 1996: 575 HL Official Report (5th series) cols 789–839.

Committee Stage 26 November 1996: 576 HL Official Report (5th series) cols 123–194, 203–256; 2 December 1996: 576 HL Official Report (5th series) cols 469–528, 544–576.

Report Stage 20 January 1997: 577 HL Official Report (5th series) cols 386–541; 21 January 1997: 577 HL Official Report (5th series) cols 668–678.

3rd Reading 28 January 1997: 577 HL Official Report (5th series) cols 1082–1128.

Consideration of Commons amendments 20 March 1997: 579 HL Official Report (5th series) col 1104.

House of Commons.

2nd Reading 12 February 1997: 290 HC Official Report (6th series) col 345.

Committee Stage 25 February–18 March 1997: HC Official Report, SC F (Police Bill).

Remaining stages 19 March 1997: 292 HC Official Report (6th series) col 888.

PART I
THE NATIONAL CRIMINAL INTELLIGENCE SERVICE

The Service Authority

1 The Service Authority for the National Criminal Intelligence Service

(1) There shall be a body corporate to be known as the Service Authority for the National Criminal Intelligence Service (in this Part referred to as "the NCIS Service Authority").

(2) Subject to the following provisions of this section, the NCIS Service Authority shall consist of nineteen members.

(3) The Secretary of State may by order provide that the number of members shall be a specified odd number greater than nineteen.

(4) Before making an order under subsection (3), the Secretary of State shall consult—

- (a) the NCIS Service Authority (if it is then in existence),
- (b) persons whom the Secretary of State considers to represent the interests of the authorities who between them maintain the police forces in Great Britain and the Royal Ulster Constabulary,
- (c) persons whom the Secretary of State considers to represent the interests of chief officers of police of police forces in England and Wales, chief constables of police forces in Scotland and the Chief Constable of the Royal Ulster Constabulary, and
- (d) the Commissioners of Customs and Excise.

(5) A statutory instrument containing an order under subsection (3) shall be laid before Parliament after being made.

(6) The NCIS Service Authority may co-opt such additional members as it thinks fit.

(7) Parts I, II and IV of Schedule 1 and Schedule 2 shall have effect in relation to the NCIS Service Authority.

References See paras 2.16, 2.19.

Functions

2 General functions of the NCIS Service Authority and NCIS

(1) The NCIS Service Authority shall maintain a body to be known as the National Criminal Intelligence Service (in this Part referred to as "NCIS").

(2) The functions of NCIS shall be—

- (a) to gather, store and analyse information in order to provide criminal intelligence,
- (b) to provide criminal intelligence to police forces in Great Britain, the Royal Ulster Constabulary, the National Crime Squad and other law enforcement agencies, and
- (c) to act in support of such police forces, the Royal Ulster Constabulary, the National Crime Squad and other law enforcement agencies carrying out their criminal intelligence activities.

(3) For the purposes of subsection (2), "law enforcement agency" includes—

- (a) any government department,
- (b) the States of Jersey Police Force, the salaried police force of the Island of Guernsey and the Isle of Man Constabulary,

(c) any other person charged with the duty of investigating offences or charging offenders, and
(d) any other person engaged outside the United Kingdom in the carrying on of activities similar to any carried on by the NCIS Service Authority, NCIS, a police authority, a police force, the NCS Service Authority or the National Crime Squad.

(4) In discharging its functions, the NCIS Service Authority shall have regard to—
(a) any objectives determined by the Secretary of State under section 26,
(b) any objectives determined by the Authority under section 3,
(c) any performance targets established by the Authority, whether in compliance with a direction under section 27 or otherwise, and
(d) any service plan issued by the Authority under section 4.

(5) In discharging any function to which a code of practice issued under section 28 relates, the NCIS Service Authority shall have regard to the code.

(6) The NCIS Service Authority shall comply with any direction given to it by the Secretary of State under section 27 or 30 or under Schedule 3.

Definitions For "NCIS Service Authority", see s 1(1); for "NCS Service Authority", see s 46.
References See paras 2.13, 2.14, 2.17, 2.18.

3 Objectives

(1) The NCIS Service Authority shall secure that NCIS is efficient and effective.

(2) The NCIS Service Authority shall, before the beginning of each financial year, determine objectives for that year for NCIS.

(3) Objectives determined under this section may relate to matters to which objectives determined under section 26 also relate, or to other matters, but in any event shall be so framed as to be consistent with the objectives determined under that section.

(4) Before determining objectives under this section, the NCIS Service Authority shall consult—
(a) the Director General of NCIS,
(b) persons whom it considers to represent the interests of the authorities who between them maintain the police forces in Great Britain and the Royal Ulster Constabulary,
(c) the NCS Service Authority, and
(d) the Commissioners of Customs and Excise.

Definitions For "NCIS Service Authority", see s 1(1); for "NCIS", see s 2; for "financial year" and "NCS Service Authority", see s 46.
References See para 2.18.

4 Service plans

(1) The NCIS Service Authority shall, before the beginning of each financial year, issue a plan setting out the proposed arrangements for the carrying out by NCIS of its functions during the year ("the service plan").

(2) The service plan shall include a statement of the Authority's priorities for the year, of the financial resources expected to be available and of the proposed allocation of those resources, and shall give particulars of—

(a) any objectives determined by the Secretary of State under section 26,
(b) any objectives determined by the Authority under section 3, and
(c) any performance targets established by the Authority, whether in compliance with a direction under section 27 or otherwise.

(3) A draft of the service plan shall be prepared by the Director General of NCIS and submitted by him to the Authority for it to consider.

(4) Before issuing a service plan which differs from the draft submitted by the Director General under subsection (3), the Authority shall consult the Director General.

(5) The Authority shall arrange for every service plan issued by it under this section to be published in such manner as appears to it to be appropriate, and shall send a copy of the plan to—
(a) the Secretary of State,
(b) each police authority for an area in Great Britain, each joint police board (within the meaning of the Police (Scotland) Act 1967) and the Police Authority for Northern Ireland,
(c) the chief officer of police of each police force in England and Wales, the chief constable of each police force in Scotland and the Chief Constable of the Royal Ulster Constabulary,
(d) the NCS Service Authority,
(e) the Director General of the National Crime Squad, and
(f) the Commissioners of Customs and Excise.

Definitions For "NCIS Service Authority", see s 1(1); for "NCIS", see s 2; for "financial year" and "NCS Service Authority", see s 46.
References See paras 2.21, 2.46.

5 Annual reports

(1) The NCIS Service Authority shall, as soon as possible after the end of each financial year, issue a report on the carrying out of its functions during that year.

(2) A report issued under this section for any year shall include an assessment of the extent to which the service plan for that year issued under section 4 has been carried out.

(3) The NCIS Service Authority shall arrange for every report issued by it under this section to be published in such manner as appears to it to be appropriate, and shall send a copy of the report to—
(a) the Secretary of State,
(b) each police authority for an area in Great Britain, each joint police board (within the meaning of the Police (Scotland) Act 1967) and the Police Authority for Northern Ireland,
(c) the chief officer of police of each police force in England and Wales, the chief constable of each police force in Scotland and the Chief Constable of the Royal Ulster Constabulary,
(d) the NCS Service Authority,
(e) the Director General of the National Crime Squad, and
(f) the Commissioners of Customs and Excise.

Definitions For "NCIS Service Authority", see s 1(1); for "financial year" and "NCS Service Authority", see s 46.
References See para 2.21.

Director General and other members

6 Appointment of Director General

(1) NCIS shall have a Director General appointed by the NCIS Service Authority on such terms and conditions as the Authority considers appropriate.

(2) The Director General shall be chosen by a panel of members of the Authority from a list of persons eligible for appointment which has been prepared by that panel and approved by the Secretary of State.

(3) A person shall be eligible for appointment as Director General for the purposes of subsection (2) if—
- (a) he holds the rank of chief constable in a police force in Great Britain or in the Royal Ulster Constabulary,
- (b) he is the Commissioner, an Assistant Commissioner or a Deputy Assistant Commissioner of Police of the Metropolis,
- (c) he is the Commissioner of Police for the City of London, or
- (d) he is, in accordance with regulations under section 50 of the Police Act 1996, section 26 of the Police (Scotland) Act 1967 or section 25 of the Police Act (Northern Ireland) 1970, a constable eligible for appointment to any of the ranks or posts mentioned in paragraphs (a) to (c).

(4) The panel mentioned in subsection (2) shall be convened by the chairman of the NCIS Service Authority and shall consist only of members of that Authority appointed—
- (a) by the Secretary of State (other than under paragraph 6, 7(f) or 8(1)(h) of Schedule 1), or
- (b) by local authority members of police authorities for areas in England and Wales (as defined in paragraph 14 of that Schedule), members of police authorities for areas in Scotland or members of the Police Authority for Northern Ireland.

(5) The Director General shall, on appointment, be attested as a constable by making a declaration in the form set out in Schedule 4 to the Police Act 1996 before a justice of the peace appointed for an area in England and Wales.

(6) Without prejudice to any other enactment conferring powers on constables for particular purposes, the Director General shall have all the powers and privileges of a constable throughout England and Wales and the adjacent United Kingdom waters.

(7) The Director General shall hold the rank of chief constable.

(8) In subsection (6)—

"powers" includes powers under any enactment, whenever passed or made;

"United Kingdom waters" means the sea and other waters within the seaward limits of the territorial sea;

and that subsection, so far as it relates to powers under any enactment, makes them exercisable throughout the United Kingdom waters whether or not the enactment applies to those waters apart from this provision.

Definitions For "NCIS Service Authority", see s 1(1); for "NCIS", see s 2.
References See paras 2.26, 2.29.

7 Removal of Director General by the Authority

(1) Without prejudice to section 21 or to any regulations under section 37 or under the Police Pensions Act 1976, the NCIS Service Authority, acting with the

approval of the Secretary of State, may call upon the Director General of NCIS to retire in the interests of efficiency or effectiveness.

(2) Before seeking the approval of the Secretary of State for the purposes of subsection (1), the Authority shall give the Director General an opportunity to make representations and shall consider any representations that he makes.

(3) A Director General who is called upon to retire under subsection (1) shall retire on such date as the Authority may specify or on such earlier date as may be agreed upon between him and the Authority.

Definitions For "NCIS Service Authority", see s 1(1); for "NCIS", see s 2.
References See paras 2.28, 2.45.

8 Deputy Director General

(1) The Director General of NCIS shall designate a member of NCIS appointed under section 9, other than a member appointed by the Director General by virtue of subsection (8) of that section, to exercise all the powers and duties of the Director General—

- (a) during any absence, incapacity or suspension from duty of the Director General, or
- (b) during any vacancy in the office of Director General.

(2) The Director General shall consult the NCIS Service Authority before designating a member under subsection (1).

(3) No more than one person shall be authorised to act by virtue of a designation under subsection (1) at any one time; and a person so authorised shall not have power to act by virtue of that subsection for a continuous period exceeding three months except with the consent of the Secretary of State.

Definitions For "NCIS Service Authority", see s 1(1); for "NCIS", see s 2.
References See paras 2.30, 2.31.

9 Members of NCIS

(1) NCIS shall consist of—

- (a) the Director General of NCIS appointed under section 6,
- (b) persons appointed by the NCIS Service Authority under this paragraph as police members of NCIS, and
- (c) other persons appointed by the NCIS Service Authority under this paragraph to be members of NCIS as employees of the Authority.

(2) A person shall be appointed as a police member of NCIS only if—

- (a) he is appointed to the rank of assistant chief constable in NCIS and he met the requirements of subsection (3) immediately prior to his being appointed, or
- (b) he is engaged with NCIS on a period of temporary service to which section 97 of the Police Act 1996, section 38A of the Police (Scotland) Act 1967 or section 21 of the Police Act (Northern Ireland) 1970 applies.

(3) A person meets the requirements of this subsection if—

- (a) he holds the rank of assistant chief constable or a higher rank in a police force in Great Britain or in the Royal Ulster Constabulary,
- (b) he holds the rank of commander or a higher rank in the metropolitan police force or in the City of London police force, or

(c) he is, in accordance with regulations under section 50 of the Police Act 1996, section 26 of the Police (Scotland) Act 1967 or section 25 of the Police Act (Northern Ireland) 1970, a constable eligible for appointment to the rank of assistant chief constable or commander in any of the police forces, or in the Constabulary, mentioned in paragraph (a) or (b).

(4) Subsections (5), (6) and (8) of section 6 apply to a police member to whom subsection (2)(a) above applies as they apply to the Director General of NCIS.

(5) A person appointed under subsection (1)(b) or (c) shall be appointed on such terms and conditions as the NCIS Service Authority considers appropriate.

(6) Before making an appointment under subsection (1)(b) or (c), or determining the terms and conditions on which such an appointment is to be made, the NCIS Service Authority shall consult the Director General of NCIS.

(7) A police member to whom subsection (2)(b) applies shall cease to be a member of NCIS at the end of his period of temporary service (unless re-appointed under this section).

(8) Where an order under section 44 authorises the NCIS Service Authority to make arrangements for the discharge of its functions by the Director General of NCIS, the Authority shall exercise its powers under that order so as to secure that, subject to subsection (9) below, the Director General appoints persons under subsection (1)(b) or (c) to be members of NCIS.

(9) Subsection (8) shall not apply to—

(a) the appointment of any person to whom subsection (2)(a) applies as a police member, or

(b) the appointment of such other persons as may be agreed between the Director General and the Authority or, in the absence of agreement, as may be determined by the Secretary of State.

(10) Section 7 applies to a member appointed under this section, other than a member appointed by the Director General by virtue of subsection (8) above, as it applies to the Director General.

Definitions For "NCIS Service Authority", see s 1(1); for "NCIS", see s 2.
References See paras 2.32, 2.35.

Functions of Director General

10 General Function of Director General

(1) NCIS shall be under the direction and control of the Director General.

(2) In discharging his functions, the Director General shall have regard to the service plan issued by the NCIS Service Authority under section 4.

Definitions For "NCIS Service Authority", see s 1(1); for "NCIS", see s 2.
References See paras 2.25, 2.27.

11 Reports by Director General to the Authority

(1) The Director General of NCIS shall, as soon as possible after the end of each financial year, submit to the NCIS Service Authority a general report on the activities of NCIS during that year.

(2) The Director General shall arrange for a report submitted by him under subsection (1) to be published in such manner as appears to him to be appropriate.

(3) The NCIS Service Authority may require the Director General to submit to it a report on such matters connected with the activities of NCIS as may be specified in the requirement.

(4) A report submitted under subsection (3) shall be in such form as the Authority may specify.

(5) If it appears to the Director General that a report in compliance with a requirement under subsection (3) would contain information which in the public interest ought not to be disclosed, or is not needed for the discharge of the functions of the Authority, he may request the Authority to refer the requirement to the Secretary of State; and in any such case the requirement shall be of no effect unless it is confirmed by the Secretary of State.

(6) The Authority may arrange, or require the Director General to arrange, for a report submitted under subsection (3) to be published in such manner as appears to the Authority to be appropriate.

Definitions For "NCIS Service Authority", see s 1(1); for "NCIS", see s 2; for "financial year", see s 46.
References See para 2.27.

12 Responsibility for co-ordination of police and Security Service activities

In section 2(2) of the Security Service Act 1989 (which imposes duties on the Director-General of the Security Service), in paragraph (c) (which provides for the Secretary of State to designate the person responsible for co-ordinating police and Security Service activities) for "a person designated by the Secretary of State" there shall be substituted "the Director General of the National Criminal Intelligence Service".

References See para 2.25.

Service Authority's officers and employees

13 Officers and employees

(1) The NCIS Service Authority may appoint officers and employees to enable it to discharge its functions.

(2) Persons appointed under this section shall be appointed on such terms and conditions as the NCIS Service Authority considers appropriate.

Definitions For "NCIS Service Authority", see s 1(1).

14 Appointment of clerk

The NCIS Service Authority shall appoint a person to be the clerk to the Authority.

Definitions For "NCIS Service Authority", see s 1(1).

15 Appointment of persons not employed by the NCIS Service Authority

Where the NCIS Service Authority is required or authorised by any Act—

(a) to appoint a person to a specified office under the Authority, or

(b) to designate a person as having specified duties or responsibilities,

then, notwithstanding any provision of that Act to the contrary, the Authority may appoint or designate either a person employed by the Authority under section 13, or a person not holding any office or employment under the Authority.

Definitions For "NCIS Service Authority", see s 1(1).

Financial provisions

16 NCIS service fund

(1) The NCIS Service Authority shall keep a fund to be known as the NCIS service fund.

(2) Subject to any regulations under the Police Pensions Act 1976 and to section 21 below, all receipts of the Authority shall be paid into the NCIS service fund and all expenditure of the Authority shall be paid out of that fund.

(3) Accounts shall be kept by the Authority of payments made into or out of the NCIS service fund.

Definitions For "NCIS Service Authority", see s 1(1).
References See para 2.37.

17 Power to issue levies

(1) The NCIS Service Authority shall, in respect of every financial year beginning after the establishment of that Authority, issue levies to—

(a) police authorities for areas in England and Wales (other than the metropolitan police district), and

(b) the Receiver for the Metropolitan Police District.

(2) The Secretary of State shall, by order, make provision in relation to the calculation, setting, collection, administration and payment of levies under this section.

(3) An order under this section may include provision—

(a) as to apportionment of levies issued under this section;

(b) conferring a right to interest on anything unpaid.

(4) An order under this section may also include provision—

(a) that the Common Council of the City of London making calculations in accordance with section 32 of the Local Government Finance Act 1992 (originally or by way of substitute) may anticipate a levy;

(b) that a police authority established under section 3 of the Police Act 1996, or the Receiver for the Metropolitan Police District, making calculations in accordance with section 43 of the Local Government Finance Act 1992 (originally or by way of substitute) may anticipate a levy;

(c) as to the treatment as special expenses of amounts so anticipated;

(d) as to the treatment of any levy actually issued.

(5) A statutory instrument containing an order under this section shall be subject to annulment in pursuance of a resolution of either House of Parliament.

(6) Schedule 3 (which makes further provision in connection with levies under this section) shall have effect.

Definitions For "NCIS Service Authority", see s 1(1); for "financial year", see s 46.
References See para 2.38.

18 Initial financing of NCIS Service Authority

The Secretary of state may make grants to the NCIS Service Authority in respect of expenditure incurred (or to be incurred) by it at any time before the financial year in which revenue is first received by it as a result of levies issued by it under section 17.

Definitions For "NCIS Service Authority", see s 1(1); for "financial year", see s 46.
References See para 2.39.

19 Charges

(1) The NCIS Service Authority may make charges in respect of the provision of any services, or an agreement for the provision of any services, to any person by the Authority or by NCIS.

(2) Any charges made under this section may include amounts calculated by reference to the expenditure incurred or expected to be incurred by the NCIS Service Authority, or by NCIS, otherwise than directly in connection with the provision of the services concerned.

Definitions For "NCIS Service Authority", see s 1(1); for "NCIS", see s 2.
References See para 2.40.

20 Acceptance of gifts and loans

(1) The NCIS Service Authority may, in connection with the discharge of any of its functions, accept gifts of money, and gifts or loans of other property, on such terms as appear to the Authority to be appropriate.

(2) The terms on which gifts or loans are accepted under subsection (1) may include terms providing for the commercial sponsorship of any activity of the Authority or of NCIS.

Definitions For "NCIS Service Authority", see s 1(1); for "NCIS", see s 2.
References See para 2.41.

21 Pensions and gratuities

(1) The NCIS Service Authority may—
- (a) pay, or make payments in respect of, pensions or gratuities to or in respect of any persons who are, or have been, its officers or employees;
- (b) provide and maintain schemes (whether contributory or not) for the payment of pensions or gratuities to or in respect of any such persons.

(2) The NCIS Service Authority may—
- (a) pay, or make payments in respect of, such pensions or gratuities as it may determine, with the consent of the Secretary of State, to or in respect of any persons who are or have been the Director General of NCIS or police members of NCIS;
- (b) provide and maintain such schemes (whether contributory or not) as it may determine, with the consent of the Secretary of State, for the payment of pensions or gratuities to or in respect of any such persons.

(3) Before exercising its powers under subsection (2), the Authority shall have regard to any provision made under the Police Pensions Act 1976 or section 25(2)(k) of the Police Act (Northern Ireland) 1970.

(4) References in this section to pensions and gratuities include references to pensions or gratuities by way of compensation to or in respect of any of the persons mentioned in subsection (1) or (2) who suffer loss of office or employment or loss or diminution of emoluments.

Definitions For "NCIS Service Authority", see s 1(1); for "NCIS", see s 2.
References See para 2.37.

General provisions

22 Collaboration agreements

(1) If it appears to the Director General of NCIS and to—

- (a) the chief officers of police of one or more police forces in England and Wales, or
- (b) the chief constables of one or more police forces in Scotland, or
- (c) the Chief Constable of the Royal Ulster Constabulary, or
- (d) the Director General of the National Crime Squad,

that any police functions can more efficiently or effectively be discharged by members of NCIS and members of their respective forces or, as the case may be, the Squad acting jointly, they may, with the approval of the appropriate authorities, enter into an agreement for that purpose.

(2) For the purposes of this section, the "appropriate authorities" means the NCIS Service Authority and—

- (a) in relation to an agreement entered by a chief officer of police of a police force in England and Wales, the police authority which maintains that force,
- (b) in relation to an agreement entered by a chief constable of a police force in Scotland, the police authority which maintains that force or, as the case may be, the police authorities for the police areas comprised in a combined area,
- (c) in relation to an agreement entered by the Chief Constable of the Royal Ulster Constabulary, the Police Authority for Northern Ireland, and
- (d) in relation to an agreement entered by the Director General of the National Crime Squad, the NCS Service Authority.

(3) In subsection (1) "police functions" includes the functions of NCIS and, in the case of an agreement entered by the Director General of the National Crime Squad, the functions of that Squad.

(4) If it appears to the NCIS Service Authority and to—

- (a) one or more police authorities for areas in England and Wales, or
- (b) one or more police authorities for areas (or combined areas) in Scotland, or
- (c) the Police Authority for Northern Ireland, or
- (d) the NCS Service Authority,

that any premises, equipment or other material or facilities can with advantage be provided jointly for NCIS and the forces maintained by the authorities concerned or, as the case may be, the National Crime Squad, they may enter an agreement for that purpose.

(5) Any expenditure incurred under an agreement made under this section shall be borne—

- (a) in the case of an agreement under subsection (1), by the appropriate authorities who approved it, and

(b) in the case of an agreement under subsection (4), by the parties to it,

in such proportions as they may agree or as may, in the absence of agreement, be determined by the Secretary of State.

(6) An agreement under subsection (1) or (4) may be varied or determined by a subsequent agreement.

(7) If it appears to the Secretary of State that any party should enter an agreement to which subsection (1), (4) or (6) applies, the Secretary of State may, after considering any representations made by the party concerned, direct the party to enter into such an agreement under those provisions as may be specified in the direction.

(8) The provisions of this section shall not prejudice the power of the NCIS Service Authority, any police authority, the Police Authority for Northern Ireland or the NCS Service Authority to act jointly, or co-operate in any other way, with any person where to do so is calculated to facilitate, or is conducive or incidental to, the discharge of any of its functions.

Definitions For "NCIS Service Authority", see s 1(1); for "NCIS", see s 2; for "NCS Service Authority", see s 46.
References See para 2.42.

23 Aid by and for NCIS

(1) The Director General of NCIS may, on the application of—

(a) the chief officer of police of a police force in England and Wales,
(b) the chief constable of a police force in Scotland,
(c) the Chief Constable of the Royal Ulster Constabulary, or
(d) the Director General of the National Crime Squad,

provide constables or other assistance for the purposes of enabling the police force or the Royal Ulster Constabulary or, as the case may, the National Crime Squad to meet any special demand on its resources.

(2) On the application of the Director General of NCIS—

(a) the chief officer of police of a police force in England and Wales,
(b) the chief constable of a police force in Scotland,
(c) the Chief Constable of the Royal Ulster Constabulary, or
(d) the Director General of the National Crime Squad,

may provide constables or other assistance for the purposes of enabling NCIS to meet any special demand on its resources.

(3) If it appears to the Secretary of State—

(a) that it is expedient in the interests of public safety or order that a police force, the Royal Ulster Constabulary, the National Crime Squad or NCIS should be reinforced or should receive other assistance for the purpose of enabling it to meet any special demand on its resources, and
(b) that satisfactory arrangements under subsection (1) or (2) cannot be made, or cannot be made in time,

he may direct the Director General of NCIS, the chief officer of police of any police force in England and Wales, the chief constable of any police force in Scotland, the chief constable of the Royal Ulster Constabulary or the Director General of the National Crime Squad to provide such constables or other assistance for that purpose as may be specified in the direction.

(4) While a constable is provided under this section for the assistance of a police force, the Royal Ulster Constabulary or the National Crime Squad he shall, notwithstanding section 10(1), be under the direction and control of the chief officer

of that force or, as the case may be, the chief constable of that force or Constabulary or the Director General of that Squad.

(5) While a constable is provided under this section for the assistance of NCIS he shall, notwithstanding section 56(1) below, section 10(1) of the Police Act 1996, section 17(2) of the Police (Scotland) Act 1967 or section 6(2) of the Police Act (Northern Ireland) 1970, be under the direction and control of the Director General of NCIS.

(6) For the purposes of this section "constable", in relation to Northern Ireland, means a member of the Royal Ulster Constabulary or the Royal Ulster Constabulary Reserve.

Definitions For "NCIS", see s 2.
References See para 2.42.

24 Provision of special services

The Director General of NCIS may, at the request of any person, provide services at any premises or in any locality in the United Kingdom, if those services are consistent with the functions of, and do not prejudice the efficiency or effectiveness of, NCIS.

Definitions For "NCIS", see s 2.
References See para 2.42.

Central supervision and direction

25 General duty of Secretary of State

The Secretary of State shall exercise his powers under this Part in such manner and to such extent as appears to him to be best calculated to promote the efficiency and effectiveness of NCIS.

Definitions For "NCIS", see s 2.
References See para 2.44.

26 Setting of objectives

(1) The Secretary of State may by order determine objectives for NCIS.

(2) Before making an order under this section, the Secretary of State shall consult—

(a) the NCIS Service Authority,
(b) the Director General of NCIS,
(c) persons whom the Secretary of State considers to represent the interests of the authorities who between them maintain the police forces in Great Britain and the Royal Ulster Constabulary,
(d) persons whom he considers to represent the interests of chief officers of police of police forces in England and Wales, the chief constables of police forces in Scotland and the Chief Constable of the Royal Ulster Constabulary,
(e) the NCS Service Authority,
(f) the Director General of the National Crime Squad, and
(g) the Commissioners of Customs and Excise.

(3) A statutory instrument containing an order under this section shall be laid before Parliament after being made.

Definitions For "NCIS Service Authority", see s 1(1); for "NCIS", see s 2; for "NCS Service Authority", see s 46.
References See paras 2.46, 2.48.

27 Setting of performance targets

(1) Where an objective has been determined under section 26, the Secretary of State may direct the NCIS Service Authority to establish levels of performance ("performance targets") to be aimed at in seeking to achieve the objective.

(2) A direction given under this section may impose conditions with which the performance targets must conform.

(3) The Secretary of State shall arrange for any direction given under this section to be published in such manner as appears to him to be appropriate.

Definitions For "NCIS Service Authority", see s 1(1).
References See para 2.20.

28 Codes of practice

(1) The Secretary of State may issue codes of practice relating to the discharge by the NCIS Service Authority of its functions.

(2) The Secretary of State may from time to time revise the whole or part of any code of practice issued under this section.

(3) The Secretary of State shall lay before Parliament a copy of any code of practice, and of any revision of a code of practice, issued by him under this section.

Definitions For "NCIS Service Authority", see s 1(1).
References See para 2.23.

29 Removal of Director General, etc

(1) The Secretary of State may require the NCIS Service Authority to exercise its power under section 7 to call upon the Director General of NCIS, or any other member (other than a member appointed by the Director General by virtue of section 9(8)), to retire in the interests of efficiency or effectiveness.

(2) Before—

(a) exercising any power conferred on him by subsection (1), or

(b) approving the exercise by the NCIS Service Authority of its power under section 7,

the Secretary of State shall give the person in relation to whom it is proposed to exercise the power (the "relevant person") an opportunity to make representations to him and shall consider any representations so made.

(3) Where representations are made under this section, the Secretary of State may, and in a case where he proposes to exercise a power conferred by subsection (1) shall, appoint one or more persons to hold an inquiry and report to him.

(4) The Secretary of State shall take account of any report made under subsection (3).

(5) The person appointed under subsection (3) (or, in a case where more than one person is so appointed, at least one of the persons so appointed) shall not be an officer of police, of a Government department, of NCIS or of the National Crime Squad.

(6) The costs incurred by a relevant person in respect of an inquiry under this section, taxed in such manner as the Secretary of State may direct, shall be defrayed out of the NCIS service fund.

Definitions For "NCIS Service Authority", see s 1(1); for "NCIS", see s 2; for "NCIS service fund", see s 46.
References See para 2.28.

30 Power to give directions after adverse report

(1) The Secretary of State may at any time—

(a) require the inspectors of constabulary appointed under section 54 of the Police Act 1996 to carry out an inspection of NCIS under that section,

(b) require the inspectors of constabulary appointed under section 33 of the Police (Scotland) Act 1967 to carry out an inspection of NCIS under that section, or

(c) require the inspectors of constabulary appointed under section 16 of the Police Act (Northern Ireland) 1970 to carry out an inspection of NCIS under that section.

(2) Where a report made to the Secretary of State on an inspection carried out in accordance with this section states—

(a) that, in the opinion of the person making the report, NCIS is not efficient or not effective, or

(b) that in his opinion, unless remedial measures are taken, NCIS will cease to be efficient or will cease to be effective,

the Secretary of State may direct the NCIS Service Authority to take such measures as may be specified in the direction.

Definitions For "NCIS Service Authority", see s 1(1); for "NCIS", see s 2.
References See para 2.47.

31 Reports from NCIS Service Authority

(1) The Secretary of State may require the NCIS Service Authority to submit to him a report on such matters connected with the discharge of the Authority's functions, or otherwise with the activities of NCIS, as may be specified in the requirement.

(2) A report submitted under subsection (1) shall be in such form as the Secretary of State may specify.

(3) The Secretary of State may arrange, or require the Authority to arrange, for a report under this section to be published in such manner as appears to him to be appropriate.

Definitions For "NCIS Service Authority", see s 1(1); for "NCIS", see s 2.
References See para 2.44.

32 Reports from Director General

(1) The Secretary of State may require the Director General of NCIS to submit to him a report on such matters connected with the activities of NCIS as may be specified in the requirement.

(2) A report submitted under subsection (1) shall be in such form as the Secretary of State may specify.

(3) The Secretary of State may arrange, or require the Director General to arrange, for a report under this section to be published in such manner as appears to the Secretary of State to be appropriate.

(4) The Director General shall, as soon as possible after the end of each financial year, submit to the Secretary of State the like report as is required by section 11 to be submitted to the NCIS Service Authority.

Definitions For "NCIS Service Authority", see s 1(1); for "NCIS", see s 2; for "financial year", see s 46.
References See para 2.45.

33 Criminal statistics

(1) The Director General of NCIS shall, at such times and in such form as the Secretary of State may direct, transmit to the Secretary of State such particulars with respect to offences, offenders, criminal proceedings and the state of crime as the Secretary of State may require.

(2) The Secretary of State shall cause a consolidated and classified abstract of the information transmitted to him under this section to be prepared and laid before Parliament.

Definitions For "NCIS", see s 2.
References See para 2.27.

34 Inquiries

(1) The Secretary of State may cause an inquiry to be held by a person appointed by him into any matter connected with NCIS.

(2) An inquiry under this section shall be held in public or in private as the Secretary of State may direct.

(3) For the purposes of an inquiry under this section, the person appointed to hold the inquiry may by summons require any person to attend, at a time and place stated in the summons, to give evidence or to produce any documents in his custody or under his control which relate to any matter in question at the inquiry, and may take evidence on oath, and for that purpose administer oaths.

(4) No person shall be required, in obedience to a summons under subsection (3), to attend to give evidence or to produce any documents, unless the necessary expenses of his attendance are paid or tendered to him.

(5) Nothing in subsection (3) shall empower a person holding an inquiry to require the production of the title, or of any instrument relating to the title, of any land not being the property of the NCIS Service Authority.

(6) Every person who refuses or deliberately fails to attend in obedience to a summons issued under this section, or to give evidence, or who deliberately alters, suppresses, conceals, destroys, or refuses to produce any book or other document which he is required or is liable to be required to produce for the purposes of this section, shall be liable on summary conviction to a fine not exceeding level 3 on the standard scale or to imprisonment for a term not exceeding six months, or to both.

(7) Where the report of the person holding an inquiry under this section is not published, a summary of his findings and conclusions shall be made known by the Secretary of State so far as appears to him consistent with the public interest.

(8) The Secretary of State may direct that the whole or part of the costs (or, in relation to any inquiry held in Scotland, the expenses) incurred by any person for the purposes of an inquiry held under this section shall be defrayed out of the NCIS service fund; and any costs (or expenses) payable under this section shall be subject to taxation in such manner as the Secretary of State may direct.

Definitions For "NCIS Service Authority", see s 1(1); for "NCIS", see s 2; for "NCIS service fund", see s 46.
References See para 2.47.

35 Regulations as to standard of equipment

The Secretary of State may make regulations requiring equipment provided or used for the purposes of NCIS to satisfy such requirements as to design and performance as may be prescribed in the regulations.

Definitions For "NCIS", see s 2.
References See para 2.47.

36 Common services

(1) The Secretary of State may, by regulations, make provision for requiring NCIS and—

(a) all police forces in England and Wales, or
(b) all police forces in Scotland, or
(c) the Royal Ulster Constabulary, or
(d) the National Crime Squad,

to use specified facilities or services, or facilities or services of a specified description, (whether or not provided under section 57(1) of the Police Act 1996 or section 36 of the Police (Scotland) Act 1967) if he considers that it would be in the interests of efficiency or effectiveness for them to do so.

(2) Before making regulations under this section the Secretary of State shall consult the NCIS Service Authority and the Director General of NCIS and—

(a) where the regulations relate to police forces in England and Wales, persons whom the Secretary of State considers to represent the interests of police authorities for areas in England and Wales and persons whom he considers to represent the interests of chief officers of police of police forces there,
(b) where the regulations relate to police forces in Scotland, persons whom the Secretary of State considers to represent the interests of police authorities for areas in Scotland and persons whom he considers to represent the interests of chief constables of police forces there,
(c) where the regulations relate to the Royal Ulster Constabulary, the Police Authority for Northern Ireland and the Chief Constable of the Royal Ulster Constabulary, and
(d) where the regulations relate to the National Crime Squad, the NCS Service Authority and the Director General of the National Crime Squad.

Definitions For "NCIS Service Authority", see s 1(1); for "NCIS", see s 2.
References See para 2.47.

Discipline and complaints

37 Discipline regulations

(1) The Secretary of State may make regulations relating to the conduct of members of NCIS and the maintenance of discipline in NCIS.

(2) In relation to any matter as to which provision may be made by regulations under this section, the regulations may—

(a) authorise or require provision to be made by, or confer discretionary powers on, the NCIS Service Authority, the Director General of NCIS or other persons, or
(b) authorise or require the delegation by any person of functions conferred on that person by or under the regulations.

(3) A statutory instrument containing regulations under this section shall be subject to annulment in pursuance of a resolution of either House of Parliament.

Definitions For "NCIS Service Authority", see s 1(1); for "NCIS", see s 2.
References See para 2.49.

38 Appeals

(1) Where the Director General of NCIS, or a police member to whom section 9(2)(a) applies, is dismissed or required to resign by a decision taken under or by virtue of regulations made under section 37, he may appeal to an appeals tribunal against the decision except where he has a right of appeal to some other person; and in that case he may appeal to an appeals tribunal from any decision of that other person as a result of which he is dismissed or required to resign.

(2) The Secretary of State shall, by order, make provision in relation to appeals tribunals and appeals under subsection (1) corresponding (with or without modification) to that which is or may be made in relation to police appeals tribunals and appeals under section 85(1) of the Police Act 1996 by, or by virtue of, section 85(2) to (4) of and Schedule 6 to that Act.

(3) A statutory instrument containing an order under this section shall be subject to annulment in pursuance of a resolution of either House of Parliament.

Definitions For "NCIS", see s 2.
References See para 2.49.

39 Complaints

(1) The Secretary of State shall, by regulations, make provision for the handling of any complaint about the conduct of any member of NCIS which is submitted by, or on behalf of, a member of the public.

(2) Regulations under subsection (1) shall, so far as the Secretary of State thinks it desirable, make provision—

(a) for the procedures for the handling of complaints relating to anything done or omitted to be done by a person in Scotland to be procedures corresponding or similar to those established by or by virtue of sections 40 and 40A of the Police (Scotland) Act 1967;

(b) for the procedures for the handling of complaints relating to anything done or omitted to be done by a person in Northern Ireland to be procedures corresponding or similar to those established by or by virtue of the Police (Amendment) (Northern Ireland) Order 1995, and for that purpose the regulations may confer additional functions on the Independent Commission for Police Complaints for Northern Ireland;

(c) for the procedures for the handling of any other complaint to be procedures corresponding or similar to those established by or by virtue of Chapter I of Part IV of the Police Act 1996 (police complaints), and for that purpose the regulations may confer additional functions on the Police Complaints Authority.

(3) The Secretary of State may issue guidance to persons on whom functions are conferred by regulations under this section concerning the performance of their functions under those regulations, and they shall have regard to any such guidance in the performance of those functions.

(4) A statutory instrument containing regulations under this section shall be subject to annulment in pursuance of a resolution of either House of Parliament.

Definitions For "NCIS", see s 2.
References See para 2.49.

40 Information as to the manner of dealing with complaints etc

The NCIS Service Authority in carrying out its duty under section 3(1), and inspectors of constabulary appointed under section 54 of the Police Act 1996, section 33 of the Police (Scotland) Act 1967 or section 16 of the Police (Scotland) Act 1967 or section 16 of the Police Act (Northern Ireland) 1970 in carrying out their duties with respect to the efficiency and effectiveness of NCIS, shall keep themselves informed as to the operation of procedures established under section 39.

Definitions For "NCIS Service Authority", see s 1(1); for "NCIS", see s 2.

Miscellaneous

41 Arrangements for consultation

(1) The NCIS Service Authority shall, after consulting the Director General of NCIS, make arrangements for obtaining the views of—

- (a) the authorities who between them maintain the police forces in Great Britain and the Royal Ulster Constabulary,
- (b) the NCS Service Authority,
- (c) the Commissioners of Customs and Excise, and
- (d) such other persons or bodies as the NCIS Service Authority considers appropriate,

about the Authority and NCIS.

(2) The Director General of NCIS shall, after consulting the Authority, make arrangements for obtaining the views of—

- (a) the chief officers of police of police forces in England and Wales,
- (b) the chief constables of police forces in Scotland,
- (c) the Chief Constable of the Royal Ulster Constabulary,
- (d) the Director General of the National Crime Squad,
- (e) the Commissioners of Customs and Excise, and
- (f) such other persons or bodies as the Director General of NCIS considers appropriate,

about NCIS.

(3) Arrangements made under subsection (1) or (2) shall be reviewed from time to time.

(4) If it appears to the Secretary of State that arrangements made for consultation by the NCIS Service Authority or the Director General under this section are not adequate for the purposes set out in subsection (1) or (2), he may require the Authority or Director General whose duty it is to make the arrangements to submit a report to him concerning the arrangements.

(5) After considering a report submitted under subsection (4), the Secretary of State may require the Authority or Director General who submitted it to review the arrangements and submit a further report to him concerning them.

(6) The Authority or Director General shall be under the same duties to consult when reviewing arrangements as when making them.

Definitions For "NCIS Service Authority", see s 1(1); for "NCIS", see s 2; for "NCS Service Authority", see s 46.
References See para 2.22.

42 Liability for wrongful acts of constables etc

(1) The Director General of NCIS shall be liable in respect of torts committed by constables under his direction and control in the performance or purported performance of their functions in like manner as a master is liable in respect of torts committed by his servants in the course of their employment, and accordingly shall in respect of any such tort be treated for all purposes as a joint tortfeasor.

(2) There shall be paid out of the NCIS service fund—

(a) any damages or costs awarded against the Director General in any proceedings brought against him by virtue of this section and any costs incurred by him in any such proceedings so far as not recovered by him in the proceedings, and

(b) any sum required in connection with the settlement of any claim made against the Director General by virtue of this section, if the settlement is approved by the NCIS Service Authority.

(3) Any proceedings in respect of a claim made by virtue of this section shall be brought against the Director General of NCIS for the time being or, in the case of a vacancy in that office, against the person for the time being performing the functions of the Director General; and references in this section to the Director General shall be construed accordingly.

(4) The NCIS Service Authority may, in such cases and to such extent as appear to it to be appropriate, pay out of the NCIS service fund—

(a) any damages or costs awarded against a person to whom this subsection applies in proceedings for a tort committed by that person,

(b) any costs incurred and not recovered by such a person in such proceedings, and

(c) any sum required in connection with the settlement of a claim that has or might have given rise to such proceedings.

(5) Subsection (4) applies to a person who is—

(a) a member of NCIS, or

(b) a constable for the time being required to serve with NCIS by virtue of section 23.

(6) In relation to Scotland—

(a) subsection (1) shall not apply but—

(i) the Director General of NCIS shall be liable in reparation in respect of any wrongful act or omission on the part of any constable under his direction and control in the performance or purported performance of his functions in the like manner as a master is so liable in respect of any wrongful act or omission on the part of his servant in the course of the servant's employment, and

(ii) subsection (4)(a) shall apply as if the reference to proceedings for a tort committed by a person were a reference to proceedings for a wrongful act or omission on the part of that person, and

(b) any reference in subsection (2) or (4) to costs shall be construed as a reference to expenses.

Definitions For "NCIS Service Authority", see s 1(1); for "NCIS", see s 2; for "NCIS service fund", see s 46.
References See para 2.29.

43 Causing disaffection

Any person who causes, or attempts to cause, or does any act calculated to cause, disaffection amongst the members of NCIS within section 9(1)(a) or (b), or induces or attempts to induce, or does any act calculated to induce, any such member to withhold his services, shall be guilty of an offence and liable—

(a) on summary conviction, to imprisonment for a term not exceeding six months or to a fine not exceeding the statutory maximum, or to both;

(b) on conviction on indictment, to imprisonment for a term not exceeding two years or to a fine, or to both.

Definitions For "NCIS", see s 2.
References See para 2.50.

44 Orders governing NCIS Service Authority

(1) The Secretary of State may by order make provision (including provision as regards Scotland and Northern Ireland) in relation to the NCIS Service Authority about matters of the kind dealt with in the enactments listed in Schedule 4 (which lists enactments which make provision about police authorities established under section 3 of the Police Act 1996).

(2) A statutory instrument containing an order under this section shall be subject to annulment in pursuance of a resolution of either House of Parliament.

Definitions For "NCIS Service Authority", see s 1(1).
References See paras 2.25, 2.32.

General

45 Orders and regulations

Any power of the Secretary of State to make orders or regulations under this Part shall be exercisable by statutory instrument.

46 Interpretation of Part I

In this Part—

"financial year" means the twelve months ending with 31st March;
"NCIS" has the meaning given in section 2;
"NCIS Service Authority" has the meaning given in section 1(1);
"NCIS service fund" means the fund established under section 16;
"NCS Service Authority" means the Service Authority for the National Crime Squad.

PART II
THE NATIONAL CRIME SQUAD

The Service Authority

47 The Service Authority for the National Crime Squad

(1) There shall be a body corporate to be known as the Service Authority for the National Crime Squad (in this Part referred to as "the NCS Service Authority").

(2) Subject to the following provisions of this section, the NCS Service Authority shall consist of seventeen members.

(3) The Secretary of State may by order provide that the number of its members shall be a specified odd number greater than seventeen.

(4) Before making an order under subsection (3), the Secretary of State shall consult—

(a) the NCS Service Authority (if it is then in existence),

(b) persons whom he considers to represent the interests of police authorities for areas in England and Wales, and

(c) persons whom he considers to represent the interests of chief officers of police of police forces in England and Wales.

(5) A statutory instrument containing an order under subsection (3) shall be laid before Parliament after being made.

(6) The NCS Service Authority may co-opt such additional members as it thinks fit.

(7) Parts I, III and IV of Schedule 1 and Schedule 2 shall have effect in relation to the NCS Service Authority.

References See para 3.6.

Functions

48 General functions of the NCS Service Authority and the National Crime Squad

(1) The NCS Service Authority shall maintain a body to be known as the National Crime Squad.

(2) The function of the National Crime Squad shall be to prevent and detect serious crime which is of relevance to more than one police area in England and Wales.

(3) The National Crime Squad may also—

(a) at the request of a chief officer of police of a police force in England and Wales, act in support of the activities of his force in the prevention and detection of serious crime;

(b) at the request of the Director General of NCIS, act in support of the activities of NCIS;

(c) institute criminal proceedings;

(d) co-operate with other police forces in the United Kingdom in the prevention and detection of serious crime;

(e) act in support of other law enforcement agencies in the prevention and detection of serious crime.

(4) For the purposes of subsection (3), "law enforcement agency" includes—

(a) any government department,

(b) the States of Jersey Police Force, the salaried police force of the Island of Guernsey and the Isle of Man Constabulary,

(c) any other person charged with the duty of investigating offences or charging offenders, and

(d) any other person engaged outside the United Kingdom in the carrying on of activities similar to any carried on by the NCS Service Authority, the National Crime Squad, a police authority, a police force, the NCIS Service Authority or NCIS.

(5) In discharging its functions, the NCS Service Authority shall have regard to—

(a) any objectives determined by the Secretary of State under section 71,
(b) any objectives determined by the Authority under section 49,
(c) any performance targets established by the Authority, whether in compliance with a direction under section 72 or otherwise, and
(d) any service plan issued by the Authority under section 50.

(6) In discharging any function to which a code of practice issued under section 73 relates, the NCS Service Authority shall have regard to the code.

(7) The NCS Service Authority shall comply with any direction given to it by the Secretary of State under section 72 or 75 or under Schedule 5.

Definitions For "NCS Service Authority", see s 47(1); for "NCIS" and "NCIS Service Authority", see s 90.
References See paras 3.4, 3.14, 3.15, 3.18.

49 Objectives

(1) The NCS Service Authority shall secure that the National Crime Squad is efficient and effective.

(2) The NCS Service Authority shall, before the beginning of each financial year, determine objectives for that year for the National Crime Squad.

(3) Objectives determined under this section may relate to matters to which objectives determined under section 71 also relate, or to other matters, but in any event shall be so framed as to be consistent with the objectives determined under that section.

(4) Before determining objectives under this section, the NCS Service Authority shall consult—

(a) the Director General of the National Crime Squad,
(b) the NCIS Service Authority, and
(c) persons whom it considers to represent the interests of police authorities for areas in England and Wales.

Definitions For "NCS Service Authority", see s 47(1); for "financial year" and "NCIS Service Authority", see s 90.
References See paras 3.7, 3.12.

50 Service plans

(1) The NCS Service Authority shall, before the beginning of each financial year, issue a plan setting out the proposed arrangements for the carrying out by the National Crime Squad of its functions during the year ("the service plan").

(2) The service plan shall include a statement of the Authority's priorities for the year, of the financial resources expected to be available and of the proposed allocation of those resources, and shall give particulars of—

(a) any objectives determined by the Secretary of State under section 71;
(b) any objectives determined by the Authority under section 49, and
(c) any performance targets established by the Authority, whether in compliance with a direction under section 72 or otherwise.

(3) A draft of the service plan shall be prepared by the Director General of the National Crime Squad and submitted by him to the Authority for it to consider.

(4) Before issuing a service plan which differs from the draft submitted by the Director General under subsection (3), the Authority shall consult the Director General.

(5) The Authority shall arrange for every service plan issued by it under this section to be published in such manner as appears to it to be appropriate, and shall send a copy of the plan to—

(a) the Secretary of State,
(b) each police authority for an area in England and Wales,
(c) the chief officer of police of each police force in England and Wales,
(d) the NCIS Service Authority, and
(e) the Director General of NCIS.

Definitions For "NCS Service Authority", see s 47(1); for "financial year", "NCIS" and "NCIS Service Authority", see s 90.
References See para 3.8.

51 Annual reports

(1) The NCS Service Authority shall, as soon as possible after the end of each financial year, issue a report on the carrying out of its functions during that year.

(2) A report issued under this section for any year shall include an assessment of the extent to which the service plan for that year issued under section 50 has been carried out.

(3) The NCS Service Authority shall arrange for every report issued by it under this section to be published in such manner as appears to it to be appropriate, and shall send a copy of the report to—

(a) the Secretary of State,
(b) each police authority for an area in England and Wales,
(c) the chief officer of police of each police force in England and Wales,
(d) the NCIS Service Authority, and
(e) the Director General of NCIS.

Definitions For "NCS Service Authority", see s 47(1); for "financial year", "NCIS" and "NCIS Service Authority", see s 90.
References See para 3.6.

Director General and other members

52 Appointment of Director General

(1) The National Crime Squad shall have a Director General appointed by the NCS Service Authority on such terms and conditions as the Authority considers appropriate.

(2) The Director General shall be chosen by a panel of members of the Authority from a list of persons eligible for appointment which has been prepared by that panel and approved by the Secretary of State.

(3) A person is eligible for appointment as Director General for the purposes of subsection (2) if—

(a) he holds the rank of chief constable in a police force in Great Britain or in the Royal Ulster Constabulary,
(b) he is the Commissioner, an Assistant Commissioner or a Deputy Assistant Commissioner of Police of the Metropolis,

(c) he is the Commissioner of Police for the City of London, or
(d) he is, in accordance with regulations under section 50 of the Police Act 1996, section 26 of the Police (Scotland) Act 1967 or section 25 of the Police Act (Northern Ireland) 1970, a constable eligible for appointment to any of the ranks or posts mentioned in paragraphs (a) to (c).

(4) The panel mentioned in subsection (2) shall be convened by the chairman of the NCS Authority and shall consist only of members of that Authority appointed—
(a) by the Secretary of State (other than under paragraph 6 of Schedule 1), or
(b) by local authority members of police authorities for areas in England and Wales (as defined in paragraph 14 of that Schedule).

(5) The Director General shall, on appointment, be attested as a constable by making a declaration in the form set out in Schedule 4 to the Police Act 1996 before a justice of the peace appointed for an area in England and Wales.

(6) Without prejudice to any other enactment conferring powers on constables for particular purposes, the Director General shall have all the powers and privileges of a constable throughout England and Wales and the adjacent United Kingdom waters.

(7) The Director General shall hold the rank of chief constable.

(8) In subsection (6)—
"powers" includes powers under any enactment, whenever passed or made;
"United Kingdom waters" means the sea and other waters within the seaward limits of the territorial sea;

and that subsection, so far as it relates to powers under any enactment, makes them exercisable throughout the United Kingdom waters whether or not the enactment applies to those waters apart from this provision.

Definitions For "NCS Service Authority", see s 47(1).
References See paras 3.22, 3.23, 3.27.

53 Removal of Director General by the Authority

(1) Without prejudice to section 66 or to any regulations under section 81 or under the Police Pensions Act 1976, the NCS Service Authority, acting with the approval of the Secretary of State, may call upon the Director General of the National Crime Squad to retire in the interests of efficiency or effectiveness.

(2) Before seeking the approval of the Secretary of State for the purposes of subsection (1), the Authority shall give the Director General an opportunity to make representations and shall consider any representations that he makes.

(3) A Director General who is called upon to retire under subsection (1) shall retire on such date as the Authority may specify or on such earlier date as may be agreed upon between him and the Authority.

Definitions For "NCS Service Authority", see s 47(1).
References See para 3.24.

54 Deputy Director General

(1) The Director General of the National Crime Squad shall designate a police member of the National Crime Squad to whom section 55(2)(a) applies to exercise all the powers and duties of the Director General—
(a) during any absence, incapacity or suspension from duty of the Director General, or
(b) during any vacancy in the office of Director General.

(2) The Director General shall consult the NCS Service Authority before designating a member under subsection (1).

(3) No more than one person shall be authorised to act by virtue of a designation under subsection (1) at any one time; and a person so authorised shall not have power to act by virtue of that subsection for a continuous period exceeding three months except with the consent of the Secretary of State.

Definitions For "NCS Service Authority", see s 47(1).
References See paras 3.25, 3.26.

55 Members of the National Crime Squad

(1) The National Crime Squad shall consist of—
- (a) the Director General appointed under section 52,
- (b) persons appointed by the NCS Service Authority under this paragraph as police members of the National Crime Squad, and
- (c) other persons appointed by the NCS Service Authority under this paragraph to be members of the National Crime Squad as employees of the Authority.

(2) A person shall be appointed as a police member of the National Crime Squad only if—
- (a) he is appointed to the rank of assistant chief constable in the National Crime Squad and he met the requirements of subsection (3) immediately prior to his being appointed, or
- (b) he is engaged with the National Crime Squad on a period of temporary service to which section 97 of the Police Act 1996 applies.

(3) A person meets the requirements of this subsection if—
- (a) he holds the rank of assistant chief constable or a higher rank in a police force in Great Britain or in the Royal Ulster Constabulary,
- (b) he holds the rank of commander or a higher rank in the metropolitan police force or in the City of London police force, or
- (c) he is, in accordance with regulations under section 50 of the Police Act 1996, section 26 of the Police (Scotland) Act 1967 or section 25 of the Police Act (Northern Ireland) 1970, a constable eligible for appointment to the rank of assistant chief constable or commander in any of the police forces, or in the Constabulary, mentioned in paragraph (a) or (b).

(4) Subsections (5), (6) and (8) of section 52 apply to a police member to whom subsection (2)(a) above applies as they apply to the Director General of the National Crime Squad.

(5) A person appointed under subsection (1)(b) or (c) shall be appointed on such terms and conditions as the NCS Service Authority considers appropriate.

(6) Before making an appointment under subsection (1)(b) or (c), or determining the terms and conditions on which such an appointment is to be made, the NCS Service Authority shall consult the Director General of the National Crime Squad.

(7) A police member to whom subsection (2)(b) applies shall cease to be a member of the National Crime Squad at the end of his period of temporary service (unless re-appointed under this section).

(8) The NCS Service Authority shall exercise its powers under section 101 (and section 107) of the Local Government Act 1972 so as to secure that, subject to subsection (9) below, the Director General of the National Crime Squad appoints persons under subsection (1)(b) or (c) to be members of the National Crime Squad.

(9) Subsection (8) shall not apply to—
 (a) the appointment of any person to whom subsection (2)(a) applies as a police member, or
 (b) the appointment of such other persons as may be agreed between the Director General and the Authority or, in the absence of agreement, as may be determined by the Secretary of State.

(10) Section 53 applies to a member appointed under this section, other than a member appointed by the Director General by virtue of subsection (8), as it applies to the Director General.

Definitions For "NCS Service Authority", see s 47(1).
References See paras 3.28–3.31.

Functions of Director General

56 General function of Director General

(1) The National Crime Squad shall be under the direction and control of the Director General.

(2) In discharging his functions, the Director General shall have regard to the service plan issued by the NCS Service Authority under section 50.

Definitions For "NCS Service Authority", see s 47(1).
References See paras 3.2, 3.21.

57 Reports by Director General to the Authority

(1) The Director General of the National Crime Squad shall, as soon as possible after the end of each financial year, submit to the NCS Service Authority a general report on the activities of the Squad during that year.

(2) The Director General shall arrange for a report submitted by him under subsection (1) to be published in such manner as appears to him to be appropriate.

(3) The NCS Service Authority may require the Director General to submit to it a report on such matters connected with the activities of the National Crime Squad as may be specified in the requirement.

(4) A report submitted under subsection (3) shall be in such form as the Authority may specify.

(5) If it appears to the Director General that a report in compliance with subsection (3) would contain information which in the public interest ought not to be disclosed, or is not needed for the discharge of the functions of the Authority, he may request the Authority to refer the requirement to the Secretary of State; and in any such case the requirement shall be of no effect unless it is confirmed by the Secretary of State.

(6) The Authority may arrange, or require the Director General to arrange, for a report submitted under subsection (3) to be published in such manner as appears to the Authority to be appropriate.

Definitions For "NCS Service Authority", see s 47(1); for "financial year", see s 90.
References See paras 3.12, 3.21.

Service Authority's officers and employees

58 Officers and employees

(1) The NCS Service Authority may appoint officers and employees to enable the Authority to discharge its functions.

(2) Persons appointed under this section shall be appointed on such terms and conditions as the NCS Service Authority considers appropriate.

Definitions For "NCS Service Authority", see s 47(1).
References See para 3.28.

59 Appointment of clerk

The NCS Service Authority shall appoint a person to be the clerk to the Authority.

Definitions For "NCS Service Authority", see s 47(1).
References See para 3.31.

60 Appointment of persons not employed by the NCS Service Authority

Where the NCS Service Authority is required or authorised by any Act—

(a) to appoint a person to a specified office under the Authority, or

(b) to designate a person as having specified duties or responsibilities,

then, notwithstanding any provision of that Act to the contrary, the Authority may appoint or designate either a person employed by the Authority under section 58, or a person not holding any office or employment under the Authority.

Definitions For "NCS Service Authority", see s 47(1).

Financial provisions

61 NCS service fund

(1) The NCS Service Authority shall keep a fund to be known as the NCS service fund.

(2) Subject to any regulations under the Police Pensions Act 1976 and to section 66 below, all receipts of the Authority shall be paid into the NCS service fund and all expenditure of the Authority shall be paid out of that fund.

(3) Accounts shall be kept by the Authority of payments made into or out of the NCS service fund.

Definitions For "NCS Service Authority", see s 47(1).
References See para 3.33.

62 Power to issue levies

(1) The NCS Service Authority shall, in respect of every financial year beginning after the establishment of that Authority, issue levies to—

(a) police authorities for areas in England and Wales (other than the metropolitan police district), and

(b) the Receiver for the Metropolitan Police District.

(2) The Secretary of State shall, by order, make provision in relation to the calculation, setting, collection, administration and payment of levies under this section.

(3) An order under this section may include provision—
- (a) as to apportionment of levies issued under this section;
- (b) conferring a right to interest on anything unpaid.

(4) An order under this section may also include provision—
- (a) that the Common Council of the City of London making calculations in accordance with section 32 of the Local Government Finance Act 1992 (originally or by way of substitute) may anticipate a levy;
- (b) that a police authority established under section 3 of the Police Act 1996, or the Receiver for the Metropolitan Police District, making calculations in accordance with section 43 of the Local Government Finance Act 1992 (originally or by way of substitute) may anticipate a levy;
- (c) as to the treatment as special expenses of amounts so anticipated;
- (d) as to the treatment of any levy actually issued.

(5) A statutory instrument containing an order under this section shall be subject to annulment in pursuance of a resolution of either House of Parliament.

(6) Schedule 5 (which makes further provision in connection with levies under this section) shall have effect.

Definitions For "NCS Service Authority", see s 47(1); for "financial year", see s 90.
References See para 3.35.

63 Initial financing of NCS Service Authority

The Secretary of State may make grants to the NCS Service Authority in respect of expenditure incurred (or to be incurred) by it at any time before the financial year in which revenue is first received by it as a result of levies issued by it under section 62.

Definitions For "NCS Service Authority", see s 47(1); for "financial year", see s 90.
References See para 3.37.

64 Charges

(1) The NCS Service Authority may make charges in respect of the provision of any services, or an agreement for the provision of any services, to any person by the Authority or by the National Crime Squad.

(2) Any charges made under this section may include amounts calculated by reference to the expenditure incurred or expected to be incurred by the NCS Service Authority, or by the National Crime Squad, otherwise than directly in connection with the provision of the services concerned.

Definitions For "NCS Service Authority", see s 47(1).
References See para 3.38.

65 Acceptance of gifts and loans

(1) The NCS Service Authority may, in connection with the discharge of any of its functions, accept gifts of money, and gifts or loans of other property, on such terms as appear to the Authority to be appropriate.

(2) The terms on which gifts or loans are accepted under subsection (1) may include terms providing for the commercial sponsorship of any activity of the Authority or of the National Crime Squad.

Definitions For "NCS Service Authority", see s 47(1).
References See para 3.38.

66 Pensions and gratuities

(1) The NCS Service Authority may—
- (a) pay, or make payments in respect of, pensions or gratuities to or in respect of any persons who are, or have been, its officers or employees;
- (b) provide and maintain schemes (whether contributory or not) for the payment of pensions or gratuities to or in respect of any such persons.

(2) The NCS Service Authority may—
- (a) pay, or make payments in respect of, such pensions or gratuities as it may determine, with the consent of the Secretary of State, to or in respect of any persons who are or have been the Director General of the National Crime Squad or police members of the Squad;
- (b) provide and maintain such schemes (whether contributory or not) as it may determine, with the consent of the Secretary of State, for the payment of pensions or gratuities to or in respect of any such persons.

(3) Before exercising its powers under subsection (2), the Authority shall have regard to any provision made under the Police Pensions Act 1976 or section 25(2)(k) of the Police Act (Northern Ireland) 1970.

(4) References in this section to pensions and gratuities include references to pensions or gratuities by way of compensation to or in respect of any of the persons mentioned in subsection (1) or (2) who suffer loss of office or employment or loss or diminution of emoluments.

Definitions For "NCS Service Authority", see s 47(1).
References See paras 3.30, 3.33.

67 Revenue accounts and capital finance

In section 39 of the Local Government and Housing Act 1989, in subsection (1) (authorities to which provisions about revenue accounts and capital finance apply), after paragraph (j) there shall be inserted—

"(ja) the Service Authority for the National Crime Squad;".

68 Financial administration

In section 111 of the Local Government Finance Act 1988, in subsection (2) (definition of "relevant authority" for the purposes of provisions regulating financial administration), after paragraph (e) there shall be inserted—

"(ea) the Service Authority for the National Crime Squad;".

Special services

69 Provision of special services

The Director General of the National Crime Squad may, at the request of any person, provide services at any premises or in any locality in England and Wales, if those services are consistent with the functions of, and do not prejudice the efficiency or effectiveness of, the Squad.

References See para 3.39.

Central supervision and direction

70 General duty of Secretary of State

The Secretary of State shall exercise his powers under this Part in such manner and to such extent as appears to him to be best calculated to promote the efficiency and effectiveness of the National Crime Squad.

References See para 3.40.

71 Setting of objectives

(1) The Secretary of State may by order determine objectives for the National Crime Squad.

(2) Before making an order under this section, the Secretary of State shall consult—

- (a) the NCS Service Authority,
- (b) the Director General of the National Crime Squad,
- (c) persons whom the Secretary of State considers to represent the interests of police authorities for areas in England and Wales,
- (d) persons whom he considers to represent the interests of chief officers of police of police forces in England and Wales,
- (e) the NCIS Service Authority, and
- (f) the Director General of NCIS.

(3) A statutory instrument containing an order under this section shall be laid before Parliament after being made.

Definitions For "NCS Service Authority", see s 47(1); for "NCIS" and "NCIS Service Authority", see s 90.
References See paras 3.42, 3.43.

72 Setting of performance targets

(1) Where an objective has been determined under section 71, the Secretary of State may direct the NCS Service Authority to establish levels of performance ("performance targets") to be aimed at in seeking to achieve the objective.

(2) A direction given under this section may impose conditions with which the performance targets must conform.

(3) The Secretary of State shall arrange for any direction given under this section to be published in such manner as appears to him to be appropriate.

Definitions For "NCS Service Authority", see s 47(1).
References See para 3.42.

73 Codes of practice

(1) The Secretary of State may issue codes of practice relating to the discharge by the NCS Service Authority of its functions.

(2) The Secretary of State may from time to time revise the whole or part of any code of practice issued under this section.

(3) The Secretary of State shall lay before Parliament a copy of any code of practice, and of any revision of a code of practice, issued by him under this section.

Definitions For "NCS Service Authority", see s 47(1).
References See para 3.13.

74 Removal of Director General etc

(1) The Secretary of State may require the NCS Service Authority to exercise its power under section 53 to call upon the Director General of the National Crime Squad, or any other member (other than a member appointed by the Director General by virtue of section 55(8)) to retire in the interests of efficiency or effectiveness.

(2) Before—

- (a) exercising any power conferred on him by subsection (1), or
- (b) approving the exercise by the NCS Service Authority of its power under section 53,

the Secretary of State shall give the person in relation to whom it is proposed to exercise the power (the "relevant person") an opportunity to make representations to him and shall consider any representations so made.

(3) Where representations are made under this section the Secretary of State may, and in a case where he proposes to exercise a power conferred by subsection (1) shall, appoint one or more persons to hold an inquiry and report to him.

(4) The Secretary of State shall take account of any report made under subsection (3).

(5) The person appointed under subsection (3) (or, in a case where more than one person is so appointed, at least one of the persons so appointed) shall not be an officer of police, of a Government department, of the National Crime Squad or of NCIS.

(6) The costs incurred by a relevant person in respect of an inquiry under this section, taxed in such manner as the Secretary of State may direct, shall be defrayed out of the NCS service fund.

Definitions For "NCS Service Authority", see s 47(1); for "NCS service fund" and "NCIS", see s 90.
References See paras 3.24, 3.41.

75 Power to give directions after adverse report

(1) The Secretary of State may at any time require the inspectors of constabulary to carry out an inspection of the National Crime Squad under section 54 of the Police Act 1996.

(2) Where a report made to the Secretary of State on an inspection carried out in accordance with this section states—

- (a) that, in the opinion of the person making the report, the National Crime Squad is not efficient or not effective, or

(b) that in his opinion, unless remedial measures are taken, the National Crime Squad will cease to be efficient or will cease to be effective,

the Secretary of State may direct the NCS Service Authority to take such measures as may be specified in the direction.

Definitions For "NCS Service Authority", see s 47(1).
References See para 3.43.

76 Reports from NCS Service Authority

(1) The Secretary of State may require the NCS Service Authority to submit to him a report on such matters connected with the discharge of the Authority's functions, or otherwise with the activities of the National Crime Squad, as may be specified in the requirement.

(2) A report submitted under subsection (1) shall be in such form as the Secretary of State may specify.

(3) The Secretary of State may arrange, or require the Authority to arrange, for a report under this section to be published in such manner as appears to him to be appropriate.

Definitions For "NCS Service Authority", see s 47(1).
References See paras 3.40, 3.41.

77 Reports from Director General

(1) The Secretary of State may require the Director General of the National Crime Squad to submit to him a report on such matters connected with the activities of the National Crime Squad as may be specified in the requirement.

(2) A report submitted under subsection (1) shall be in such form as the Secretary of State may specify.

(3) The Secretary of State may arrange, or require the Director General to arrange, for a report under this section to be published in such manner as appears to the Secretary of State to be appropriate.

(4) The Director General shall, as soon as possible after the end of each financial year, submit to the Secretary of State the like report as is required by section 57 to be submitted to the NCS Service Authority.

Definitions For "NCS Service Authority", see s 47(1); for "financial year", see s 90.

78 Criminal statistics

(1) The Director General of the National Crime Squad shall, at such times and in such form as the Secretary of State may direct, transmit to the Secretary of State such particulars with respect to offences, offenders, criminal proceedings and the state of crime as the Secretary of State may require.

(2) The Secretary of State shall cause a consolidated and classified abstract of the information transmitted to him under this section to be included in the abstract laid before Parliament under section 45 of the Police Act 1996.

References See para 3.21.

79 Inquiries

(1) The Secretary of State may cause an inquiry to be held by a person appointed by him into any matter connected with the National Crime Squad.

(2) An inquiry under this section shall be held in public or in private as the Secretary of State may direct.

(3) Subsections (2) and (3) of section 250 of the Local Government Act 1972 (power to summon and examine witnesses) shall apply to an inquiry held under this section as they apply to an inquiry held under that section.

(4) Where the report of the person holding an inquiry under this section is not published, a summary of his findings and conclusions shall be made known by the Secretary of State so far as appears to him consistent with the public interest.

(5) The Secretary of State may direct that the whole or part of the costs incurred by any person for the purposes of an inquiry held under this section shall be defrayed out of the NCS service fund; and any costs payable under this section shall be subject to taxation in such manner as the Secretary of State may direct.

Definitions For "NCS service fund", see s 90.
References See para 3.45.

80 Regulations as to standard of equipment

The Secretary of State may make regulations requiring equipment provided or used for the purposes of the National Crime Squad to satisfy such requirements as to design and performance as may be prescribed in the regulations.

References See para 3.43.

Discipline and complaints

81 Discipline regulations

(1) The Secretary of State may make regulations as to the conduct of members of the National Crime Squad and the maintenance of discipline in that Squad.

(2) In relation to any matter as to which provision may be made by regulations under this section, the regulations may—

- (a) authorise or require provision to be made by, or confer discretionary powers on, the NCS Service Authority, the Director General of the National Crime Squad or other persons, or
- (b) authorise or require the delegation by any person of functions conferred on that person by or under the regulations.

(3) A statutory instrument containing regulations under this section shall be subject to annulment in pursuance of a resolution of either House of Parliament.

Definitions For "NCS Service Authority", see s 47(1).

82 Appeals

(1) Where the Director General of the National Crime Squad, or a police member to whom section 55(2)(a) applies, is dismissed or required to resign by a decision taken under or by virtue of regulations made under section 81, he may appeal to an appeals tribunal against the decision except where he has a right of

appeal to some other person; and in that case he may appeal to an appeals tribunal from any decision of that other person as a result of which he is dismissed or required to resign.

(2) Section 85(2) to (5) of, and Schedule 6 to, the Police Act 1996 (police appeals tribunals) shall apply, subject to such modifications as the Secretary of State may by order prescribe, in relation to an appeals tribunal and an appeal under subsection (1) above as they apply in relation to a police appeals tribunal and an appeal under section 85(1) of that Act.

(3) A statutory instrument containing an order under this section shall be subject to annulment in pursuance of a resolution of either House of Parliament.

References See para 3.46.

83 Complaints

(1) The Secretary of State shall, by regulations, make provision for the handling of any complaint about the conduct of any member of the National Crime Squad which is submitted by, or on behalf of, a member of the public.

(2) The procedures established by virtue of subsection (1) shall, so far as the Secretary of State thinks it desirable, be procedures corresponding or similar to those established by or by virtue of Chapter I of Part IV of the Police Act 1996 (police complaints), and for that purpose regulations may confer additional functions on the Police Complaints Authority.

(3) The Secretary of State may issue guidance to persons on whom functions are conferred by regulations under this section concerning the performance of their functions under those regulations, and they shall have regard to any such guidance in the performance of those functions.

(4) A statutory instrument containing regulations under this section shall be subject to annulment in pursuance of a resolution of either House of Parliament.

References See para 3.46.

84 Information as to the manner of dealing with complaints etc

The NCS Service Authority in carrying out its duty under section 49(1), and the inspectors of constabulary in carrying out their duties with respect to the efficiency and effectiveness of the National Crime Squad, shall keep themselves informed as to the operation of procedures established under section 83.

Definitions For "NCS Service Authority", see s 47(1).

Miscellaneous

85 Arrangements for consultation

(1) The NCS Service Authority shall, after consulting the Director General of the National Crime Squad, make arrangements for obtaining the views of—

(a) police authorities for areas in England and Wales,

(b) the NCIS Service Authority, and

(c) such other persons or bodies as the NCS Service Authority considers appropriate,

about the Authority and the National Crime Squad.

(2) The Director General of the National Crime Squad shall, after consulting the Authority, make arrangements for obtaining the views of—

(a) the chief officers of police of police forces in England and Wales,

(b) the Director General of NCIS, and

(c) such other persons or bodies as the Director General of the National Crime Squad considers appropriate,

about the National Crime Squad.

(3) Arrangements made under subsection (1) or (2) shall be reviewed from time to time.

(4) If it appears to the Secretary of State that arrangements made for consultation by the NCS Service Authority or the Director General under this section are not adequate for the purposes set out in subsection (1) or (2), he may require the Authority or Director General whose duty it is to make the arrangements to submit a report to him concerning the arrangements.

(5) After considering a report submitted under subsection (4), the Secretary of State may require the Authority or Director General who submitted it to review the arrangements and submit a further report to him concerning them.

(6) The Authority or Director General shall be under the same duties to consult when reviewing arrangements as when making them.

Definitions For "NCS Service Authority", see s 47(1); for "NCIS" and "NCIS Service Authority" see s 90.
References See para 3.43.

86 Liability for wrongful acts of constables etc

(1) The Director General of the National Crime Squad shall be liable in respect of torts committed by constables under his direction and control in the performance or purported performance of their functions in like manner as a master is liable in respect of torts committed by his servants in the course of their employment, and accordingly shall in respect of any such tort be treated for all purposes as a joint tortfeasor.

(2) There shall be paid out of the NCS service fund—

(a) any damages or costs awarded against the Director General in any proceedings brought against him by virtue of this section and any costs incurred by him in any such proceedings so far as not recovered by him in the proceedings, and

(b) any sum required in connection with the settlement of any claim made against the Director General by virtue of this section, if the settlement is approved by the NCS Service Authority.

(3) Any proceedings in respect of a claim made by virtue of this section shall be brought against the Director General of the National Crime Squad for the time being or, in the case of a vacancy in that office, against the person for the time being performing the functions of the Director General; and references in subsections (1) and (2) to the Director General shall be construed accordingly.

(4) The NCS Service Authority may, in such cases and to such extent as appear to it to be appropriate, pay out of the NCS service fund—

(a) any damages or costs awarded against a person to whom this subsection applies in proceedings for a tort committed by that person,

(b) any costs incurred and not recovered by such a person in such proceedings, and
(c) any sum required in connection with the settlement of a claim that has or might have given rise to such proceedings.

(5) Subsection (4) applies to a person who is—
(a) a member of the National Crime Squad, or
(b) a constable for the time being required to serve with the National Crime Squad by virtue of section 23 above or section 24 or 98 of the Police Act 1996.

Definitions For "NCS Service Authority", see s 47(1); for "NCS service fund", see s 90.
References See para 3.27.

87 Causing disaffection

Any person who causes, or attempts to cause, or does any act calculated to cause, disaffection amongst the members of the National Crime Squad within section 55(1)(a) or (b), or induces or attempts to induce, or does any act calculated to induce, any such member to withhold his services, shall be guilty of an offence and liable—
(a) on summary conviction, to imprisonment for a term not exceeding six months or to a fine not exceeding the statutory maximum, or to both;
(b) on conviction on indictment, to imprisonment for a term not exceeding two years or to a fine, or to both.

References See para 3.47.

88 Application to NCS Service Authority of local authority enactments

Schedule 6 (which amends local authority enactments applying to police authorities so as to apply those enactments in a similar way to the NCS Service Authority) shall have effect.

General

89 Orders and regulations

Any power of the Secretary of State to make orders or regulations under this Part shall be exercisable by statutory instrument.

90 Interpretation of Part II

In this Part—
"financial year" means the twelve months ending with 31st March;
"NCIS" means the National Criminal Intelligence Service;
"NCIS Service Authority" means the Service Authority for the National Criminal Intelligence Service;
"NCS Service Authority" has the meaning given in section 47(1);
"NCS service fund" means the fund established under section 61.

PART III
AUTHORISATION OF ACTION IN RESPECT OF PROPERTY

The Commissioners

91 The Commissioners

(1) The Prime Minister shall appoint for the purposes of this Part—
  (a) a Chief Commissioner, and
  (b) such number of other Commissioners as the Prime Minister thinks fit.

(2) The persons appointed under subsection (1) shall be persons who hold or have held high judicial office within the meaning of the Appellate Jurisdiction Act 1876.

(3) Subject to subsections (4) to (7), each Commissioner shall hold and vacate office in accordance with the terms of his appointment.

(4) Each Commissioner shall be appointed for a term of three years.

(5) A person who ceases to be a Commissioner (otherwise than under subsection (7)) may be reappointed under this section.

(6) Subject to subsection (7), a Commissioner shall not be removed from office before the end of the term for which he is appointed unless a resolution approving his removal has been passed by each House of Parliament.

(7) A Commissioner may be removed from office by the Prime Minister if after his appointment—
  (a) a bankruptcy order is made against him or his estate is sequestrated or he makes a composition or arrangement with, or grants a trust deed for, his creditors;
  (b) a disqualification order under the Company Directors Disqualification Act 1986 or Part II of the Companies (Northern Ireland) Order 1989, or an order under section 429(2)(b) of the Insolvency Act 1986 (failure to pay under county court administration order), is made against him; or
  (c) he is convicted in the United Kingdom, the Channel Islands or the Isle of Man of an offence and has passed on him a sentence of imprisonment (whether suspended or not).

(8) The Secretary of State shall pay to each Commissioner such allowances as the Secretary of State considers appropriate.

(9) The Secretary of State shall, after consultation with the Chief Commissioner, provide the Commissioners with such staff as the Secretary of State considers necessary for the discharge of their functions.

(10) The decisions of the Chief Commissioner or, subject to sections 104 and 106, any other Commissioner (including decisions as to his jurisdiction) shall not be subject to appeal or liable to be questioned in any court.

References See paras 4.60, 4.61, 4.114.

Authorisations

92 Effect of authorisation under Part III

No entry on or interference with property or with wireless telegraphy shall be unlawful if it is authorised by an authorisation having effect under this Part.

Definitions For "authorisation", see s 93; for "wireless telegraphy", see s 108(1).

93 Authorisations to interfere with property etc

(1) Where subsection (2) applies, an authorising officer may authorise—

(a) the taking of such action, in respect of such property in the relevant area, as he may specify, or

(b) the taking of such action in the relevant area as he may specify, in respect of wireless telegraphy.

(2) This subsection applies where the authorising officer believes—

(a) that it is necessary for the action specified to be taken on the ground that it is likely to be of substantial value in the prevention or detection of serious crime, and

(b) that what the action seeks to achieve cannot reasonably be achieved by other means.

(3) An authorising officer shall not give an authorisation under this section except on an application made—

(a) if the authorising officer is within subsection (5)(a) to (e), by a member of his police force,

(b) if the authorising officer is within subsection (5)(f), by a member of the National Criminal Intelligence Service,

(c) if the authorising officer is within subsection (5)(g), by a member of the National Crime Squad, or

(d) if the authorising officer is within subsection (5)(h), by a customs officer.

(4) For the purposes of subsection (2), conduct which constitutes one or more offences shall be regarded as serious crime if, and only if,—

(a) it involves the use of violence, results in substantial financial gain or is conduct by a large number of persons in pursuit of a common purpose, or

(b) the offence or one of the offences is an offence for which a person who has attained the age of twenty-one and has no previous convictions could reasonably be expected to be sentenced to imprisonment for a term of three years or more,

and, where the authorising officer is within subsection (5)(h), it relates to an assigned matter within the meaning of section 1(1) of the Customs and Excise Management Act 1979.

(5) In this section "authorising officer" means—

(a) the chief constable of a police force maintained under section 2 of the Police Act 1996 (maintenance of police forces for areas in England and Wales except London);

(b) the Commissioner, or an Assistant Commissioner, of Police of the Metropolis;

(c) the Commissioner of Police for the City of London;

(d) the chief constable of a police force maintained under or by virtue of section 1 of the Police (Scotland) Act 1967 (maintenance of police forces for areas in Scotland);

(e) the Chief Constable or a Deputy Chief Constable of the Royal Ulster Constabulary;

(f) the Director General of the National Criminal Intelligence Service;

(g) the Director General of the National Crime Squad; or

(h) the customs officer designated by the Commissioners of Customs and Excise for the purposes of this paragraph.

(6) In this section "relevant area"—

(a) in relation to a person within paragraph (a), (b) or (c) of subsection (5), means the area in England and Wales for which his police force is maintained;

(b) in relation to a person within paragraph (d) of that subsection means the area in Scotland for which his police force is maintained;

(c) in relation to a person within paragraph (e) of that subsection, means Northern Ireland;

(d) in relation to the Director General of the National Criminal Intelligence Service, means the United Kingdom;

(e) in relation to the Director General of the National Crime Squad, means England and Wales; and

(f) in relation to the customs officer designated for the purposes of paragraph (h) of that subsection, means the United Kingdom,

and in each case includes the adjacent United Kingdom waters.

(7) The powers conferred by, or by virtue of, this section are additional to any other powers which a person has as a constable either at common law or under or by virtue of any other enactment and are not to be taken to affect any of those other powers.

Definitions For "customs officer", "interference", "United Kingdom waters" and "wireless telegraphy", see s 108(1).
References See paras 4.43–4.54.

94 Authorisations given in absence of authorising officer

(1) Subsection (2) applies where it is not reasonably practicable for an authorising officer to consider an application for an authorisation under section 93 and—

(a) if the authorising officer is within paragraph (b) or (e) of section 93(5), it is also not reasonably practicable for the application to be considered by any of the other persons within the paragraph concerned; or

(b) if the authorising officer is within paragraph (a), (c), (d), (f) or (g) of section 93(5), it is also not reasonably practicable for the application to be considered by his designated deputy.

(2) Where this subsection applies, the powers conferred on the authorising officer by section 93 may, in an urgent case, be exercised—

(a) where the authorising officer is within paragraph (a) or (d) of subsection (5) of that section, by a person holding the rank of assistant chief constable in his force;

(b) where the authorising officer is within paragraph (b) of that subsection, by a person holding the rank of commander in the metropolitan police force;

(c) where the authorising officer is within paragraph (c) of that subsection, by a person holding the rank of commander in the City of London police force;

(d) where the authorising officer is within paragraph (e) of that subsection, by a person holding the rank of assistant chief constable in the Royal Ulster Constabulary;

(e) where the authorising officer is within paragraph (f) or (g) of that subsection by a person designated for the purposes of this section by the Director General of the National Criminal Intelligence Service or, as the case may be, of the National Crime Squad;

(f) where the authorising officer is within paragraph (h) of that subsection, by a customs officer designated by the Commissioners of Customs and Excise for the purposes of this section.

(3) A police member of the National Criminal Intelligence Service or the National Crime Squad appointed under section 9(1)(b) or 55(1)(b) may not be designated under subsection (2)(e) unless—

(a) he has held the rank of assistant chief constable in a police force maintained under section 2 of the Police Act 1996 or under or by virtue of section 1 of the Police (Scotland) Act 1967, or in the Royal Ulster Constabulary, or

(b) he has held the rank of commander in the metropolitan police force or the City of London police force.

(4) In subsection (1), "designated deputy"—

(a) in the case of an authorising officer within paragraph (a) or (d) of section 93(5), means the person holding the rank of assistant chief constable designated to act in his absence under section 12(4) of the Police Act 1996 or, as the case may be, section 5(4) of the Police (Scotland) Act 1967;

(b) in the case of an authorising officer within paragraph (c) of section 93(5), means the person authorised to act in his absence under section 25 of the City of London Police Act 1839; and 1839.

(c) in the case of an authorising officer within paragraph (f) or (g) of section 93(5), means the person designated to act in his absence under section 8 or 54.

Definitions For "authorisation", see s 93; for "authorising officer", see s 93(5); for "customs officer" see s 108(1).
References See paras 4.36, 4.37, 4.56, 4.58.

95 Authorisations: form and duration etc

(1) An authorisation shall be in writing, except that in an urgent case an authorisation (other than one given by virtue of section 94) may be given orally.

(2) An authorisation shall, unless renewed under subsection (3), cease to have effect—

(a) if given orally or by virtue of section 94, at the end of the period of 72 hours beginning with the time when it took effect;

(b) in any other case, at the end of the period of three months beginning with the day on which it took effect.

(3) If at any time before an authorisation would cease to have effect the authorising officer who gave the authorisation, or in whose absence it was given, considers it necessary for the authorisation to continue to have effect for the purpose for which it was issued, he may, in writing, renew it for a period of three months beginning with the day on which it would cease to have effect.

(4) A person shall cancel an authorisation given by him if satisfied that the action authorised by it is no longer necessary.

(5) An authorising officer shall cancel an authorisation given in his absence if satisfied that the action authorised by it is no longer necessary.

(6) If the authorising officer who gave the authorisation is within paragraph (b) or (e) of section 93(5), the power conferred on that person by subsections (3) and (4) above shall also be exercisable by each of the other persons within the paragraph concerned.

(7) Nothing in this section shall prevent a designated deputy from exercising the powers conferred on an authorising officer within paragraph (a), (c), (d), (f) or (g) of section 93(5) by subsections (3), (4) and (5) above.

Definitions For "authorisation", see s 93; for "authorising officer", see s 93(5); for "designated deputy", see s 94(4).
References See paras 4.35, 4.55–4.58.

96 Notification of authorisations etc

(1) Where a person gives, renews or cancels an authorisation, he shall, as soon as is reasonably practicable and in accordance with arrangements made by the Chief Commissioner, give notice in writing that he has done so to a Commissioner appointed under section 91(1)(b).

(2) Subject to subsection (3), a notice under this section shall specify such matters as the Secretary of State may by order prescribe.

(3) A notice under this section of the giving or renewal of an authorisation shall specify—

(a) whether section 97 applies to the authorisation or renewal, and

(b) where that section does not apply by virtue of subsection (3) of that section, the grounds on which the case is believed to be one of urgency.

(4) Where a notice is given to a Commissioner under this section, he shall, as soon as is reasonably practicable, scrutinise the notice.

(5) An order under subsection (2) shall be made by statutory instrument.

(6) A statutory instrument which contains an order under subsection (2) shall not be made unless a draft has been laid before, and approved by a resolution of, each House of Parliament.

Definitions For "authorisation", see s 93.
References See paras 4.59, 4.62, 4.63.

Authorisations requiring approval

97 Authorisations requiring approval

(1) An authorisation to which this section applies shall not take effect until—

(a) it has been approved in accordance with this section by a Commissioner appointed under section 91(1)(b), and

(b) the person who gave the authorisation has been notified under subsection (4).

(2) Subject to subsection (3), this section applies to an authorisation if, at the time it is given, the person who gives it believes—

(a) that any of the property specified in the authorisation—

(i) is used wholly or mainly as a dwelling or as a bedroom in a hotel, or

(ii) constitutes office premises, or

(b) that the action authorised by it is likely to result in any person acquiring knowledge of—

(i) matters subject to legal privilege,

(ii) confidential personal information, or

(iii) confidential journalistic material.

(3) This section does not apply to an authorisation where the person who gives it believes that the case is one of urgency.

(4) Where a Commissioner receives a notice under section 96 which specifies that this section applies to the authorisation, he shall as soon as is reasonably practicable—

(a) decide whether to approve the authorisation or refuse approval, and

(b) give written notice of his decision to the person who gave the authorisation.

(5) A Commissioner shall approve an authorisation if, and only if, he is satisfied that there are reasonable grounds for believing the matters specified in section 93(2).

(6) Where a Commissioner refuses to approve an authorisation, he shall, as soon as is reasonably practicable, make a report of his findings to the authorising officer who gave it or in whose absence it was given (and paragraph 7 of Schedule 7 shall apply for the purposes of this subsection as it applies for the purposes of that Schedule).

(7) This section shall apply in relation to a renewal of an authorisation as it applies in relation to an authorisation (the references in subsection (2)(a) and (b) to the authorisation being construed as references to the authorisation renewed).

(8) In this section—

"office premises" has the meaning given in section 1(2) of the Offices, Shops and Railway Premises Act 1963;

"hotel" means premises used for the reception of guests who desire to sleep in the premises.

Definitions For "authorisation", see s 93; for "authorising officer", see s 93(5).
References See paras 4.62–4.66.

98 Matters subject to legal privilege

(1) Subject to subsection (5) below, in section 97 "matters subject to legal privilege" means matters to which subsection (2), (3) or (4) below applies.

(2) This subsection applies to communications between a professional legal adviser and—

(a) his client, or
(b) any person representing his client,

which are made in connection with the giving of legal advice to the client.

(3) This subsection applies to communications—

(a) between a professional legal adviser and his client or any person representing his client, or
(b) between a professional legal adviser or his client or any such representative and any other person,

which are made in connection with or in contemplation of legal proceedings and for the purposes of such proceedings.

(4) This subsection applies to items enclosed with or referred to in communications of the kind mentioned in subsection (2) or (3) and made—

(a) in connection with the giving of legal advice, or
(b) in connection with or in contemplation of legal proceedings and for the purposes of such proceedings.

(5) For the purposes of section 97—

(a) communications and items are not matters subject to legal privilege when they are in the possession of a person who is not entitled to possession of them, and
(b) communications and items held, or oral communications made, with the intention of furthering a criminal purpose are not matters subject to legal privilege.

References See paras 4.67–4.71.

99 Confidential personal information

(1) In section 97 "confidential personal information" means—

(a) personal information which a person has acquired or created in the course of any trade, business, profession or other occupation or for the purposes of any paid or unpaid office, and which he holds in confidence, and

(b) communications as a result of which personal information—

(i) is acquired or created as mentioned in paragraph (a), and

(ii) is held in confidence.

(2) For the purposes of this section "personal information" means information concerning an individual (whether living or dead) who can be identified from it and relating—

(a) to his physical or mental health, or

(b) to spiritual counselling or assistance given or to be given to him.

(3) A person holds information in confidence for the purposes of this section if he holds it subject—

(a) to an express or implied undertaking to hold it in confidence, or

(b) to a restriction on disclosure or an obligation of secrecy contained in any enactment (including an enactment contained in an Act passed after this Act).

References See paras 4.72–4.77.

100 Confidential journalistic material

(1) In section 97 "confidential journalistic material" means—

(a) material acquired or created for the purposes of journalism which—

(i) is in the possession of persons who acquired or created it for those purposes,

(ii) is held subject to an undertaking, restriction or obligation of the kind mentioned in section 99(3), and

(iii) has been continuously held (by one or more persons) subject to such an undertaking, restriction or obligation since it was first acquired or created for the purposes of journalism, and

(b) communications as a result of which information is acquired for the purposes of journalism and held as mentioned in paragraph (a)(ii).

(2) For the purposes of subsection (1), a person who receives material, or acquires information, from someone who intends that the recipient shall use it for the purposes of journalism is to be taken to have acquired it for those purposes.

References See paras 4.78–4.87.

Code of Practice

101 Code of Practice

(1) The Secretary of State shall issue a code of practice in connection with the performance of functions under this Part by persons other than Commissioners appointed under section 91.

(2) Before issuing a code of practice under subsection (1), the Secretary of State shall prepare and publish a draft of that code, shall consider any representations made to him about the draft and may modify the draft accordingly.

(3) The Secretary of State shall lay before both Houses of Parliament a draft of the code of practice prepared by him under this section.

(4) The code of practice laid before Parliament in draft under subsection (3) shall not be brought into operation except in accordance with an order made by the Secretary of State by statutory instrument.

(5) A statutory instrument which contains an order under subsection (4) shall not be made unless a draft has been laid before, and approved by a resolution of, each House of Parliament.

(6) An order bringing the code into operation may contain such transitional provisions or savings as appear to the Secretary of State to be necessary or expedient in connection with the bringing into operation of that code.

(7) The Secretary of State may from time to time revise the whole or any part of a code to which this section applies and issue that revised code; and the foregoing provision of this section shall apply (with appropriate modifications) to such a revised code as they apply to the first issue of the code.

(8) Persons, other than Commissioners appointed under section 91, shall have regard to any code of practice issued under this section in the performance of their functions under this Part.

(9) A failure on the part of any person to comply with any provision of a code of practice issued under this section shall not of itself render him liable to any criminal or civil proceedings.

(10) A code issued under this section shall be admissible in evidence in criminal and civil proceedings; and if any provision of such a code appears to the court or tribunal conducting the proceedings to be relevant to any question arising in the proceedings it shall be taken into account in determining that question.

Definitions For "criminal proceedings", see s 108(1).
References See paras 4.115–4.117.

Complaints etc

102 Complaints

(1) Where a complaint is made, in accordance with arrangements made by the Chief Commissioner, to a Commissioner appointed under section 91(1)(b), the Commissioner shall investigate the complaint if and so far as it alleges that anything has been done in relation to any property of the complainant in pursuance of an authorisation under section 93(1)(a) or (b).

(2) For the purposes of subsection (1), a place where the complainant works or resides shall be treated as property of the complainant.

(3) A Commissioner's duty under this section does not extend to a complaint if he considers that it is frivolous or vexatious.

(4) Schedule 7 makes further provision in relation to the investigation of complaints by a Commissioner.

Definitions For "authorisation", see s 93.
References See paras 4.99–4.103.

103 Quashing of authorisations etc

(1) Where, at any time, a Commissioner appointed under section 91(1)(b) is satisfied that, at the time an authorisation was given or renewed, there were no reasonable grounds for believing the matters specified in section 93(2), he may quash the authorisation or, as the case may be, renewal.

(2) Where, in the case of an authorisation or renewal to which section 97 does not apply, a Commissioner appointed under section 91(1)(b) is at any time satisfied that, at the time the authorisation was given or, as the case may be, renewed,—

- (a) there were reasonable grounds for believing any of the matters specified in subsection (2) of section 97, and
- (b) there were no reasonable grounds for believing the case to be one of urgency for the purposes of subsection (3) of that section,

he may quash the authorisation or, as the case may be, renewal.

(3) Where a Commissioner quashes an authorisation or renewal under subsection (1) or (2), he may order the destruction of any records relating to information obtained by virtue of the authorisation (or, in the case of a renewal, relating wholly or partly to information so obtained after the renewal) other than records required for pending criminal or civil proceedings.

(4) If a Commissioner appointed under section 91(1)(b) is satisfied that, at any time after an authorisation was given or, in the case of an authorisation renewed under section 95, after it was renewed, there were no reasonable grounds for believing the matters specified in section 93(2), he may cancel the authorisation.

(5) Where—

- (a) an authorisation has ceased to have effect (otherwise than by virtue of subsection (1) or (2)), and
- (b) a Commissioner appointed under section 91(1)(b) is satisfied that, at any time during the period of the authorisation, there were no reasonable grounds for believing the matters specified in section 93(2),

he may order the destruction of any records relating, wholly or partly, to information which was obtained by virtue of the authorisation after that time (other than records required for pending criminal or civil proceedings).

(6) Where a Commissioner exercises his powers under subsection (1), (2) or (4), he shall, if he is satisfied that there are reasonable grounds for doing so, order that the authorisation shall be effective, for such period as he shall specify, so far as it authorises the taking of action to retrieve anything left on property in accordance with the authorisation.

(7) Where a Commissioner exercises a power conferred by this section, he shall, as soon as is reasonably practicable, make a report of his findings—

- (a) to the authorising officer who gave the authorisation or in whose absence it was given, and
- (b) to the Chief Commissioner;

and paragraph 7 of Schedule 7 shall apply for the purposes of this subsection as it applies for the purposes of that Schedule.

(8) Where—

- (a) a decision is made under subsection (1) or (2) and an order for the destruction of records is made under subsection (3), or
- (b) a decision to order the destruction of records is made under subsection (5),

the order shall not become operative until the period for appealing against the decision has expired and, where an appeal is made, a decision dismissing it has been made by the Chief Commissioner.

(9) A Commissioner may exercise any of the powers conferred by this section notwithstanding any approval given under section 97.

Definitions For "authorisation", see s 93; for "authorising officer", see s 93(5); for "criminal proceedings", see s 108(1).
References See paras 4.88–4.103.

Appeals

104 Appeals by authorising officers

(1) An authorising officer who gives an authorisation, or in whose absence it is given, may, within the prescribed period, appeal to the Chief Commissioner against—

- (a) any refusal to approve the authorisation or any renewal of it under section 97;
- (b) any decision to quash the authorisation, or any renewal of it, under subsection (1) of section 103;
- (c) any decision to quash the authorisation, or any renewal of it, under subsection (2) of that section;
- (d) any decision to cancel the authorisation under subsection (4) of that section;
- (e) any decision to order the destruction of records under subsection (5) of that section;
- (f) any refusal to make an order under subsection (6) of that section;
- (g) any determination in favour of a complainant under Schedule 7.

(2) In subsection (1), "the prescribed period" means the period of seven days beginning with the day on which the refusal, decision or, as the case may be, determination appealed against is reported to the authorising officer.

(3) In determining an appeal within subsection (1)(a), the Chief Commissioner shall, if he is satisfied that there are reasonable grounds for believing the matters specified in section 93(2), allow the appeal and direct the Commissioner to approve the authorisation or renewal under that section.

(4) In determining—

- (a) an appeal within subsection (1)(b), or
- (b) an appeal within subsection (1)(g), in a case where paragraph 2(2) of Schedule 7 applies,

the Chief Commissioner shall allow the appeal unless he is satisfied that, at the time the authorisation was given or, as the case may be, renewed there were no reasonable grounds for believing the matters specified in section 93(2).

(5) In determining—

- (a) an appeal within subsection (1)(c), or
- (b) an appeal within subsection (1)(g), in a case where paragraph 2(3) of Schedule 7 applies,

the Chief Commissioner shall allow the appeal unless he is satisfied as mentioned in section 103(2).

(6) In determining—

- (a) an appeal within subsection (1)(d) or (e), or
- (b) an appeal within subsection (1)(g), in a case where paragraph 2(4) of Schedule 7 applies,

the Chief Commissioner shall allow the appeal unless he is satisfied that at the time to which the decision relates there were no reasonable grounds for believing the matters specified in section 93(2).

(7) In determining an appeal within subsection (1)(f), the Chief Commissioner shall allow the appeal and order that the authorisation shall be effective to the extent mentioned in section 103(6), for such period as he shall specify, if he is satisfied that there are reasonable grounds for making such an order.

(8) Where an appeal is allowed under this section, the Chief Commissioner shall—

- (a) in the case of an appeal within subsection (1)(b) or (c), also quash any order made by the Commissioner to destroy records relating to information obtained by virtue of the authorisation concerned, and
- (b) in the case of an appeal within subsection (1)(g), also quash any direction to pay compensation to the complainant.

Definitions For "authorisation", see s 93; for "authorising officer", see s 93(5).
References See paras 4.106–4.111.

105 Appeals by authorising officers: supplementary

(1) Where the Chief Commissioner determines an appeal under section 104—

- (a) he shall give notice of his determination—
  - (i) to the authorising officer concerned,
  - (ii) to the Commissioner against whose refusal, decision or determination the appeal was made, and
  - (iii) in the case of an appeal within subsection (1)(g) of that section, to the complainant, and
- (b) if he dismisses the appeal, he shall make a report of his findings—
  - (i) to the authorising officer concerned,
  - (ii) to the Commissioner against whose refusal, decision or determination the appeal was made, and
  - (iii) under section 107(2), to the Prime Minister.

(2) Subject to subsection (1)(b), the Chief Commissioner shall not give any reasons for a determination under section 104.

(3) Nothing in section 104 shall prevent a designated deputy from exercising the powers conferred by subsection (1) of that section on an authorising officer within paragraph (a), (c), (d), (f) or (g) of section 93(5).

Definitions For "authorising officer", see s 93(5); for "designated deputy", see s 94(4).
References See para 4.112.

106 Appeals by complainants

(1) Where a complainant is notified under paragraph 3(2) of Schedule 7 that no determination in his favour has been made on a complaint, he may, within the period of seven days beginning with the day on which he receives the notice, appeal to the Chief Commissioner against the decision.

(2) Where a complainant appeals under this section, the Chief Commissioner shall have—

- (a) all the powers and duties conferred by Schedule 7 on a Commissioner appointed under section 91(1)(b) who is required to investigate a complaint, and
- (b) where the Chief Commissioner makes a determination in favour of the complainant by virtue of paragraph (a), all the powers and duties conferred by section 103.

(3) Where, by virtue of subsection (2), the Chief Commissioner makes an order to destroy records under section 103 or directs the payment of compensation under Schedule 7, subsection (8) of that section and paragraph 5(2) of that Schedule shall not apply.

(4) The Chief Commissioner shall make a report of his findings on an appeal under this section—

(a) to the Commissioner who made the decision appealed against, and
(b) where he allows the appeal, to the Prime Minister under section 107(2).

References See para 4.113.

General

107 Supplementary provisions relating to Commissioners

(1) The Chief Commissioner shall keep under review the performance of functions under this Part.

(2) The Chief Commissioner shall make an annual report on the discharge of functions under this Part to the Prime Minister and may at any time report to him on any matter relating to those functions.

(3) The Prime Minister shall lay before each House of Parliament a copy of each annual report made by the Chief Commissioner under subsection (2) together with a statement as to whether any matter has been excluded from that copy in pursuance of subsection (4) below.

(4) The Prime Minister may exclude a matter from the copy of a report as laid before each House of Parliament, if it appears to him, after consultation with the Chief Commissioner, that the publication of that matter in the report would be prejudicial to the prevention or detection of serious crime or otherwise to the discharge of—

(a) the functions of any police authority,
(b) the functions of the Service Authority for the National Criminal Intelligence Service or the Service Authority for the National Crime Squad, or
(c) the duties of the Commissioners of Customs and Excise.

(5) Any person having functions under this Part, and any person taking action in relation to which an authorisation was given, shall comply with any request of a Commissioner for documents or information required by him for the purpose of enabling him to discharge his functions.

(6) In this section, "serious crime" shall be construed in accordance with section 93(4).

Definitions For "authorisation", see s 93.
References See paras 4.103, 4.104.

108 Interpretation of Part III

(1) In this Part—

"authorisation" means an authorisation under section 93;
"authorising officer" has the meaning given by section 93(5);
"criminal proceedings" includes—

(a) proceedings in the United Kingdom or elsewhere before a court-martial constituted under the Army Act 1955, the Air Force Act 1955 or the Naval Discipline Act 1957 or a disciplinary court constituted under section 50 of the Act of 1957,

(b) proceedings before the Courts-Martial Appeal Court, and
(c) proceedings before a Standing Civilian Court;

"customs officer" means an officer commissioned by the Commissioners of Customs and Excise under section 6(3) of the Customs and Excise Management Act 1979;

"designated deputy" has the meaning given in section 94(4);

"United Kingdom waters" has the meaning given in section 30(5) of the Police Act 1996; and

"wireless telegraphy" has the same meaning as in the Wireless Telegraphy Act 1949 and, in relation to wireless telegraphy, "interfere" has the same meaning as in that Act.

(2) Where, under this Part, notice of any matter is required to be given in writing, the notice may be transmitted by electronic means.

(3) For the purposes of this Part, an authorisation (or renewal) given—
(a) by the designated deputy of an authorising officer, or
(b) by a person on whom an authorising officer's powers are conferred by section 94,

shall be treated as an authorisation (or renewal) given in the absence of the authorising officer concerned; and references to the authorising officer in whose absence an authorisation (or renewal) was given shall be construed accordingly.

PART IV
POLICE INFORMATION TECHNOLOGY ORGANISATION

109 Police Information Technology Organisation

(1) There shall be a body corporate to be known as the Police Information Technology Organisation ("the Organisation").

(2) Schedule 8 (which makes provision about the Organisation) shall have effect.

(3) The Organisation may carry out activities (including the commissioning of research) relating to information technology equipment and systems for the use of—
(a) police authorities and police forces, and
(b) such other bodies as the Secretary of State may determine by order made by statutory instrument.

(4) The Organisation may also procure or assist in procuring other equipment, systems and services for any body falling within subsection (3)(a) or (b).

(5) Any statutory instrument made by virtue of subsection (3)(b) shall be subject to annulment in pursuance of a resolution of either House of Parliament.

(6) In this Part "information technology" includes any computer or other technology by means of which information or other matter may be recorded or communicated without being reduced to documentary form.

Definitions For "police authority", see s 111(1); for "police force", see s 111(3).
References See paras 5.9–5.17.

---

110 Relationship between the Organisation and the Secretary of State

(1) In exercising its functions the Organisation shall comply with any general or specific directions given in writing by the Secretary of State.

(2) Before giving directions under subsection (1), the Secretary of State shall consult the Organisation.

(3) The Organisation shall provide the Secretary of State with such information about its activities as he may request.

Definitions For "the Organisation", see s 109(1).
References See para 5.26.

111 Interpretation of Part IV

(1) In this Part, except where the context otherwise requires, "police authority" means—

- (a) a police authority for an area in Great Britain or a joint police board (within the meaning of the Police (Scotland) Act 1967),
- (b) the Police Authority for Northern Ireland,
- (c) the Service Authority for the National Criminal Intelligence Service, and
- (d) the Service Authority for the National Crime Squad.

(2) In this Part, except where the context otherwise requires, "chief officer of police" means—

- (a) a chief officer of police of a police force in England and Wales,
- (b) a chief constable of a police force in Scotland,
- (c) the Chief Constable of the Royal Ulster Constabulary,
- (d) the Director General of the National Criminal Intelligence Service, and
- (e) the Director General of the National Crime Squad.

(3) In this Part "police force" means—

- (a) a police force in Great Britain,
- (b) the Royal Ulster Constabulary and the Royal Ulster Constabulary Reserve,
- (c) the National Criminal Intelligence Service, and
- (d) the National Crime Squad.

References See para 5.13.

PART V
CERTIFICATES OF CRIMINAL RECORDS, &C

112 Criminal conviction certificates

(1) The Secretary of State shall issue a criminal conviction certificate to any individual who—

- (a) makes an application in the prescribed form, and
- (b) pays any fee that is payable in relation to the application under regulations made by the Secretary of State.

(2) A criminal conviction certificate is a certificate which—

- (a) gives the prescribed details of every conviction of the applicant which is recorded in central records, or
- (b) states that there is no such conviction.

(3) In this section—

"central records" means such records of convictions held for the use of police forces generally as may be prescribed;

"conviction" means a conviction within the meaning of the Rehabilitation of Offenders Act 1974, other than a spent conviction.

(4) Where an applicant has received a criminal conviction certificate, the Secretary of State may refuse to issue another certificate to that applicant during such period as may be prescribed.

Definitions For "prescribed", see s 125(1); for "certificate" and "police force", see s 126(1).
References See paras 6.25, 6.26.

113 Criminal record certificates

(1) The Secretary of State shall issue a criminal record certificate to any individual who—

(a) makes an application under this section in the prescribed form countersigned by a registered person, and

(b) pays any fee that is payable in relation to the application under regulations made by the Secretary of State.

(2) An application under this section must be accompanied by a statement by the registered person that the certificate is required for the purposes of an exempted question.

(3) A criminal record certificate is a certificate which—

(a) gives the prescribed details of every relevant matter relating to the applicant which is recorded in central records, or

(b) states that there is no such matter.

(4) The Secretary of State shall send a copy of a criminal record certificate to the registered person who countersigned the application.

(5) In this section—

"central records" means such records of convictions and cautions held for the use of police forces generally as may be prescribed;

"exempted question" means a question in relation to which section 4(2)(a) or (b) of the Rehabilitation of Offenders Act 1974 (effect of rehabilitation) has been excluded by an order of the Secretary of State under section 4(4);

"relevant matter" means—

(i) a conviction within the meaning of the Rehabilitation of Offenders Act 1974, including a spent conviction, and

(ii) a caution.

Definitions For "registered person", see s 120(1); for "prescribed", see s 125(1); for "caution", "certificate" and "police force", see s 126(1).
References See paras 6.27–6.34.

114 Criminal record certificates: Crown employment

(1) The Secretary of State shall issue a criminal record certificate to any individual who—

(a) makes an application under this section in the prescribed form, and

(b) pays any fee that is payable in relation to the application under regulations made by the Secretary of State.

(2) An application under this section must be accompanied by a statement by a Minister of the Crown that the certificate is required for the purposes of an exempted question asked in the course of considering the applicant's suitability for an appointment by or under the Crown.

(3) Section 113(3) to (5) shall apply in relation to this section with any necessary modifications.

Definitions For "prescribed", see s 125(1); for "certificate", "Minister of the Crown", see s 126(1).
References See para 6.36.

115 Enhanced criminal record certificates

(1) The Secretary of State shall issue an enhanced criminal record certificate to any individual who—

(a) makes an application under this section in the prescribed form countersigned by a registered person, and

(b) pays any fee that is payable in relation to the application under regulations made by the Secretary of State.

(2) An application under this section must be accompanied by a statement by the registered person that the certificate is required for the purposes of an exempted question asked—

(a) in the course of considering the applicant's suitability for a position (whether paid or unpaid) within subsection (3) or (4), or

(b) for a purpose relating to any of the matters listed in subsection (5).

(3) A position is within this subsection if it involves regularly caring for, training, supervising or being in sole charge of persons aged under 18.

(4) A position is within this subsection if—

(a) it is of a kind specified in regulations made by the Secretary of State, and

(b) it involves regularly caring for, training, supervising or being in sole charge of persons aged 18 or over.

(5) The matters referred to in subsection (2)(b) are—

(a) a certificate for the purposes of sections 19 or 27(1) or (5) of the Gaming Act 1968 (gaming);

(b) a certificate of consent, or a licence, for any purpose of Schedule 2 to that Act (licences);

(c) registration or certification in accordance with Schedule 1A, 2 or 2A to the Lotteries and Amusements Act 1976 (societies, schemes and lottery managers);

(d) a licence under section 5 or 6 of the National Lottery etc Act 1993 (running or promoting lotteries);

(e) registration under section 71 of the Children Act 1989 or Article 118 of the Children (Northern Ireland) Order 1995 (child minding and day care);

(f) the placing of children with foster parents in accordance with any provision of, or made by virtue of, the Children Act 1989 or the Children (Northern Ireland) Order 1995 or the exercise of any duty under or by virtue of section 67 of that Act or Article 108 of that Order (welfare of privately fostered children);

(g) the approval of any person as a foster carer by virtue of section 5(2), (3) and (4) of the Social Work (Scotland) Act 1968, the exercise by a local authority of their functions under the Foster Children (Scotland) Act 1984 or the placing of children with foster parents by virtue of section 70 of the Children (Scotland) Act 1995 (disposal of referral by children's hearing).

(6) An enhanced criminal record certificate is a certificate which—

(a) gives—

(i) the prescribed details of every relevant matter relating to the applicant which is recorded in central records, and

(ii) any information provided in accordance with subsection (7), or

(b) states that there is no such matter or information.

(7) Before issuing an enhanced criminal record certificate the Secretary of State shall request the chief officer of every relevant police force to provide any information which, in the chief officer's opinion—

(a) might be relevant for the purpose described in the statement under subsection (2), and

(b) ought to be included in the certificate.

(8) The Secretary of State shall also request the chief officer of every relevant police force to provide any information which, in the chief officer's opinion—

(a) might be relevant for the purpose described in the statement under subsection (2),

(b) ought not to be included in the certificate, in the interests of the prevention or detection of crime, and

(c) can, without harming those interests, be disclosed to the registered person.

(9) The Secretary of State shall send to the registered person who countersigned an application under this section—

(a) a copy of the enhanced criminal record certificate, and

(b) any information provided in accordance with subsection (8).

(10) In this section—

"central records", "exempted question" and "relevant matter" have the same meaning as in section 113; and

"relevant police force", in relation to an application under this section, means a police force which is a relevant police force in relation to that application under regulations made by the Secretary of State.

Definitions For "registered person", see s 120(1); for "prescribed", see s 125(1); for "certificate", "chief officer" and "police force", see s 126(1).
References See para 6.38–6.47.

116 Enhanced criminal record certificates: judicial appointments and Crown employment

(1) The Secretary of State shall issue an enhanced criminal record certificate to any individual who—

(a) makes an application under this section in the prescribed form, and

(b) pays any fee that is payable in relation to the application under regulations made by the Secretary of State.

(2) An application under this section must be accompanied by a statement by a Minister of the Crown, or a person nominated by a Minister of the Crown, that the certificate is required for the purposes of an exempted question asked in the course of considering the applicant's suitability for—

(a) a judicial appointment, or

(b) an appointment by or under the Crown to a position to which subsection (3) or (4) of section 115 applies.

(3) Section 115(6) to (10) shall apply in relation to this section with any necessary modifications.

Definitions For "registered person", see s 120(1); for "prescribed", see s 125(1); for "certificate", "Minister of the Crown", see s 126(1).
References See para 6.48.

117 Disputes about accuracy of certificates

(1) Where an applicant for a certificate under any of sections 112 to 116 believes that the information contained in the certificate is inaccurate he may make an application in writing to the Secretary of State for a new certificate.

(2) The Secretary of State shall consider any application under this section; and where he is of the opinion that the information in the certificate is inaccurate he shall issue a new certificate.

Definitions For "certificate", see s 126(1).
References See para 6.49.

118 Evidence of identity

(1) The Secretary of State may refuse to issue a certificate under this Part, or to consider an application under section 117, unless the application is supported by such evidence of identity as he may require.

(2) In particular, the Secretary of State may refuse to issue a certificate or consider an application unless the applicant—

(a) has his fingerprints taken at such place and in such manner as may be prescribed, and

(b) pays the prescribed fee to such person as may be prescribed.

(3) Regulations dealing with the taking of fingerprints may make provision requiring their destruction in specified circumstances and by specified persons.

(4) Regulations prescribing a fee for the purposes of subsection (2)(b) shall make provision for a refund in cases of an application under section 117 where a new certificate is issued.

Definitions For "prescribed", see s 125(1); for "certificate", see s 126(1).
References See paras 6.49–6.50.

119 Sources of information

(1) Any person who holds records of convictions or cautions for the use of police forces generally shall make those records available to the Secretary of State for the purposes of an application under this Part.

(2) Where the chief officer of a police force receives a request under section 115 or 116 he shall comply with it as soon as practicable.

(3) The Secretary of State shall pay to the appropriate police authority, or, in the case of the metropolitan police force, the Receiver for the Metropolitan Police District, the prescribed fee for information provided in accordance with subsection (2).

(4) Any person who holds records of fingerprints for the use of police forces generally shall make those records available to the Secretary of State for the purposes of an application under this Part.

(5) No proceedings shall lie against the Secretary of State by reason of an inaccuracy in the information made available or provided to him in accordance with this section.

Definitions For "prescribed", see s 125(1); for "caution", "chief officer", "police authority" and "police force", see s 126(1).
References See paras 6.47, 6.56, 6.65.

120 Registered persons

(1) For the purposes of this Part a registered person is a person who is listed in a register to be maintained by the Secretary of State for the purposes of this Part.

(2) Subject to regulations under subsection (3), the Secretary of State shall include in the register any person who applies to him in writing to be registered and satisfies the conditions in subsections (4) to (6).

(3) The Secretary of State may make regulations about the maintenance of the register; and regulations may, in particular, provide for—

(a) the information to be included in the register,

(b) the removal from the register of persons who are, in the opinion of the Secretary of State, no longer likely to wish to countersign applications under section 113 or 115, and

(c) the payment of fees.

(4) A person applying for registration under this section must be—

(a) a body corporate or unincorporate,

(b) a person appointed to an office by virtue of any enactment, or

(c) an individual who employs others in the course of a business.

(5) A body applying for registration under this section must satisfy the Secretary of State that it—

(a) is likely to ask exempted questions, or

(b) is likely to countersign applications under section 113 or 115 at the request of bodies or individuals asking exempted questions.

(6) A person, other than a body, applying for registration under this section must satisfy the Secretary of State that he is likely to ask exempted questions.

(7) In this section "exempted question" has the same meaning as in section 113.

Definitions For "prescribed", see s 125(1).
References See paras 6.33, 6.34.

121 Performance by constables on central service in Scotland of functions under this Part

In Scotland a constable engaged on central service (within the meaning of section 38 of the Police (Scotland) Act 1967) may perform functions under this Part (other than functions under section 114(2), 115(4) or (10), 116(2), 122(1) or (2) or 125) on behalf of the Secretary of State; and without prejudice to the application of subsection (5) of section 119 in respect of any other person performing functions on behalf of the Secretary of State, that subsection shall apply in respect of any constable performing functions by virtue of this section as the subsection applies in respect of the Secretary of State.

References See para 6.56.

122 Code of practice

(1) The Secretary of State shall publish, and may from time to time revise, a code of practice in connection with the use of information provided to registered persons under this Part.

(2) The Secretary of State shall lay before Parliament the code of practice under this section as soon as practicable after publication and after revision.

(3) The Secretary of State may refuse to issue a certificate under section 113 or 115 if he believes that the registered person who countersigned the application—

(a) has failed to comply with the code of practice under this section, or

(b) countersigned at the request of a body which, or individual who, has failed to comply with the code of practice.

Definitions For "registered persons", see s 120(1); for "certificate", see s 126(1).
References See paras 6.52–6.55.

123 Offences: falsification, &c

(1) A person commits an offence if, with intent to deceive, he—

(a) makes a false certificate under this Part,

(b) alters a certificate under this Part,

(c) uses a certificate under this Part which relates to another person in a way which suggests that it relates to himself, or

(d) allows a certificate under this Part which relates to him to be used by another person in a way which suggests that it relates to that other person.

(2) A person commits an offence if he knowingly makes a false statement for the purpose of obtaining, or enabling another person to obtain, a certificate under this Part.

(3) A person who is guilty of an offence under this section shall be liable on summary conviction to imprisonment for a term not exceeding six months or to a fine not exceeding level 5 on the standard scale, or to both.

Definitions For "certificate", see s 126(1).
References See paras 6.57–6.60.

124 Offences: disclosure

(1) A member, officer or employee of a body registered under section 120 commits an offence if he discloses information provided following an application under section 113 or 115 unless he discloses it, in the course of his duties,—

(a) to another member, officer or employee of the registered body,

(b) to a member, officer or employee of a body at the request of which the registered body countersigned the application, or

(c) to an individual at whose request the registered body countersigned the relevant application.

(2) Where information is provided under section 113 or 115 following an application countersigned at the request of a body which is not registered under section 120, a member, officer or employee of the body commits an offence if he discloses the information unless he discloses it, in the course of his duties, to another member, officer or employee of that body.

(3) Where information is provided under section 113 or 115 following an application countersigned by or at the request of an individual—

(a) the individual commits an offence if he discloses the information unless he discloses it to an employee of his for the purpose of the employee's duties, and

(b) an employee of the individual commits an offence if he discloses the information unless he discloses it, in the course of his duties, to another employee of the individual.

(4) Where information provided under section 113 or 115 is disclosed to a person and the disclosure—

(a) is an offence under this section, or

(b) would be an offence under this section but for subsection (5) or (6)(a), (d), (e) or (f),

the person to whom the information is disclosed commits an offence (subject to subsections (5) and (6)) if he discloses it to any other person.

(5) Subsections (1) to (4) do not apply to a disclosure of information provided in accordance with section 115(8) which is made with the written consent of the chief officer who provided the information.

(6) Subsections (1) to (4) do not apply to a disclosure of information contained in a certificate under section 113 or 115 which is made—

(a) with the written consent of the applicant for the certificate, or

(b) to a government department, or

(c) to a person appointed to an office by virtue of any enactment, or

(d) in accordance with an obligation to provide information under or by virtue of any enactment, or

(e) for the purposes of answering an exempted question (within the meaning of section 113) of a kind specified in regulations made by the Secretary of State, or

(f) for some other purpose specified in regulations made by the Secretary of State.

(7) A person who is guilty of an offence under this section shall be liable on summary conviction to imprisonment for a term not exceeding six months or to a fine not exceeding level 3 on the standard scale, or to both.

Definitions For "Registered body", see s 120; for "certificate", see s 126(1).
References See paras 6.61–6.64.

125 Regulations

(1) Anything authorised or required by any provision of this Part to be prescribed shall be prescribed by regulations made by the Secretary of State.

(2) Regulations under this Part shall be made by statutory instrument.

(3) A statutory instrument which contains (whether alone or with other provisions) regulations made by virtue of section 115(4) shall not be made unless a draft has been laid before, and approved by resolution of, each House of Parliament.

(4) A statutory instrument to which subsection (3) does not apply shall be subject to annulment pursuant to a resolution of either House of Parliament.

(5) Regulations under this Part may make different provision for different cases.

126 Interpretation of Part V

(1) In this Part—

"caution" means a caution given to a person in England and Wales or Northern Ireland in respect of an offence which, at the time when the caution is given, he has admitted;

"certificate" means any one or more documents issued in response to a particular application;

"chief officer" means—

(i) a chief officer of police of a police force in England and Wales,

(ii) a chief constable of a police force in Scotland, and

(iii) the Chief Constable of the Royal Ulster Constabulary;

"government department" includes a Northern Ireland department;

"Minister of the Crown" includes a Northern Ireland department;

"police authority" means—

(i) a police authority for an area in Great Britain or a joint police board (within the meaning of the Police (Scotland) Act 1967), and

(ii) the Police Authority for Northern Ireland;

"police force" means—

(i) a police force in Great Britain, and

(ii) the Royal Ulster Constabulary and the Royal Ulster Constabulary Reserve;

"prescribed" shall be construed in accordance with section 125(1).

(2) In the application of this Part to Northern Ireland, a reference to the Rehabilitation of Offenders Act 1974, or to a provision of that Act, shall be construed as a reference to the Rehabilitation of Offenders (Northern Ireland) Order 1978 or, as the case may be, to the corresponding provision of that order.

127 Saving: disclosure of information and records

Nothing in sections 112 to 119 shall be taken to prejudice any power which exists apart from this Act to disclose information or to make records available.

PART VI
MISCELLANEOUS

Amendments of Police Act 1996

128 Regulations for special constables and police cadets

(1) In section 51 of the Police Act 1996 (regulations for special constables), after subsection (3) there shall be inserted—

"(3A) In relation to any matter as to which provision may be made by regulations under this section, the regulations may—

(a) authorise or require provision to be made by, or confer discretionary powers on, the Secretary of State, police authorities, chief officers of police or other persons, or

(b) authorise or require the delegation by any person of functions conferred on that person by or under the regulations.".

(2) In section 52 of that Act (regulations for police cadets) after subsection (1) there shall be inserted—

"(1A) In relation to any matter as to which provision may be made by regulations under this section, the regulations may—

(a) authorise or require provision to be made by, or confer discretionary powers on, the Secretary of State, police authorities, chief officers of police or other persons, or

(b) authorise or require the delegation by any person of functions conferred on that person by or under the regulations.".

Definitions For "chief officer of police" and "police authority", see the Police Act 1996, s 101(1).

129 Change of name or description of certain police areas

In Schedule 1 to the Police Act 1996 (police areas for England and Wales except London)—

(a) in the entry in the first column for "Humberside" there shall be substituted "Humber";

(b) in the entry in the second column opposite the name of the Dyfed Powys police area for "Cardiganshire" there shall be substituted "Ceredigion";

(c) for the entry in that column opposite the name of the North Wales police area there shall be substituted—

"The counties of the Isle of Anglesey, Gwynedd, Denbighshire and Flintshire and the county boroughs of Conwy and Wrexham.";

(d) in the entry in that column opposite the name of the South Wales police area for "Neath and Port Talbot" there shall be substituted "Neath Port Talbot".

Amendments of Police Act (Northern Ireland) 1970

130 Members of RUC engaged on service outside their force

For section 21 of the Police Act (Northern Ireland) 1970 there shall be substituted—

"21 Members of RUC engaged in service outside their force

(1) For the purposes of this section "relevant service" means—

(a) service in a police force in England and Wales or a police force in Scotland on which a member of the Royal Ulster Constabulary (other than the Chief Constable) is engaged with the consent of the Secretary of State and the Chief Constable;

(b) temporary service with the National Criminal Intelligence Service on which a member of the Royal Ulster Constabulary (other than the Chief Constable) is engaged with the consent of the Chief Constable; or

(c) temporary service with the Police Information Technology Organisation on which a member of the Royal Ulster Constabulary (other than the Chief Constable) is engaged with the consent of the Chief Constable.

(2) Subject to the following provisions of this section, a member of the Royal Ulster Constabulary engaged on relevant service shall be treated as if he were not a member of that Constabulary during that service; but, except where a pension, allowance or gratuity becomes payable to him by virtue of regulations under section 25—

(a) he shall be entitled at the end of the period of relevant service to revert to that Constabulary in the rank in which he was serving immediately before that period began; and

(b) he shall be treated as if he had been serving in that Constabulary during the period of relevant service for the purpose of any scale prescribed by or under regulations made under section 25 fixing his rate of pay by reference to his length of service.

(3) A member of the Royal Ulster Constabulary may, when engaged on relevant service, be promoted in that Constabulary, as if he were serving in it; and in any such case—

(a) the reference in paragraph (a) of subsection (2) to the rank in which he was serving immediately before the period of relevant service began shall be construed as a reference to the rank to which he is promoted; and

(b) for the purposes mentioned in paragraph (b) of that subsection he shall be treated as having served in that rank from the time of his promotion.

(4) A member of the Royal Ulster Constabulary who—

(a) while engaged on relevant service within subsection (1)(a), is dismissed from that service or is required to resign as an alternative to dismissal, or

(b) has completed a period of relevant service within subsection (1)(b) or (c),

may be dealt with under regulations under section 25(3) for anything done or omitted while he was engaged on that service as if that service had been service in the Royal Ulster Constabulary.

(5) For the purposes of subsection (4)(a), a certificate certifying that a person has been dismissed, or required to resign as an alternative to dismissal, shall be evidence of the fact so certified if it is given by or on behalf of the chief officer of the police force in which that person was engaged in relevant service.

(6) A member of the Royal Ulster Constabulary engaged on relevant service within subsection (1)(b) or (c)—

(a) shall continue to be a constable; and

(b) shall be treated for the purposes of—

(i) section 17 of this Act; and

(ii) sections 2 and 8 of the Constabulary and Police (Ireland) Act 1919,

as if he were a member of that Constabulary.".

131 Regulations requiring use of specified facilities or services

In the Police Act (Northern Ireland) 1970 at the end of section 27 (regulations as to standards of equipment) (which becomes subsection (1)) there shall be added—

"(2) The Secretary of State may by regulations make provision for requiring the police force to use specified facilities or services, or facilities or services of a specified description, if he considers that it would be in the interests of the efficiency and effectiveness of the police force for it to do so.

(3) The Secretary of State shall consult the Police Information Technology Organisation before making regulations under this section relating to information technology.

(4) In subsection (3) "information technology" includes any computer or other technology by means of which information or other matter may be recorded or communicated without being reduced to documentary form.".

132 Expenditure by Secretary of State for police purposes

After section 31 of the Police Act (Northern Ireland) 1970 there shall be inserted—

"31A Expenditure by Secretary of State for police purposes

The Secretary of State may—

(a) make such contribution to the provision or maintenance of such organisations, facilities and services; and

(b) make such other payments,

as he thinks necessary or expedient for promoting the efficiency and effectiveness of the police force.".

Rehabilitation of Offenders

133 Rehabilitation of Offenders

The following provisions (which restrict the effect of the Rehabilitation of Offenders Act 1974 and the Rehabilitation of Offenders (Northern Ireland) Order 1978) shall cease to have effect—

(a) section 189 of, and Schedule 14 to, the Financial Services Act 1986;

(b) section 95 of the Banking Act 1987;

(c) section 39 of the Osteopaths Act 1993;

(d) section 19 of the National Lottery etc Act 1993;

(e) section 40 of the Chiropractors Act 1994.

PART VII

GENERAL

134 Amendments and repeals

(1) Schedule 9 (minor and consequential amendments) shall have effect.

(2) The enactments mentioned in Schedule 10 are hereby repealed to the extent specified in the third column of that Schedule.

135 Commencement

(1) The preceding provisions of this Act shall come into force on such day as the Secretary of State may by order made by statutory instrument appoint.

(2) An order under this section may—

(a) appoint different days for different purposes or different areas, and

(b) make transitional provision and savings (including provision modifying this Act).

(3) An order under this section may, in relation to Part I, II or IV make provision—

(a) for the transfer and apportionment of property and for the transfer, apportionment and creation of rights and liabilities;

(b) for the transfer of members of police forces in Great Britain, members of the Royal Ulster Constabulary and other persons;
(c) for the Secretary of State, or any other person nominated by or in accordance with the order, to determine any matter requiring determination under or in consequence of the order;
(d) as to the payment of fees charged, or expenses incurred, by any person nominated to determine any matter by virtue of paragraph (c).

(4) Any day appointed by an order under this section for the coming into force of section 93, 94 or 95 of this Act shall not be earlier than the day on which a code of practice issued under section 101 comes into operation.

(5) A statutory instrument containing provisions made by virtue of subsection (2)(b) or (3) shall be subject to annulment in pursuance of a resolution of either House of Parliament.

136 Police: co-operation on implementation

It shall be the duty of police authorities for areas in Great Britain, and the Police Authority for Northern Ireland, and their staff to co-operate with each other, and generally to exercise their functions, so as to facilitate the implementation of Parts I and II of this Act and any transfer of property or staff made by an order under section 135.

137 Extent

(1) Subject to subsections (2) to (4), this Act extends throughout the United Kingdom.

(2) The following provisions of this Act extend to England and Wales only—
(a) Part II;
(b) Part III of Schedule 1;
(c) Parts I and IV of Schedule 1, and Schedule 2, so far as they relate to the Service Authority for the National Crime Squad;
(d) Schedule 5;
(e) sections 128 and 129.

(3) Sections 130 to 132 extend to Northern Ireland only.

(4) The amendments in Schedules 6 and 9, and the repeals in Schedule 10, have the same extent as the enactments to which they refer.

138 Short title

This Act may be cited as the Police Act 1997.

SCHEDULES

SCHEDULE 1

Sections 1(7) and 47(7)

APPOINTMENT OF MEMBERS OF THE SERVICE AUTHORITIES

PART I

CORE MEMBERS

1.—(1) The NCS Service Authority and the NCIS Service Authority shall have a common core membership consisting of ten members ("the core members") appointed in accordance with this Part.

2.—(1) Three of the core members shall be persons appointed by the Secretary of State under this paragraph.

(2) A person shall not be appointed under this paragraph if he is—

(a) a member of a police force in Great Britain or of the Royal Ulster Constabulary,

(b) a Crown servant, or

(c) a local authority member of a police authority for an area in England and Wales, a member of a police authority for an area in Scotland or a member of the Police Authority for Northern Ireland.

(3) One of the core members appointed under this paragraph shall be appointed by the Secretary of State to be the chairman of both the NCS Service Authority and the NCIS Service Authority.

3.—(1) Two of the core members shall be appointed by the chief officers of police of forces in England and Wales and the Assistant Commissioners of Police of the Metropolis ("the relevant police officers"), from among their number.

(2) The relevant police officers shall exercise their powers under sub-paragraph (1) so as to ensure that—

(a) one of the members appointed by them is the chief constable of a police force maintained under section 2 of the Police Act 1996 (forces in England and Wales outside London), and

(b) the other is the Commissioner or an Assistant Commissioner of Police of the Metropolis or the Commissioner of Police for the City of London.

4. Three of the core members shall be appointed by the local authority members of police authorities for areas in England and Wales, from among their number.

5. One of the core members shall be a person (other than a member of a police force) appointed by the Secretary of State under this paragraph to represent the Secretary of State in his capacity as police authority for the metropolitan police district.

6. One of the core members shall be a Crown servant appointed by the Secretary of State under this paragraph.

Definitions For "NCIS Service Authority", see s 1(1); for "NCS Service Authority", see ss 46, 90; for "local authority members of police authorities", see Pt IV, para 14 of this Schedule.
References See paras 2.7, 2.44.

PART II

ADDITIONAL MEMBERS OF NCIS SERVICE AUTHORITY

7. Where the NCIS Service Authority is to consist of nineteen members by virtue of section 1, then in addition to the ten core members—

(a) one of the members shall be appointed by the chief constables of police forces in Scotland, from among their number;

(b) one shall be a person holding at least the rank of deputy chief constable in the Royal Ulster Constabulary, appointed by the Chief Constable of that Constabulary;
(c) two shall be appointed by the local authority members of police authorities for areas in England and Wales, from among their number;
(d) one shall be appointed by the members of police authorities for areas in Scotland, from among their number;
(e) one shall be appointed by the members of the Police Authority for Northern Ireland, from among their number;
(f) two shall be Crown servants appointed by the Secretary of State under this paragraph; and
(g) one shall be a customs officer appointed by the Commissioners of Customs and Excise.

8.—(1) Where the Authority is to consist of more than nineteen members by virtue of an order under section 1(3), then in addition to the ten core members—
(a) a prescribed number of members shall be appointed by the Secretary of State under this paragraph;
(b) a prescribed number shall be appointed by the relevant police officers, from among their number;
(c) a prescribed number of members shall be appointed by the chief constables of police forces in Scotland, from among their number;
(d) one shall be a person holding at least the rank of deputy chief constable in the Royal Ulster Constabulary, appointed by the Chief Constable of that Constabulary;
(e) a prescribed number (being not less than two) shall be appointed by the local authority members of police authorities for areas in England and Wales, from among their number;
(f) a prescribed number shall be appointed by the members of police authorities for areas in Scotland, from among their number;
(g) a prescribed number shall be appointed by the members of the Police Authority for Northern Ireland, from among their number;
(h) two shall be Crown servants appointed by the Secretary of State under this paragraph; and
(i) one shall be a customs officer appointed by the Commissioners of Customs and Excise.

(2) An order under section 1(3) shall ensure—
(a) that a majority of the members of the Authority are members appointed—
  (i) by the Secretary of State (other than under sub-paragraph (1)(h) or paragraph 6),
  (ii) by local authority members of police authorities for areas in England and Wales,
  (iii) by members of police authorities for areas in Scotland, or
  (iv) by members of the Police Authority for Northern Ireland, and
(b) that the number of members appointed by local authority members of police authorities in England and Wales is—
  (i) greater than the total number appointed under sub-paragraph (1)(a) or paragraph 2,
  (ii) greater than the total number appointed under sub-paragraph (1)(b), (c) or (d) or paragraph 3, and
  (iii) greater than the number appointed under each of paragraphs (f) and (g) of sub-paragraph (1).

(3) Paragraph 2(2) applies in relation to appointments under sub-paragraph (1)(a), as it applies to appointments under paragraph 2.

(4) A person appointed under sub-paragraph (1)(a) shall not be so appointed to represent the Secretary of State in his capacity as police authority for the metropolitan police district.

(5) The power to make an order under section 1(3) includes power to prescribe anything which is require to be prescribed for the purposes of this paragraph.

Definitions For "NCIS Service Authority", see s 1(1); for "relevant police officers", see Pt I, para 3(1) of this Schedule; for "local authority members of police authorities", see Pt IV, para 14 of this Schedule; for "customs officer", see Pt IV, para 15(b) of this Schedule.
References See para 2.8.

PART III

ADDITIONAL MEMBERS OF NCS SERVICE AUTHORITY

9. Where the NCS Service Authority is to consist of seventeen members by virtue of section 47, then in addition to the ten core members—

(a) one member shall be appointed by the relevant police officers, from among their number; and

(b) six shall be appointed by the local authority members of police authorities for areas in England and Wales, from among their number.

10.—(1) Where the Authority is to consist of more than seventeen members by virtue of an order under section 47(3), then in addition to the ten core members—

(a) a prescribed number of members shall be appointed by the Secretary of State;

(b) a prescribed number shall be appointed by the relevant police officers, from among their number; and

(c) a prescribed number (being not less than six) shall be appointed by the local authority members of police authorities for areas in England and Wales, from among their number.

(2) An order under section 47(3) shall ensure—

(a) that a majority of the members of the Authority are members appointed—

(i) by the Secretary of State (other than under paragraph 6), or

(ii) by local authority members of police authorities for areas in England and Wales, and

(b) that the number of members appointed by such local authority members of police authorities is—

(i) greater than the total number appointed under sub-paragraph (1)(a) or paragraph 2, and

(ii) greater than the total number appointed under sub-paragraph (1)(b) or paragraph 3.

(3) Paragraph 2(2) applies in relation to appointments under sub-paragraph (1)(a), as it applies to appointments under paragraph 2.

(4) A person appointed under sub-paragraph (1)(a) shall not be so appointed to represent the Secretary of State in his capacity as the police authority for the metropolitan police district.

(5) The power to make an order under section 47(3) includes power to prescribe anything which is required to be prescribed for the purposes of this paragraph.

Definitions For "NCS Service Authority", see s 47(1); for "relevant police officers", see Pt I, para 3(1) of this Schedule; for "local authority members of police authorities", see Pt IV, para 14 of this Schedule.

PART IV

GENERAL

Membership of more than one Service Authority by non-core members

11.—(1) Nothing in this Schedule shall prevent a member of the NCS Service Authority appointed under Part III from being appointed as a member of the NCIS Service Authority under Part II.

(2) Nothing in this Schedule shall prevent a member of the NCIS Service Authority appointed under Part II from being appointed as a member of the NCS Service Authority under Part III.

Local authority members

12. Local authority members of police authorities for areas in England and Wales shall exercise—

(a) their powers to appoint members of the NCIS Service Authority under paragraphs 4, 7(c) and 8(1)(e), and

(b) their powers to appoint members of the NCS Service Authority under paragraphs 4, 9(b) and 10(1)(c),

so as to ensure that, so far as practicable, the members of the Authority appointed by them reflect the balance of parties for the time being prevailing among the local authority members of such police authorities taken as a whole.

13. The clerk to a Service Authority shall make such arrangements as he considers necessary to facilitate the appointment to the Authority, in accordance with this Schedule, of—

(a) local authority members of police authorities for areas in England and Wales, and

(b) in the case of the clerk to the NCIS Service Authority, members of police authorities for areas in Scotland and members of the Police Authority for Northern Ireland.

Interpretation

14. In this Schedule "local authority members of police authorities", in relation to areas in England and Wales, means—

(a) the members of police authorities appointed under paragraph 2 of Schedule 2 to the Police Act 1996 (local authority members), and

(b) the members of the Common Council of the City of London who are members of any committee appointed under section 26 of the City of London Police Act 1839.

15. In this Schedule—

(a) "the relevant police officers" shall be construed in accordance with paragraph 3(1), and

(b) "customs officer" means an officer commissioned by the Commissioners of Customs and Excise under section 6(3) of the Customs and Excise Management Act 1979.

16. For the purposes of this Schedule, the Commissioner and Assistant Commissioners of Police of the Metropolis and the Commissioner of Police for the City of London shall be treated as if they were members of the metropolitan police force and the City of London police force respectively.

Definitions For "NCIS Service Authority" and "NCS Service Authority", see ss 46, 90.
References See para 2.8.

SCHEDULE 2

Sections 1(7) and 47(7)

OTHER PROVISIONS ABOUT MEMBERS OF SERVICE AUTHORITIES

Disqualification

1. A person shall be disqualified for being appointed as a member of a Service Authority if—

(a) he has not yet attained the age of twenty-one years, or

(b) he has attained the age of seventy years.

2.—(1) A person shall be disqualified for being appointed as a member of a Service Authority if neither his principal or only place of work, nor his principal or only place of residence, has been in the relevant area during the whole of the period of twelve months ending with the day of appointment.

(2) A person shall be disqualified for being a member of a Service Authority if, at any time, neither his principal or only place of work, nor his principal or only place of residence, is within the relevant area.

(3) In this paragraph "relevant area"—

(a) in relation to appointments under Part I or III of Schedule 1, means England and Wales, and

(b) in relation to appointments under Part II of that Schedule, means the United Kingdom.

3.—(1) Subject to sub-paragraphs (2) and (3), a person shall be disqualified for being appointed as or being a member of a Service Authority if—

(a) he holds any paid office or employment appointments to which are or may be made or confirmed by the Service Authority or any committee or sub-committee of the Authority, or by a joint committee on which the Authority is represented, or by any person holding any such office or employment;

(b) a bankruptcy order has been made against him or his estate has been sequestrated or he has made a composition or arrangement with, or granted a trust deed for, his creditors;

(c) he is subject to a disqualification order under the Company Directors Disqualification Act 1986 or Part II of the Companies (Northern Ireland) Order 1989, or to an order made under section 429(2)(b) of the Insolvency Act 1986 (failure to pay under county court administration order); or

(d) he has within five years before the date of his appointment or since his appointment been convicted in the United Kingdom, the Channel Islands or the Isle of Man of an offence, and has had passed on him a sentence of imprisonment (whether suspended or not) for a period of not less than three months.

(2) Where a person is disqualified under sub-paragraph (1)(b) by reason that a bankruptcy order has been made against him or his estate has been sequestrated, the disqualification shall cease—

(a) unless the bankruptcy order is previously annulled or the sequestration of his estate is recalled or reduced, on his obtaining a discharge, and

(b) if the bankruptcy order is annulled or the sequestration of his estate is recalled or reduced, on the date of that event.

(3) Where a person is disqualified under sub-paragraph (1)(b) by reason of his having made a composition or arrangement with, or granted a trust deed for, his creditors and he pays his debts in full, the disqualification shall cease on the date on which the payment is completed, and in any other case it shall cease at the end of the period of five years beginning with the date on which the terms of the deed of composition or arrangement or trust deed are fulfilled.

(4) For the purposes of sub-paragraph (1)(d), the date of a conviction shall be taken to be the ordinary date on which the period allowed for making an appeal or application expires or, if an appeal or application is made, the date on which the appeal or application is finally disposed of or abandoned or fails by reason of its non-prosecution.

Tenure of office

4. Subject to the following paragraphs (and to the provisions of any order under section 1(3) or 47(3)) a person shall hold and vacate office as a member of a Service Authority in accordance with the terms of his appointment.

5. A person shall be appointed to hold office as a member for—

(a) a term of four years or a term expiring on his attaining the age of seventy years, whichever is the shorter, or

(b) such shorter term as the person or persons appointing him may determine in any particular case.

6.—(1) A person may at any time—

(a) resign his office as chairman or as a core member by notice in writing to both of the Service Authorities, or

(b) resign his office as a member of a Service Authority appointed under Part II or III of Schedule 1 by notice in writing to that Service Authority.

(2) Where a member resigns his office as a member or as chairman under subparagraph (1), he shall send a copy of the notice—

(a) to the Secretary of State, and

(b) if he was appointed under paragraph 7(g) or 8(1)(i) of Schedule 1, to the Commissioners of Customs and Excise.

7.—(1) A member of a police authority appointed to be a member of a Service Authority under paragraph 4, 7(c), (d) or (e), 8(1)(e), (f) or (g), 9(b) or 10(1)(c), of Schedule 1 shall cease to be a member of the Service Authority if he ceases to be a member of the police authority eligible for appointment under the paragraph concerned (unless re-elected or re-appointed on the same day).

(2) A member of a Service Authority appointed other than as mentioned in sub-paragraph (1) shall cease to be a member if he becomes a member of a police authority for an area in Great Britain, or of the Police Authority for Northern Ireland, eligible for appointment under one of the paragraphs mentioned in subparagraph (1).

(3) A Crown servant appointed to be a member of a Service Authority under paragraph 6, 7(f) or 8(1)(h) of Schedule 1 shall cease to be a member of the Service Authority if he ceases to be a Crown servant.

(4) A person appointed to be a member of a Service Authority in accordance with paragraph 3, 7(a) or (b), 8(1)(b), (c) or (d), 9(a) or 10(1)(b) of Schedule 1 (appointment of senior police officers) shall cease to be a member of the Service Authority if he ceases to be a person eligible for appointment under the paragraph concerned.

(5) A person appointed to be a member of the NCIS Service Authority under paragraph 7(g) or 8(1)(i) of Schedule 1 shall cease to be a member if he ceases to be a customs officer within the meaning of paragraph 15 of that Schedule.

8.—(1) Subject to sub-paragraph (3), a member of a Service Authority may be removed from office as such a member or as chairman by the authorised person, by notice in writing, if—

- (a) he has been absent from meetings of the Service Authority for a period longer than four consecutive months without the consent of the Authority,
- (b) he has been convicted of a criminal offence (but is not disqualified for being a member under paragraph 3),
- (c) the authorised person is satisfied that the member is incapacitated by physical or mental illness, or
- (d) the authorised person is satisfied that the member is otherwise unable or unfit to discharge his functions as a member.

(2) For the purposes of sub-paragraph (1) "the authorised person", in relation to a member of a Service Authority, means—

- (a) the Service Authority, or
- (b) the person or persons who would be required to appoint his successor.

(3) A Service Authority shall not, under sub-paragraph (1), remove its chairman from office as chairman or as a member of the Service Authority.

(4) Where a Service Authority removes a member under sub-paragraph (1), it shall give notice of that fact—

- (a) to the person or persons who are required to appoint his successor, and
- (b) if the member was appointed under Part I of Schedule 1, to the other Service Authority.

(5) Where a member of a Service Authority is removed under sub-paragraph (1) by the person mentioned in sub-paragraph (2)(b), that person shall give notice of that fact—

- (a) to the Service Authority, and
- (b) if he is a member appointed under Part I of Schedule 1 and is not also removed from the other Service Authority, to that other Authority.

9.—(1) A member of a Service Authority appointed under paragraph 4, 7(c), 8(1)(e), 9(b) or 10(1)(c) of Schedule 1 may be removed from office by the persons responsible for appointing his successor if those persons consider that his removal, and the appointment of another person in his place, would further the object provided for by paragraph 12 of that Schedule.

(2) Persons who remove a member under this paragraph shall—

- (a) if the member was a core member, give notice to both Service Authorities, and
- (b) in any other case, give notice to the Service Authority of which he was a member.

10. Where a core member appointed under Part I of Schedule 1 is removed from a Service Authority under paragraph 8 or 9, he shall cease to be a member of the other Service Authority.

Chairman

11.—(1) On being notified of a casual vacancy occurring in the office of chairman of the Service Authorities, the Secretary of State—

(a) shall take such steps as are reasonably practicable to fill the vacancy, and

(b) shall appoint a core member appointed under paragraph 2 of Schedule 1 to be the temporary chairman of the Service Authorities.

(2) A temporary chairman appointed in accordance with this paragraph—

(a) shall not continue in office as chairman for a period exceeding six months, and

(b) shall cease to hold that office on the appointment, by the Secretary of State, of a person to the office of chairman.

Eligibility for re-appointment

12. A person who ceases to be a member or to be chairman, otherwise than by virtue of paragraph 8(1)(a), (b) or (d), may (if otherwise eligible) be re-appointed.

Eligibility to vote

13. A member of a Service Authority appointed under paragraph 3, 7(a) or (b), 8(1)(b), (c) or (d), 9(a) or 10(1)(b) of Schedule 1 (appointment of senior police officers) shall not be entitled to vote on any decision taken by the Authority—

(a) on a motion of censure of the Director General or of any other member of NCIS or, as the case may be, the National Crime Squad (other than a member appointed by the Director General by virtue of section 9(8) or 55(8)), including any motion on disciplinary action to be taken against him, or

(b) relating to the exercise by the Authority of its power under section 7 or, as the case may be, 53 to require the Director General, or any other member, to resign in the interests of efficiency or effectiveness.

14. A member of a Service Authority appointed under paragraph 6, 7(f) or 8(1)(h) of Schedule 1 shall not be entitled to vote at any meeting of the Service Authority, or of any committee of that Authority.

Validity of acts

15. The acts and proceedings of any person appointed to be a member or chairman of a Service Authority and acting in that office shall, notwithstanding his disqualification or want of qualification, be as valid and effectual as if he had been qualified.

16. The proceedings of a Service Authority shall not be invalidated by a vacancy in the membership of the Authority or in the office of chairman or by any defect in the appointment of a person as a member or as chairman.

Allowances

17.—(1) Subject to sub-paragraph (2), a Service Authority may make to its chairman and other members such payments by way of reimbursement of expenses and allowances as the Secretary of State may determine.

(2) No payments by way of allowances shall be made under sub-paragraph (1) to a member of a Service Authority appointed under paragraph 3, 6, 7(a), (b), (f) or (g), 8(1)(b), (c), (d), (h) or (i), 9(a) or 10(1)(b) of Schedule 1.

(3) Payments made under sub-paragraph (1) may differ according to whether the recipient is the chairman, a core member or another member.

Co-opted Members

18.—(1) Paragraphs 1 to 3 apply to a person co-opted as a member of a Service Authority as they apply to a person appointed as such a member.

(2) Except as provided by sub-paragraph (1), the preceding paragraphs of this Schedule do not apply to a person co-opted as a member of a Service Authority.

(3) A customs officer (within the meaning of paragraph 15 of Schedule 1) shall be disqualified for being co-opted as a member of the NCS Service Authority; and a person shall cease to be a co-opted member of that Authority if he becomes a customs officer.

(4) A person co-opted as a member of a Service Authority shall be co-opted to serve as such a member for a term not exceeding twelve months, but may (if otherwise eligible) again be co-opted.

(5) A person co-opted as a member of a Service Authority shall not be entitled to vote at any meeting of the Authority, or of any committee of that Authority.

(6) A Service Authority may make to a person co-opted to serve as a member of the Authority such payments by way of reimbursement of expenses as the Secretary of State may determine.

Interpretation

19. For the purposes of this Schedule—
- (a) "Service Authority" means—
  - (i) the NCS Service Authority, or
  - (ii) the NCIS Service Authority, and
- (b) "core member" means a member appointed under Part I of Schedule 1.

Definitions For "NCIS Service Authority", "NCIS" and "NCS Service Authority", see ss 46, 90.
References See paras 2.9–2.12.

SCHEDULE 3

Section 17(6)

LEVIES ISSUED BY NCIS SERVICE AUTHORITY

Decisions of Service Authority

1.—(1) Where an order under section 17 requires the NCIS Service Authority to determine the total amount of the levies which it proposes to issue under that section for any financial year, that determination shall not be made except by a decision which—
- (a) is made only by independent members and police authority members of the NCIS Service Authority, and
- (b) complies with sub-paragraphs (2) and (3).

(2) A decision complies with this sub-paragraph only if a majority of the members making the decision (whether or not approving it) are police authority members of the Authority.

(3) A decision complies with this sub-paragraph only if the members approving it include more than half of the independent members and more than half of the police authority members of the Authority at the time of the decision.

(4) Before making such a determination as is mentioned in sub-paragraph (1) in respect of any financial year, the independent members and police authority members of the Authority shall take account of—
- (a) the expenditure which the Director General of NCIS estimates will be incurred in connection with NCIS in the year,
- (b) any income which it is estimated will be received by way of charges imposed by the Authority under section 19, or otherwise, in the year,
- (c) the financial reserves of the Authority and the reserves which it estimates it will be appropriate to raise in the year for meeting its estimated future expenditure,
- (d) the current and proposed level of borrowing of the Authority,
- (e) the views of all members of the Authority, and
- (f) such other matters as may be prescribed.

(5) In this paragraph "independent members" means members of the Authority appointed by the Secretary of State under paragraph 2 or 8(1)(a) of Schedule 1.

(6) In this paragraph "police authority members" means members appointed—
- (a) by the local authority members of police authorities for areas in England and Wales (as defined by paragraph 14 of Schedule 1), or
- (b) by the Secretary of State under paragraph 5 of that Schedule.

Approval by Secretary of State

2.—(1) Subject to paragraph 3, a levy shall not be issued by the NCIS Service Authority under section 17 in respect of a financial year, unless the Secretary of State has notified the Authority in writing that he approves the total amount of the levies the Authority proposes to issue for that year.

(2) Where the Secretary of State gives an approval under sub-paragraph (1), levies shall not be issued by the Authority in respect of the financial year concerned in excess of the amount so approved.

(3) Before deciding whether to give an approval under sub-paragraph (1), the Secretary of State shall consult—

(a) persons whom he considers to represent the interests of chief officers of police of police forces in England and Wales, and

(b) persons whom he considers to represent the interests of police authorities for areas in England and Wales.

(4) The Secretary of State shall give a copy of any notice sent to the NCIS Service Authority under sub-paragraph (1) to—

(a) each police authority for an area in England and Wales (other than the authority for the metropolitan police district), and

(b) the Receiver for the Metropolitan Police District.

Directions

3.—(1) Where the Secretary of State does not approve, under paragraph 2, the total amount of the levies the NCIS Service Authority proposes to issue for a financial year—

(a) he shall notify the Authority of his decision, and

(b) he may direct the Authority to issue such levies under section 17 for that year as he considers appropriate.

(2) Where the NCIS Service Authority does not, within the prescribed period, make a determination of the total amount of levies it proposes to issue under section 17 in respect of a financial year, the Secretary of State may direct the Authority to issue, under that section, such levies as he considers appropriate.

(3) The NCIS Service Authority shall provide the Secretary of State with such information as he may require to enable him to give a direction under this paragraph.

(4) Before giving a direction under this paragraph, the Secretary of State may take into account any matter he considers relevant.

(5) A direction under this paragraph shall be in writing.

(6) The Secretary of State shall send a copy of any direction under this paragraph to—

(a) each police authority for an area in England and Wales (other than the authority for the metropolitan police district), and

(b) the Receiver for the Metropolitan Police District.

Notices

4.—(1) The NCIS Service Authority shall, within the prescribed period, give notice of any levy to be issued under section 17 to—

(a) the Secretary of State,

(b) each police authority for an area in England and Wales (other than the authority for the metropolitan police district), and

(c) the Receiver for the Metropolitan Police District.

(2) A notice under this paragraph shall contain such information as may be prescribed.

Interpretation

5. In this Schedule "prescribed" means prescribed by an order under section 17.

Definitions For "NCIS Service Authority", see s 1(1); for "NCIS", see s 2; and for "financial year", see s 46.
References See para 2.38.

SCHEDULE 4

Section 44(1)

SUBJECT-MATTER OF ORDERS ABOUT NCIS SERVICE AUTHORITY

The enactments referred to in section 44 are—

(a) in the Local Government Act 1972—
  (i) sections 94 to 98 (restrictions on voting);
  (ii) section 99 and Schedule 12 (meetings and proceedings);
  (iii) Part VA (regulation of access to meetings and documents);
  (iv) Part VI (discharge of functions by local authorities);
  (v) section 111 (subsidiary powers of local authorities);
  (vi) sections 113 to 119 (provision regarding officers of local authorities);
  (vii) sections 120 (except subsection (1)(b)), 121, 123 and 128 to 131 (land transactions);
  (viii) section 135 (making of contracts);
  (ix) section 136 (contribution towards expenditure on concurrent functions);
  (x) section 140 (personal injury insurance in respect of members);
  (xi) section 143 (subscription to local government associations);
  (xii) section 223 (appearance of local authorities in legal proceedings);
  (xiii) sections 228 and 229 (inspection of documents and status of photocopies);
  (xiv) sections 231 to 234 (notices);

(b) Part III of the Local Government Act 1974 (investigation of complaints about maladministration etc);

(c) in the Local Government (Miscellaneous Provisions) Act 1976—
  (i) sections 13 to 16 and 29 (land);
  (ii) section 30 (power to forgo repayment of advances of remuneration paid to deceased employees);
  (iii) section 38 (use of spare capacity of computers);
  (iv) section 39 (personal liability insurance);
  (v) section 41 (evidence of resolutions and minutes of proceedings);

(d) in the Local Government, Planning and Land Act 1980—
  (i) Part III (direct labour organisations); and
  (ii) Part X (land held by public bodies);

(e) in the Local Government (Miscellaneous Provisions) Act 1982—
  (i) section 33 (covenants relating to land);
  (ii) section 41 (lost and uncollected property);

(f) Part III of the Local Government Finance Act 1982 (accounts and audit);

(g) in the Local Government Act 1986—
  (i) Part II (local authority publicity);
  (ii) Part III (transfer of local authority mortgages);

(h) in the Local Government Act 1988—
  (i) Part I (competition);
  (ii) Part II (public supply or works contracts);

(i) Part VIII of the Local Government Finance Act 1988 (financial administration);

(j) in the Local Government and Housing Act 1989—
  (i) Part I (local authority members, officers, staff and committees, etc);
  (ii) Part IV (revenue accounts and capital finance);
  (iii) Part V (companies in which local authorities have interests);
  (iv) section 155 (emergency financial assistance to local authorities);
  (v) section 157 (commutation of, and interest on, periodic payments of grants, etc).

SCHEDULE 5

Section 62(6)

LEVIES ISSUED BY NCS SERVICE AUTHORITY

Decisions of Service Authority

1.—(1) Where an order under section 62 requires the NCS Service Authority to determine the total amount of the levies which it proposes to issue under that section for any financial year, that determination shall not be made except by a decision which—

(a) is made only by independent members and police authority members of the Authority, and

(b) complies with sub-paragraphs (2) and (3).

(2) A decision complies with this sub-paragraph only if a majority of the members making the decision (whether or not approving it) are police authority members of the Authority.

(3) A decision complies with this sub-paragraph only if the members approving it include more than half of the independent members and more than half of the police authority members of the Authority at the time of the decision.

(4) Before making such a determination as is mentioned in sub-paragraph (1) in respect of any financial year, the independent members and police authority members of the Authority shall take account of—

(a) the expenditure which the Director General of the National Crime Squad estimates will be incurred in connection with the Squad in the year,

(b) any income which it is estimated will be received by way of charges imposed by the NCS Service Authority under section 64, or otherwise, in the year,

(c) the financial reserves of the Authority and the reserves which it estimates it will be appropriate to raise in the year for meeting its estimated future expenditure,

(d) the current and proposed level of borrowing of the Authority,

(e) the views of all members of the Authority, and

(f) such other matters as may be prescribed.

(5) In this paragraph "independent members" means members of the Authority appointed by the Secretary of State under paragraph 2 or 10(1)(a) of Schedule 1.

(6) In this paragraph "police authority members" means members appointed—

(a) by the local authority members of police authorities for areas in England and Wales (as defined by paragraph 14 of Schedule 1), or

(b) by the Secretary of State under paragraph 5 of that Schedule.

Approval by Secretary of State

2.—(1) Subject to paragraph 3, a levy shall not be issued by the NCS Service Authority under section 62 in respect of a financial year, unless the Secretary of State has notified the Authority in writing that he approves the total amount of the levies the Authority proposes to issue for that year.

(2) Where the Secretary of State gives an approval under sub-paragraph (1), levies shall not be issued by the Authority in respect of the financial year concerned in excess of the amount so approved.

(3) Before deciding whether to give an approval under sub-paragraph (1), the Secretary of State shall consult—

(a) persons whom he considers to represent the interests of chief officers of police of police forces in England and Wales, and

(b) persons whom he considers to represent the interests of police authorities for areas in England and Wales.

(4) The Secretary of State shall give a copy of any notice sent to the Authority under sub-paragraph (1) to—

(a) each police authority for an area in England and Wales (other than the authority for the metropolitan police district), and

(b) the Receiver for the Metropolitan Police District.

Directions

3.—(1) Where the Secretary of State does not approve, under paragraph 2, the total amount of the levies the Authority proposes to issue for a financial year—
- (a) he shall notify the Authority of his decision, and
- (b) he may direct the Authority to issue such levies under section 62 for that year as he considers appropriate.

(2) Where the NCS Service Authority does not, within the prescribed period, make a determination of the total amount of levies it proposes to issue under section 62 in respect of a financial year, the Secretary of State may direct the Authority to issue, under that section, such levies as he considers appropriate.

(3) The Authority shall provide the Secretary of State with such information as he may require to enable him to give a direction under this paragraph.

(4) Before giving a direction under this paragraph, the Secretary of State may take into account any matter he considers relevant.

(5) A direction under this paragraph shall be in writing.

(6) The Secretary of State shall send a copy of any direction under this paragraph to—
- (a) each police authority for an area in England and Wales (other than the authority for the metropolitan police district), and
- (b) the Receiver for the Metropolitan Police District.

Notices

4.—(1) The NCS Service Authority shall, within the prescribed period, give notice of any levy to be issued under section 62 to—
- (a) the Secretary of State,
- (b) each police authority for an area in England and Wales (other than the authority for the metropolitan police district), and
- (c) the Receiver for the Metropolitan Police District.

(2) A notice under this paragraph shall contain such information as may be prescribed.

Interpretation

5. In this Schedule "prescribed" means prescribed by an order under section 62.

Definitions For "NCS Service Authority", see s 47(1); for "financial year", see s 90.
References See paras 3.35, 3.36.

SCHEDULE 6

Section 88

APPLICATION TO NCS SERVICE AUTHORITY OF LOCAL GOVERNMENT ENACTMENTS

Local Government Act 1972 (c 70)

1. In section 94 of the Local Government Act 1972 (disability of members of authorities for voting on account of interest in contracts, etc), in subsection (5)(b) (receipt of certain allowances not to be treated as a pecuniary interest) after "1996" there shall be inserted "or paragraph 17 of Schedule 2 to the Police Act 1997".

2. In section 98—
- (a) in subsection (1A) (application to joint authorities of provisions about members' interests) after "1996" there shall be inserted "and the Service Authority for the National Crime Squad", and
- (b) after subsection (1A) there shall be inserted—

"(1B) In the application of section 97 above to a member of the Service Authority for the National Crime Squad, subsection (1) of that section shall apply as if the words from "or in any other case" to the end were omitted."

3. In section 99 (meetings and proceedings of local authorities) after "1996" there shall be inserted ", the Service Authority for the National Crime Squad".

4.—(1) Section 100J (application to joint authorities etc of provisions relating to access to meetings and documents) shall be amended as follows.

(2) In subsection (1), after paragraph (e) there shall be inserted—

"(ea) the Service Authority for the National Crime Squad;".

(3) In subsection (3), after "(e)" there shall be inserted ", (ea)".

(4) After subsection (3) there shall be inserted—

"(3A) In its application by virtue of subsection (1) above in relation to the Service Authority for the National Crime Squad, section 100A(6)(a) shall also have effect with the substitution for the word "three" of the word "seven"."

(5) In subsection (4), in paragraph (a), after "1996" there shall be inserted "or the Service Authority for the National Crime Squad".

5.—(1) Section 107 (application to police authorities of provisions relating to the discharge of functions by local authorities) shall be amended as follows.

(2) In subsection (7) for "(a) and (b)" there shall be substituted "(a), (aa) and (b)".

(3) After subsection (8) there shall be inserted—

"(8A) References in this section to a police authority, a police force, a chief officer of police or his deputy include references to the Service Authority for the National Crime Squad, the National Crime Squad, the Director General of that Squad and his deputy respectively."

6.—(1) Section 146A (application to police authorities of miscellaneous powers of local authorities) shall be amended as follows.

(2) In subsection (1)—

(a) for "subsection (1A)" there shall be substituted "subsections (1A) and (1AA)", and

(b) for "shall be" there shall be substituted "and the Service Authority for the National Crime Squad shall each be".

(3) In subsection (1A)—

(a) for "A" there shall be substituted "Neither a",

(b) after "1996" there shall be inserted "nor the Service Authority for the National Crime Squad", and

(c) the word "not" shall be omitted.

(4) After subsection (1A) there shall be inserted—

"(1AA) The Service Authority for the National Crime Squad shall not be treated as a local authority for the purposes of section 146 above."

7. In section 223 (appearance of local authorities in legal proceedings), in subsection (2), after "1996" there shall be inserted "and the Service Authority for the National Crime Squad".

8. In section 228 (inspection of documents), in subsection (7A), after "1996" there shall be inserted "or the Service Authority for the National Crime Squad".

9. The words "and the Service Authority for the National Crime Squad" shall be inserted after "1996"—

(a) in section 229 (photographic copies of documents), in subsection (8);

(b) in section 231 (service of notices on local authorities, etc), in subsection (4);

(c) in section 232 (public notices), in subsection (1A);

(d) in section 233 (service of notices by local authorities), in subsection (11); and

(e) in section 234 (authentication of documents), in subsection (4).

10.—(1) Schedule 12 (meetings and proceedings of local authorities) shall be amended as follows.

(2) In paragraph 6A, in sub-paragraph (1), after "1996" there shall be inserted "or the Service Authority for the National Crime Squad".

(3) In paragraph 6B—

(a) in sub-paragraph (b), after "1996" there shall be inserted ", or of the Service Authority for the National Crime Squad,", and

(b) at the end of sub-paragraph (b) there shall be added

", and

(c) in the case of the Service Authority for the National Crime Squad, paragraph 4(2) shall apply as if the reference to three clear days were a reference to seven clear days."

(4) In paragraph 46, after "1996" there shall be inserted "and the Service Authority for the National Crime Squad".

Local Government Act 1974 (c 7)

11. In section 25 of the Local Government Act 1974 (authorities subject to investigation by Commission for Local Administration), in subsection (1) after paragraph (ca) there shall be inserted—

"(caa) the Service Authority for the National Crime Squad;".

Local Government (Miscellaneous Provisions) Act 1976 (c 57)

12. In section 30 of the Local Government (Miscellaneous Provisions) Act 1976 (power to forgo repayment of remuneration paid to deceased employees), in subsection (3), after "the authority" there shall be inserted ", and a member of the National Crime Squad within section 55(1)(a) or (b) of the Police Act 1997 shall be treated as employed by the Service Authority for the National Crime Squad,".

13. In section 44 (interpretation), in subsection (1), in paragraph (a) of the definition of "local authority", after "1996" there shall be inserted ", the Service Authority for the National Crime Squad".

Local Government, Planning and Land Act 1980 (c 65)

14. In section 20 of the Local Government, Planning and Land Act 1980 (interpretation of provisions relating to direct labour organisations), in subsection (1)—

(a) in paragraph (a) of the definition of "local authority", in sub-paragraph (i), after "1996" there shall be inserted ", the Service Authority for the National Crime Squad", and

(b) in paragraph (aa) of the definition, after "1996" there shall be inserted "or the Service Authority for the National Crime Squad".

15. In section 99 (directions to dispose of land), in subsection (4), after paragraph (dc) there shall be inserted—

"(dd) the Service Authority for the National Crime Squad;".

16. In Schedule 16 (bodies to whom provisions of Part X relating to registration of land apply), after paragraph 5C there shall be inserted—

"5D. The Service Authority for the National Crime Squad.".

Local Government (Miscellaneous Provisions) Act 1982 (c 30)

17. In section 33 of the Local Government (Miscellaneous Provisions) Act 1982 (enforceability by local authorities of certain covenants relating to land), in subsection (9)(a), after "1996" there shall be inserted ", the Service Authority for the National Crime Squad".

18. In section 41 (lost and uncollected property), in subsection (13), in the definition of "local authority", for "and" at the end of paragraph (ca) there shall be substituted—

"(cb) the Service Authority for the National Crime Squad; and".

Local Government Finance Act 1982 (c 32)

19. In section 12 of the Local Government Finance Act 1982 (accounts subject to audit), in subsection (2), after paragraph (g) there shall be inserted—

"(ga) the Service Authority for the National Crime Squad;".

20. In section 19 (declaration that item of account is unlawful), at the end of subsection (7) there shall be added "and the Service Authority for the National Crime Squad".

21. In section 20 (recovery of amount not accounted for etc), at the end of subsection (10) there shall be added "and the Service Authority for the National Crime Squad".

22. For section 28B (delivery of documents relating to police authorities to Secretary of State), as inserted by paragraph 28 of Schedule 4 to the Police and Magistrates' Courts Act 1994, there shall be substituted—

"28F Delivery of documents relating to police authorities etc to Secretary of State

(1) The Commission shall send to the Secretary of State a copy of any report of which a copy is sent to the Commission under section 18(4) above and which relates—

(a) to a police authority established under section 3 of the Police Act 1996, or

(b) to the Service Authority for the National Crime Squad.

(2) If it appears to the Commission appropriate to do so, it may send to the Secretary of State a copy of any document—

(a) which relates to one or more police authorities established under section 3 of the Police Act 1996 or to the Service Authority for the National Crime Squad, and

(b) which has been sent (or a copy of which has been sent) by the Commission to a police authority established under that section or to that Authority."

Local Government Act 1986 (c 10)

23. In section 6 of the Local Government Act 1986 (interpretation of provisions relating to publicity and promotion of homosexuality), in subsection (2)(a), after "1996," there shall be inserted—

"the Service Authority for the National Crime Squad,".

24. In section 9 (interpretation of provisions relating to the transfer of mortgages), in subsection (1)(a), after "1996," there shall be inserted—

"the Service Authority for the National Crime Squad,".

Local Government Act 1988 (c 9)

25. In section 1 of the Local Government Act 1988 (defined authorities for provisions on competition), in subsection (1), after paragraph (e) there shall be inserted—

"(ea) the Service Authority for the National Crime Squad,".

26. In Schedule 2, in the list of public authorities to which provisions on public supply or works contracts apply, after the entry relating to police authorities there shall be inserted—

"The Service Authority for the National Crime Squad."

Local Government Finance Act 1988 (c 41)

27. In section 112 of the Local Government Finance Act 1988 (financial administration as to certain police and fire authorities), in subsection (2), for "and" at the end of paragraph (c) there shall be substituted—

"(ab) the Service Authority for the National Crime Squad, and".

28. In section 114 (functions of the chief finance officer as regards reports), at the end there shall be added—

"(9) The National Crime Squad shall be treated as a police force for the purposes of subsection (2) above."

Local Government and Housing Act 1989 (c 42)

29. In section 21 of the Local Government and Housing Act 1989, in subsection (1) (definition of local authority for purposes of various provisions relating to their members, officers, staff and committees etc), in paragraph (g), after "1996" there shall be inserted "or the Service Authority for the National Crime Squad".

30. In section 67 (application of provisions relating to companies in which local authorities have interests), in subsection (3) (definition of local authority), in paragraph (i), after "1996" there shall be inserted "or the Service Authority for the National Crime Squad".

31. In section 155 (emergency assistance to local authorities), after subsection (4)(ea) there shall be inserted—

"(eb) the Service Authority for the National Crime Squad;".

32. In section 157 (commutation of, and interest on, periodic payments of grants etc), in subsection (6), after paragraph (g) there shall be inserted—

"(ga) the Service Authority for the National Crime Squad;".

Definitions In the Local Government Finance Act 1982, for "the Commission", see s 36(1) thereof.

SCHEDULE 7

Section 102(4)

INVESTIGATION OF COMPLAINTS BY COMMISSIONERS ETC

Investigation

1. Where a Commissioner appointed under section 91(1)(b) is required by virtue of section 102 to investigate a complaint, he shall investigate whether an authorisation was given under section 93 in relation to the doing of the act or acts in question in relation to the property concerned ("a relevant authorisation").

2.—(1) In a case where the Commissioner determines that a relevant authorisation was given he shall, if sub-paragraph (2), (3) or (4) applies, make a determination in favour of the complainant.

(2) This sub-paragraph applies if the Commissioner is satisfied that there were, at the time the relevant authorisation was given or renewed, no reasonable grounds for believing the matters specified in section 93(2).

(3) This sub-paragraph applies where section 97 did not apply to the relevant authorisation or its renewal, but the Commissioner is satisfied as mentioned in section 103(2).

(4) This sub-paragraph applies if the Commissioner is satisfied that anything has been done in relation to any property of the complainant in pursuance of the relevant authorisation (other than by virtue of section 103(6) or section 104(7)) at a time when there were no reasonable grounds for believing the matters specified in section 93(2).

Report of conclusions

3.—(1) If the Commissioner makes a determination in favour of the complainant under paragraph 2, he shall—

(a) give notice to the complainant that he has done so, and
(b) make a report of his findings to the authorising officer who gave the authorisation, or in whose absence it was given, and to the Chief Commissioner.

(2) In any other case, the Commissioner shall give notice to the complainant that no determination in his favour has been made on the complaint.

(3) Subject to sub-paragraph (1)(b), the Commissioner shall not give any reasons for the making of, or any refusal to make, a determination in favour of the complainant.

4. Where—

(a) the Chief Commissioner receives a report of the Commissioner's findings under paragraph 3(1)(b), and
(b) no appeal is made against the determination in favour of the complainant,

the Chief Commissioner shall, under section 107(2), make a report of those findings to the Prime Minister.

Remedies

5.—(1) Where the Commissioner gives a complainant notice that a determination in his favour has been made on the complaint, he may (whether or not he has exercised, or intends to exercise, any of the powers under section 103) direct the authorising officer who gave the authorisation, or in whose absence it was given, to pay the complainant such sum by way of compensation as may be specified in the direction.

(2) Where a direction to pay compensation has been made under subparagraph (1), it shall not become operative until—

(a) the period for appealing against the determination in favour of the complainant has expired, and

(b) where such an appeal is made, a decision dismissing it has been made by the Chief Commissioner.

6. Any compensation which the Commissioner directs the authorising officer to pay under paragraph 5 shall be paid—

(a) in the case of an authorising officer within paragraph (a), (b) or (c) of subsection (5) of section 93, out of the police fund,

(b) in the case of an authorising officer within paragraph (d) of that subsection, by the police authority or, as the case may be, the joint police board (within the meaning of the Police (Scotland) Act 1967),

(c) in the case of an authorising officer within paragraph (e) of that subsection, by the Police Authority for Northern Ireland,

(d) in the case of an authorising officer within paragraph (f) or (g) of that subsection, out of the appropriate service fund established under section 16 or 61, and

(e) in the case of an authorising officer within paragraph (h) of section 93(5), by the Commissioners of Customs and Excise.

Interpretation

7. The references in this Schedule to the authorising officer who gave the authorisation or in whose absence it was given shall, in the case of an authorisation given by or in the absence of a person within paragraph (b) or (e) of section 93(5), be construed as references to the Commissioner of Police or, as the case may be, the Chief Constable mentioned in the paragraph concerned.

References See paras 4.100–4.103.

SCHEDULE 8

Section 109(2)

THE POLICE INFORMATION TECHNOLOGY ORGANISATION

Constitution

1.—(1) The Police Information Technology Organisation ("the Organisation") shall consist of a chairman and other members appointed by the Secretary of State.

(2) Before appointing the chairman the Secretary of State shall consult—

(a) persons whom he considers to represent the interests of police authorities, and

(b) persons whom he considers to represent the interests of chief officers of police.

(3) The members apart from the chairman at any time shall include—

(a) at least three members nominated by persons whom the Secretary of State considers to represent police authorities for areas in England and Wales;

(b) at least three members nominated by persons whom the Secretary of State considers to represent chief officers of police of police forces in England and Wales;

(c) at least one member nominated by persons whom the Secretary of State considers to represent police authorities for areas in Scotland;

(d) at least one member nominated by persons whom the Secretary of State considers to represent the interests of chief constables of police forces in Scotland;

(e) at least one member nominated by the Police Authority for Northern Ireland;

(f) at least one member nominated by the Chief Constable of the Royal Ulster Constabulary; and

(g) at least one other member.

Members

2.—(1) Subject to the provisions of this Schedule, a member of the Organisation shall hold office in accordance with the terms of his appointment.

(2) A member shall not be appointed for more than five years at a time.

(3) A person may at any time resign as a member or as chairman by notice in writing to the Secretary of State.

(4) The Secretary of State may remove a person from office as a member or as chairman if satisfied that—

(a) he has without reasonable excuse failed to discharge his functions for a continuous period of three months;
(b) he has without reasonable excuse been absent from three consecutive meetings of the Organisation;
(c) he has been convicted of a criminal offence;
(d) he has become bankrupt, his estate has been sequestrated or he has made an arrangement with or granted a trust deed for his creditors;
(e) he has failed to comply with the terms of his appointment; or
(f) he is otherwise unable or unfit to discharge his functions.

(5) The Secretary of State shall not remove from office a member nominated by persons representing certain interests in accordance with paragraph 1(3)(a) to (d) unless he has first consulted persons whom he considers to represent those interests.

(6) The Secretary of State shall not remove from office a member nominated in accordance with paragraph 1(3)(e) or (f) unless he has first consulted the Police Authority for Northern Ireland or, as the case may be, the Chief Constable of the Royal Ulster Constabulary.

3.—(1) The Organisation shall pay to its members such remuneration and allowances as the Secretary of State may determine.

(2) The Organisation shall, as regards any member or former member in whose case the Secretary of State may so determine, pay or make payments in respect of such pension or gratuity as the Secretary of State may determine.

(3) If a person ceases to be a member, or ceases to be chairman, and it appears to the Secretary of State that there are special circumstances which make it right that he should receive compensation, the Secretary of State may direct the Organisation to make a payment of such amount as he may determine.

Staff, &c

4.—(1) The Organisation shall not appoint employees except with the approval of the Secretary of State as to numbers and as to terms and conditions of service.

(2) No person shall be appointed to act as the chief executive of the Organisation unless the Secretary of State has consented to the appointment.

5.—(1) The Organisation shall pay to its employees such remuneration and allowances as it may, with the consent of the Secretary of State, determine.

(2) The Organisation shall—

(a) pay, or make payments in respect of, such pensions or gratuities to or in respect of employees or former employees as it may, with the consent of the Secretary of State, determine;
(b) provide and maintain such schemes (whether contributory or not) as it may determine, with the consent of the Secretary of State, for the payment of pensions or gratuities in respect of employees or former employees.

(3) References in this paragraph to pensions and gratuities include references to pensions or gratuities by way of compensation to or in respect of employees who suffer loss of employment or loss or diminution of emoluments.

(4) If any person—

(a) on ceasing to be employed by the Organisation, becomes or continues to be one of its members, and

(b) was, by reference to his employment, a participant in a pension scheme maintained by the Organisation,

the Organisation may, with the consent of the Secretary of State, make provision for that person to continue to participate in that scheme, on such terms and conditions as it may with the consent of the Secretary of State determine, as if his service as a member were service as an employee; and any such provision shall be without prejudice to paragraph 3.

6.—(1) Employment with the Organisation shall be included among the kinds of employment to which a scheme under section 1 of the Superannuation Act 1972 can apply.

(2) The Organisation shall pay to the Minister for the Civil Service, at such times as he may direct, such sums as he may determine in respect of the increase attributable to sub-paragraph (1) in the sums payable out of money provided by Parliament under that Act.

(3) Where an employee of the Organisation is, by reference to that employment, a participant in a scheme under section 1 of that Act and is also a member of the Organisation, the Minister for the Civil Service may determine that his service as a member shall be treated for the purposes of the scheme as service as an employee (whether or not any benefits are payable to or in respect of him by virtue of paragraph 3 above).

7.—(1) The Organisation shall be liable in respect of a tort committed by a member of a police force engaged on service with the Organisation in the performance or purported performance of his functions in like manner as a master is liable in respect of torts committed by his servants in the course of their employment, and shall in respect of any such tort be treated for all purposes as a joint tortfeasor.

(2) In relation to Scotland, sub-paragraph (1) shall not apply but the Organisation shall be liable in reparation in respect of a wrongful act or omission on the part of a member of a police force engaged on service with the Organisation in the performance or purported performance of his functions in like manner as a master is so liable in respect of any wrongful act or omission on the part of his servant in the course of the servant's employment.

Committees

8.—(1) No person who is not a member of the Organisation shall be appointed to a committee or sub-committee of the Organisation unless the Secretary of State has consented to the appointment.

(2) Remuneration and allowances paid to members of committees and subcommittees of the Organisation who are not members of the Organisation shall be of such amounts as the Secretary of State may determine.

Proceedings

9. Subject to the provisions of this Schedule, the Organisation shall regulate its own procedure.

10.—(1) The Organisation shall make provision for a quorum for its meetings to include at least—

(a) one member appointed in accordance with paragraph 1(3)(a), (c) or (e);
(b) one member appointed in accordance with paragraph 1(3)(b), (d) or (f); and
(c) one member appointed in accordance with paragraph 1(3)(g).

(2) The Organisation shall make provision for a quorum for meetings of any committee or sub-committee to include at least one member or employee of the Organisation.

11. The validity of the proceedings of the Organisation (or any committee or sub-committee) shall not be affected by—

(a) any vacancy among the members of the Organisation or in the office of chairman of the Organisation, or
(b) any defect in the appointment of any person as a member of the Organisation or as chairman of the Organisation.

Evidence

12. A document purporting to be—

(a) duly executed under the seal of the Organisation, or
(b) signed on behalf of the Organisation,

shall be received in evidence and, unless the contrary is proved, deemed to be so executed or signed.

Money

13. The Secretary of State may make payments to the Organisation out of money provided by Parliament.

14.—(1) The Organisation may impose such charges as it considers appropriate for the provision of goods and services in accordance with section 109(3) and (4).

(2) The Organisation shall pay any sums received in the course of carrying out its functions to the Secretary of State.

(3) Sub-paragraph (2) shall not apply where the Secretary of State, with the consent of the Treasury, so directs.

(4) Any sums received by the Secretary of State under sub-paragraph (2) shall be paid into the Consolidated Fund.

15. The Organisation may, for purposes related to information technology, make payments to any police authority.

16.—(1) The Organisation shall keep proper accounts and records in relation to the accounts.

(2) The Organisation shall prepare in respect of each financial year a statement of accounts.

(3) The statement shall be in such form, and shall contain such information, as the Secretary of State may, with the consent of the Treasury, direct.

(4) The Organisation shall send copies of the statement to the Secretary of State and to the Comptroller and Auditor General within such period after the end of the financial year to which the statement relates as the Secretary of State may direct.

(5) The Comptroller and Auditor General shall examine, certify and report on each statement received by him in accordance with this paragraph and shall lay copies of the statement and his report before each House of Parliament.

(6) In this paragraph "financial year" means the period of twelve months ending with 31st March; but the first financial year shall be the period beginning with the establishment of the Organisation and ending with the next 31st March.

Annual report

17.—(1) As soon as possible after the end of each financial year, the Organisation shall send to the Secretary of State a report on the discharge of its functions during that year.

(2) The Secretary of State shall lay a copy of each report before each House of Parliament.

(3) In this paragraph, "financial year" has the same meaning as in paragraph 16.

Status of the Organisation

18. The Organisation shall not be regarded as the servant or agent of the Crown or as enjoying any status, immunity or privilege of the Crown; and the property of the Organisation shall not be regarded as property of, or property held on behalf of, the Crown.

Definitions For "police authority", see s 101(1); for "chief officer of police", see s 111(2); for "police force", see s 101(3).
References See paras 5.18–5.32.

SCHEDULE 9

Section 134(1)

MINOR AND CONSEQUENTIAL AMENDMENTS

Explosives Act 1875 (c 17)

1. In the Explosives Act 1875, at the end of section 75 (inspections of ships with explosives on board, etc) (which becomes subsection (1)) there shall be added—

"(2) In subsection (1)—

(a) "officer of police" includes any member of the National Criminal Intelligence Service appointed under section 9(1)(b) of the Police Act 1997 (police members) and any member of the National Crime Squad appointed under section 55(1)(b) of that Act (police members), and

(b) "chief officer of police" includes the Director General of that Service and the Director General of that Squad.".

Civil Defence Act 1948 (c 5)

2. In section 9 of the Civil Defence Act 1948 (interpretation etc), after subsection (3) there shall be inserted—

"(3A) For the purposes of this Act (other than section 3(3)) the Service Authority for the National Criminal Intelligence Service and the Service Authority for the National Crime Squad shall be treated as police authorities and the National Criminal Intelligence Service and the National Crime Squad as police forces.".

Public Records Act 1958 (c 51)

3. In Schedule 1 to the Public Records Act 1958 (definition of public records), in Part II of the Table at the end of paragraph 3 there shall be inserted at the appropriate place—

"Police Information Technology Organisation".

Trustee Investments Act 1961 (c 62)

4. In section 11 of the Trustee Investments Act 1961 (local authority investment schemes), in subsection (4)—

(a) in paragraph (a) after "1996" there shall be inserted ", the Service Authority for the National Crime Squad", and

(b) after paragraph (d) there shall be added—

"(e) in any part of the United Kingdom, the Service Authority for the National Criminal Intelligence Service.".

5. In Schedule 1, in Part II (narrower-range investments requiring advice), in paragraph 9, after sub-paragraph (d) there shall be inserted—

"(da) the Service Authority for the National Criminal Intelligence Service or the Service Authority for the National Crime Squad;".

Offices, Shops and Railway Premises Act 1963 (c 41)

6. In section 90 of the Offices, Shops and Railway Premises Act 1963 (interpretation), in subsection (4) (persons treated as employed for purposes of that Act), after paragraph (c) there shall be added—

"(d) a member of the National Criminal Intelligence Service within section 9(1)(a) or (b) of the Police Act 1997 or a member of the National Crime Squad within section 55(1)(a) or (b) of that Act (police members).".

Parliamentary Commissioner Act 1967 (c 13)

7. In Schedule 2 to the Parliamentary Commissioner Act 1967 (departments etc subject to investigation), there shall be inserted at the appropriate place—

"Police Information Technology Organisation."

Police (Scotland) Act 1967 (c 77)

8. The Police (Scotland) Act 1967 shall be amended as follows.

9. In section 27(3) (regulations as to police cadets), after "(1A)," there shall be inserted "(2B),".

10. At the end of section 28 (regulations as to standards of equipment) (which becomes subsection (1)) there shall be added—

"(2) The Secretary of State shall consult the Police Information Technology Organisation before making regulations under this section relating to information technology.

(3) In subsection (2) of this section "information technology" includes any computer or other technology by means of which information or other matter may be recorded or communicated without being reduced to documentary form.".

11. In section 33 (inspectors of constabulary), in each of subsections (3) and (4), after "generally" there shall be inserted "and the National Criminal Intelligence Service".

12. At the end of section 36 (common services) there shall be added—

"(7) The Secretary of State shall consult the Police Information Technology Organisation before making regulations under this section relating to information technology.

(8) In subsection (7) of this section "information technology" includes any computer or other technology by means of which information or other matter may be recorded or communicated without being reduced to documentary form.".

13. In section 38 (constables engaged on central service and certain temporary service), in subsection (3A), after "service" there shall be inserted ", or on temporary service such as is mentioned in paragraph (ba) or (bb) of the said section 38A(1),".

14. In section 38A (constables engaged on service outside their force)—

(a) in subsection (1), after paragraph (b) there shall be inserted—

"(ba) temporary service with the National Criminal Intelligence Service on which a person is engaged with the consent of the appropriate authority;

(bb) temporary service with the Police Information Technology Organisation on which a person is engaged with the consent of the appropriate authority;"

; and

(b) in subsection (6)(a), after "(b)," there shall be inserted "(ba) or (bb)".

15. In section 39 (liability for wrongful acts of constables), in subsection (4), after "1996" there shall be inserted "or section 23 of the Police Act 1997".

Leasehold Reform Act 1967 (c 88)

16. In section 28 of the Leasehold Reform Act 1967 (retention or resumption of land required for public purposes), in subsection (5), after paragraph (bb) there shall be inserted—

"(bc) the Service Authority for the National Crime Squad and the Service Authority for the National Criminal Intelligence Service;".

Public Expenditure and Receipts Act 1968 (c 14)

17. In section 4 of the Public Expenditure and Receipts Act 1968 (compensation to civil defence employees for loss of employment etc) after subsection (6) (interpretation) there shall be added—

"(7) For the purposes of this section, the Service Authority for the National Criminal Intelligence Service and the Service Authority for the National Crime Squad shall be treated as police authorities.".

Firearms Act 1968 (c 27)

18. In section 54 of the Firearms Act 1968 (application of Act to Crown servants), in subsection (3) (which provides that members of police forces and certain employees of police authorities are deemed to be in the service of Her Majesty), at the end of paragraph (b) there shall be inserted

", or

(c) a member of the National Criminal Intelligence Service or the National Crime Squad.".

Post Office Act 1969 (c 48)

19. In section 7 of the Post Office Act 1969 (powers of the Post Office), in subsection (1AA), after "1996" there shall be inserted ", the Service Authority for the National Criminal Intelligence Service and the Service Authority for the National Crime Squad".

Employers' Liability (Compulsory Insurance) Act 1969 (c 57)

20. In section 3 of the Employers' Liability (Compulsory Insurance) Act 1969 (employers exempted from insurance), in subsection (2)(b) for "and any police authority" there shall be substituted ", any police authority, the Service Authority for the National Criminal Intelligence Service and the Service Authority for the National Crime Squad".

Police Act (Northern Ireland) 1970 (c 9 (NI))

21. In section 14 of the Police Act (Northern Ireland) 1970 (liability for wrongful acts of members of the police force), in subsection (5), after "Police Act 1996" there shall be inserted "or section 23 of the Police Act 1997".

22. In section 16(1) of that Act (appointment and functions of inspectors of constabulary) at the end there shall be added "and the National Criminal Intelligence Service".

Local Authorities (Goods and Services) Act 1970 (c 39)

23. In section 1 of the Local Authorities (Goods and Services) Act 1970 (supply of goods and services by local authorities), in subsection (4), in the definition of "public body", after "1996" there shall be inserted ", the Service Authority for the National Crime Squad, the Service Authority for the National Criminal Intelligence Service".

Superannuation Act 1972 (c 11)

24. The following entry shall be inserted at the appropriate place in the list of "Other Bodies" in Schedule 1 to the Superannuation Act 1972 (kinds of employment to which schemes may apply)—

"Police Information Technology Organisation".

Employers' Liability (Defective Equipment and Compulsory Insurance) (Northern Ireland) Order 1972 (NI 6)

25. In Article 7 of the Employers' Liability (Defective Equipment and Compulsory Insurance) (Northern Ireland) Order 1972 (employers exempted from insurance), after paragraph (aa) there shall be inserted—

"(ab) the Service Authority for the National Criminal Intelligence Service;".

Employment Agencies Act 1973 (c 35)

26. In section 13 of the Employment Agencies Act 1973, in subsection (7) (cases in which the Act is not to apply), in paragraph (f), after "1996" there shall be inserted ", the Service Authority for the National Criminal Intelligence Service, the Service Authority for the National Crime Squad".

Juries Act 1974 (c 23)

27. In Part I of Schedule 1 to the Juries Act 1974, in Group B (ineligibility for jury service of certain persons concerned with the administration of justice), after the entry for civilians employed for police purposes and members of the metropolitan civil staffs there shall be inserted—

"A member of the National Criminal Intelligence Service or the National Crime Squad.

A member of the Service Authority for the National Criminal Intelligence Service; a member of the Service Authority for the National Crime Squad; a person employed by the Service Authority for the National Criminal Intelligence Service under section 13 of the Police Act 1997 or by the Service Authority for the National Crime Squad under section 58 of that Act.".

District Courts (Scotland) Act 1975 (c 20)

28. In subsection (2) of section 12 of the District Courts (Scotland) Act 1975 (disqualification in certain cases of justices who are members of local authorities), the following shall be inserted as the first paragraph—

"(aa) any reference to a local authority includes a reference to the Service Authority for the National Criminal Intelligence Service;".

House of Commons Disqualification Act 1975 (c 24)

29.—(1) The House of Commons Disqualification Act 1975 shall be amended as follows.

(2) In section 1(1) (disqualification of certain office holders and places), after paragraph (d) there shall be inserted—

"(da) is a member of the National Criminal Intelligence Service or the National Crime Squad;".

(3) In Part III of Schedule 1 (disqualifying offices), there shall be inserted at the appropriate place—

"Any member of the Police Information Technology Organisation in receipt of remuneration.".

Northern Ireland Assembly Disqualification Act 1975 (c 25)

30.—(1) The Northern Ireland Assembly Disqualification Act 1975 shall be amended as follows.

(2) In section 1(1) (disqualification of certain office holders and places), after paragraph (d) there shall be inserted—

"(da) is a member of the National Criminal Intelligence Service or the National Crime Squad;".

(3) In Part III of Schedule 1 (disqualifying offices), there shall be inserted at the appropriate place—

"Any member of the Police Information Technology Organisation in receipt of remuneration.".

Sex Discrimination Act 1975 (c 65)

31. In section 17 of the Sex Discrimination Act 1975 (police), in subsection (7)—

(a) in the definition of "chief officer of police", after paragraph (a) there shall be inserted—

"(aa) in relation to a person appointed, or an appointment falling to be made, under section 9(1)(b) or 55(1)(b) of the Police Act 1997 (police members of the National Criminal Intelligence Service and the National Crime Squad) means the Director General of the National Criminal Intelligence Service or, as the case may be, the Director General of the National Crime Squad,",

and

(b) in the definition of "police fund" after "1996" there shall be inserted ", in relation to a chief officer of police within paragraph (aa) of that definition means the service fund established under section 16 or, as the case may be, 61 of the Police Act 1997".

Fair Employment (Northern Ireland) Act 1976 (c 25)

32. In section 53 of the Fair Employment (Northern Ireland) Act 1976 (police), in subsection (6), in the definition of "chief officer of police", after paragraph (a) there shall be inserted—

"(aa) in relation to a person appointed, or to an appointment falling to be made, under section 9(1)(b) of the Police Act 1997 (police members of the National Criminal Intelligence Service) means the Director General of the National Criminal Intelligence Service;".

Police Pensions Act 1976 (c 35)

33.—(1) Section 11 of the Police Pensions Act 1976 (interpretation) shall be amended as follows.

(2) In subsection (2)—

(a) the word "and" after paragraph (a) shall be omitted,

(b) in paragraph (b) after "it means" there shall be inserted ", subject to paragraphs (c) to (e) below,", and

(c) after paragraph (b) there shall be added—

"(c) in relation to service of the kind described in section 97(1)(ca) of the Police Act 1996 or section 38A(1)(ba) of the Police (Scotland) Act 1967, it means the Service Authority for the National Criminal Intelligence Service,

(d) in relation to service of the kind described in section 97(1)(cb) of the Police Act 1996, it means the Service Authority for the National Crime Squad and

(e) in relation to service of the kind described in section 97(1)(cc) of the Police Act 1996 or section 38A(1)(bb) of the Police (Scotland) Act 1967, it means the Police Information Technology Organisation.".

(3) In subsection (5), in the definition of "central service"—

(a) after "within paragraph (b), (c)" there shall be inserted ", (ca), (cb), (cc)", and

(b) after "1967" there shall be inserted "or means relevant service within paragraph (ba) or (bb) of section 38A(1) of the said Act of 1967".

Local Government (Miscellaneous Provisions) Act 1976 (c 57)

34. In each of sections 51 and 59 of the Local Government (Miscellaneous Provisions) Act 1976 (licensing of drivers of private hire vehicles and hackney carriages), subsection (1A) shall be omitted.

Race Relations Act 1976 (c 74)

35. In section 16 of the Race Relations Act 1976 (police), in subsection (5)—

(a) in the definition of "chief officer of police", after paragraph (a) there shall be inserted—

"(aa) in relation to a person appointed, or an appointment falling to be made, under section 9(1)(b) or 55(1)(b) of the Police Act 1997 (police members of the National Criminal Intelligence Service and the National Crime Squad) means the Director General of the National Criminal Intelligence Service or, as the case may be, the Director General of the National Crime Squad,",

and,

(b) in the definition of "police fund" after "Act" there shall be inserted," in relation to a chief officer of police within paragraph (aa) of that definition means the service fund established under section 16 or, as the case may be, 61 of the Police Act 1997".

36. In section 71 of that Act (local authorities: general statutory duty) after "1996" there shall be inserted ", the Service Authority for the National Criminal Intelligence Service, the Service Authority for the National Crime Squad".

Sex Discrimination (Northern Ireland) Order 1976 (NI 15)

37. In Article 19 of the Sex Discrimination (Northern Ireland) Order 1976 (police), in paragraph (6), in the definition of "chief officer of police", after subparagraph (a) there shall be inserted—

"(aa) in relation to a person appointed, or to an appointment falling to be made, under section 9(1)(b) of the Police Act 1997 (police members of the National Criminal Intelligence Service) means the Director General of the National Criminal Intelligence Service;".

Rent (Agriculture) Act 1976 (c 80)

38. In section 5 of the Rent (Agriculture) Act 1976 (no statutory tenancy where landlord's interest belongs to Crown or to local authority, etc), in subsection (3), in paragraph (baa), after "1996" there shall be added ", the Service Authority for the National Crime Squad and the Service Authority for the National Criminal Intelligence Service".

Rent Act 1977 (c 42)

39. In section 14 of the Rent Act 1977 (landlord's interest belonging to local authority, etc), after paragraph (caa) there shall be inserted—

"(caaa) the Service Authority for the National Criminal Intelligence Service or the Service Authority for the National Crime Squad;".

Justices of the Peace Act 1979 (c 55)

40. In section 64 of the Justices of the Peace Act 1979 (disqualification in certain cases of justices who are members of local authorities), in subsection (6) (definition of local authority), after "1996" there shall be inserted ", the Service Authority for the National Criminal Intelligence Service, the Service Authority for the National Crime Squad".

Law Reform (Miscellaneous Provisions) (Scotland) Act 1980 (c 55)

41. In Part I of Schedule 1 to the Law Reform (Miscellaneous Provisions) (Scotland) Act 1980, in Group B (ineligibility for jury service of certain persons concerned with the administration of justice), after paragraph (n) there shall be inserted—

"(na) members of the National Criminal Intelligence Service;

(nb) members of the Service Authority for the National Criminal Intelligence Service and persons employed by that Authority under section 13 of the Police Act 1997;".

Finance Act 1981 (c 35)

42. In section 107 of the Finance Act 1981 (sale of houses at discount by local authorities etc), after subsection (3)(k) there shall be inserted—

"(ka) the Service Authority for the National Crime Squad or the Service Authority for the National Criminal Intelligence Service;".

Acquisition of Land Act 1981 (c 67)

43. In section 17 of the Acquisition of Land Act 1981 (compulsory purchase of local authority and statutory undertakers' land), in subsection (4), in the definition (for the purposes of subsection (3)) of "local authority"—

(a) in paragraph (a), after "1996" there shall be inserted ", the Service Authority for the National Crime Squad, the Service Authority for the National Criminal Intelligence Service"; and

(b) in paragraph (b), after "1996" there shall be inserted ", the Service Authority for the National Crime Squad or the Service Authority for the National Criminal Intelligence Service".

Stock Transfer Act 1982 (c 41)

44. In Schedule 1 to the Stock Transfer Act 1982 (securities that can be transferred through a computerised system), in paragraph 7(1), for "or" at the end of paragraph (ba) there shall be substituted—

"(bb) the Service Authority for the National Criminal Intelligence Service or the Service Authority for the National Crime Squad; or".

County Courts Act 1984 (c 28)

45. In section 60 of the County Courts Act 1984 (right of audience for officer of local authority in proceedings brought by authority), in subsection (3), in the definition of "local authority", after "1996" there shall be inserted ", the Service Authority for the National Criminal Intelligence Service, the Service Authority for the National Crime Squad".

Police and Criminal Evidence Act 1984 (c 60)

46. In section 5 of the Police and Criminal Evidence Act 1984 (reports of recorded searches and of road checks), after subsection (1) there shall be inserted—

"(1A) Every annual report under section 57 of the Police Act 1997 (reports by Director General of the National Crime Squad) shall contain information—

(a) about searches recorded under section 3 above which have been carried out by members of the National Crime Squad during the period to which the report relates, and

(b) about road checks authorised by members of the National Crime Squad during that period under section 4 above;".

47. In section 55 (intimate searches), after subsection (14) there shall be inserted—

"(14A)Every annual report under section 57 of the Police Act 1997 (reports by Director General of the National Crime Squad) shall contain information about searches authorised under this section by members of the National Crime Squad during the period to which the report relates.".

Prosecution of Offences Act 1985 (c 23)

48. In section 3 of the Prosecution of Offences Act 1985 (functions of Director), in subsection (3), in the definition of "police force", after "1996" there shall be inserted ", the National Crime Squad".

Housing Act 1985 (c 51)

49. In section 4 of the Housing Act 1985 (interpretation), in paragraph (e) (definition of "local authority"), after "1996" there shall be inserted ", the Service Authority for the National Criminal Intelligence Service, the Service Authority for the National Crime Squad".

Housing Associations Act 1985 (c 69)

50. In section 106 of the Housing Associations Act 1985 (minor definitions), in subsection (1), in the definition of "local authority", after "1996" there shall be inserted "and the Service Authority for the National Crime Squad and the Service Authority for the National Criminal Intelligence Service".

Landlord and Tenant Act 1985 (c 70)

51. In section 38 of the Landlord and Tenant Act 1985 (minor definitions), in the definition of "local authority", after "1996" there shall be inserted ", the Service Authority for the National Criminal Intelligence Service, the Service Authority for the National Crime Squad".

Landlord And Tenant Act 1987 (c 31)

52. In section 58 of the Landlord and Tenant Act 1987, in subsection (1) (definition of "exempt landlord"), in paragraph (a), after "1996" there shall be inserted ", the Service Authority for the National Criminal Intelligence Service, the Service Authority for the National Crime Squad".

Income and Corporation Taxes Act 1988 (c 1)

53. In section 842A of the Income and Corporation Taxes Act 1988, in subsection (1)—

(a) in paragraph (a), after "paragraph" there shall be inserted "or the Service Authority for the National Criminal Intelligence Service or the Service Authority for the National Crime Squad",

(b) in paragraph (b), after "paragraph" there shall be inserted "or the Service Authority for the National Criminal Intelligence Service", and

(c) in paragraph (c), after "paragraph" there shall be inserted "or the Service Authority for the National Criminal Intelligence Service".

Dartford-Thurrock Crossing Act 1988 (c 20)

54. In section 19 of the Dartford-Thurrock Crossing Act 1988 (exemption from tolls), in paragraph (a), after sub-paragraph (i) there shall be inserted—

"(ia) the Service Authority for the National Criminal Intelligence Service or the Service Authority for the National Crime Squad;".

Local Government Finance Act 1988 (c 41)

55. In section 64 of the Local Government Finance Act 1988, in subsection (7) (exclusion from Crown exemption of hereditaments of certain authorities), after paragraph (d) there shall be inserted—

"(da) the Service Authority for the National Criminal Intelligence Service;

(db) the Service Authority for the National Crime Squad;".

56. In section 65A (which was inserted by section 3 of the Local Government and Rating Act 1997 and makes provision about Crown property), in subsection (4)(b) for the words from "or by a police authority" to the end there shall be substituted ", a police authority established under section 3 of the Police Act 1996, the Service Authority for the National Criminal Intelligence Service or the Service Authority for the National Crime Squad".

Housing Act 1988 (c 50)

57. In Schedule 1 to the Housing Act 1988 (tenancies which cannot be assured tenancies), in paragraph 12 (local authority tenancies, etc), in sub-paragraph (2)(g), after "1996" there shall be inserted—

", the Service Authority for the National Criminal Intelligence Service and the Service Authority for the National Crime Squad."

Road Traffic Act 1988 (c 52)

58. In section 124 of the Road Traffic Act 1988 (exemption of police instructors from prohibition imposed by section 123), in subsection (2), after "section—" there shall be inserted—

""chief officer of police" includes the Director General of the National Criminal Intelligence Service and the Director General of the National Crime Squad;

"police authority" includes the Service Authority for the National Criminal Intelligence Service and the Service Authority for the National Crime Squad;

"police force" includes the National Criminal Intelligence Service and the National Crime Squad;".

59. In section 144 (exceptions from requirement of third-party insurance or security), after subsection (2)(b) there shall be inserted—

"(ba) to a vehicle owned by the Service Authority for the National Criminal Intelligence Service or the Service Authority for the National Crime Squad, at a time when it is being driven under the owner's control, or to a vehicle at a time when it is being driven for the purposes of the body maintained by such an Authority by or under the direction of a constable, or by a person employed by such an Authority;".

Security Service Act 1989 (c 5)

60. In section 1 of the Security Service Act 1989, in subsection (4) (Security Service to act in support of police forces etc), after "forces" there shall be inserted ", the National Criminal Intelligence Service, the National Crime Squad".

61. In section 2 (which imposes duties on the Director General of the Security Service), in subsection (2)(c), after "forces" there shall be inserted ", the National Criminal Intelligence Service, the National Crime Squad".

Official Secrets Act 1989 (c 6)

62. In section 12 of the Official Secrets Act 1989, in subsection (1) (meaning of "Crown servant" for purposes of that Act), in paragraph (e) after "1970)" there shall be inserted "or of the National Criminal Intelligence Service or the National Crime Squad".

Town and Country Planning Act 1990 (c 8)

63. In section 252 of the Town and Country Planning Act 1990 (procedure for making of orders relating to highways), in subsection (12), in the definition of "local authority", after "1996" there shall be inserted ", the Service Authority for the National Crime Squad, the Service Authority for the National Criminal Intelligence Service".

Aviation and Maritime Security Act 1990 (c 31)

64. In section 22 of the Aviation and Maritime Security Act 1990 (power to require harbour authorities to promote searches in harbour areas), in subsection (4)(b)—

(a) the words "who is a member of a body of constables maintained" shall be omitted,

(b) at the beginning of both sub-paragraph (i) and sub-paragraph (ii) there shall be inserted "who is a member of a body of constables maintained", and

(c) at the end of sub-paragraph (ii) there shall be inserted—

", or

(iii) who is a member of the National Criminal Intelligence Service within section 9(1)(a) or (b) of the Police Act 1997 or a member of the National Crime Squad within section 55(1)(a) or (b) of that Act."

Road Traffic Act 1991 (c 40)

65. Section 47 of the Road Traffic Act 1991 (applications for licences to drive hackney carriages etc) shall cease to have effect.

Local Government Finance Act 1992 (c 14)

66. In section 19 of the Local Government Finance Act 1992 (exclusion of Crown exemption in certain cases), in subsection (3), for "and" at the end of paragraph (c) there shall be substituted—

"(ca) the Service Authority for the National Criminal Intelligence Service;
(cb) the Service Authority for the National Crime Squad;".

67. In section 32 (calculation of budget requirement by billing authorities), after subsection (6) there shall be inserted—

"(6A) In estimating under subsection (2)(a) above, the Common Council shall take into account the amount of any levy issued to it under section 17 or 62 of the Police Act 1997 (levies issued by the Service Authority for the National Criminal Intelligence Service and the Service Authority for the National Crime Squad) for the year, but (except as provided by an order under either of those sections) shall not anticipate a levy not issued.".

68.—(1) Section 43 (calculation of budget requirement by major precepting authorities) shall be amended as follows.

(2) After subsection (5) there shall be inserted—

"(5A) In estimating under subsection (2)(a) above—
(a) a police authority established under section 3 of the Police Act 1996 (authorities for areas outside London), and
(b) the Receiver for the Metropolitan Police District,
shall take into account the amount of any levy issued to it under section 17 or 62 of the Police Act 1997 (levies issued by the Service Authority for the National Criminal Intelligence Service and the Service Authority for the National Crime Squad) for the year, but (except as provided by an order under either of those sections) shall not anticipate a levy not issued.".

(3) In subsection (7)(b), after "subsections (5)" there shall be inserted ",(5A)".

Tribunals and Inquiries Act 1992 (c 53)

69.—(1) In section 7 of the Tribunals and Inquiries Act 1992, in subsection (2), after "36A" there shall be inserted "(a) or (b)".

70. In Schedule 1 to that Act, in Part I, at the end of paragraph 36A (which becomes sub-paragraph (a)) there shall be inserted—

"(b) An appeals tribunal constituted in accordance with an order under section 38(2) of the Police Act 1997 (c 50) and an appeals tribunal constituted in accordance with Schedule 6 to the Police Act 1996 as applied by section 82(2) of the Police Act 1997.".

Criminal Appeals Act 1995 (c 35)

71.—(1) Section 22 of the Criminal Appeals Act 1995 (meaning of "public body" etc) shall be amended as follows.

(2) In subsection (2)—
(a) in paragraph (a) (meaning of "police force"), after "Reserve" there shall be inserted ", the National Crime Squad",
(b) for paragraph (b) (meaning of "chief officer of police") there shall be substituted—
"(b) references to the chief officer of police—
(i) in relation to the Royal Ulster Constabulary and the Royal Ulster Constabulary Reserve, are to the Chief Constable of the Constabulary,
(ii) in relation to the National Crime Squad, are to the Director General of the Squad, and
(iii) in relation to any other police force maintained otherwise than by a police authority, are to the chief constable,",
(c) in paragraph (c) for "or the City of London police force" there shall be substituted ", the City of London police force or the National Crime Squad", and

(d) after paragraph (c) there shall be added—

"(d) "police authority" includes the Service Authority for the National Crime Squad, and

(e) references to a person serving in a police force or to a member of a police force, in relation to the National Crime Squad, mean a police member of that Squad appointed under section 55(1)(b) of the Police Act 1997.".

(3) In subsection (4) (meaning of "appropriate person"), after paragraph (a) there shall be inserted—

"(aa) in relation to the National Criminal Intelligence Service, the Director General of that Service,".

Police Act 1996 (c 16)

72. The Police Act 1996 shall be amended as follows.

73. At the end of section 23 (collaboration agreements) there shall be added—

"(8) For the purposes of this section, the Service Authority for the National Crime Squad, the National Crime Squad and the Director General of that Squad shall be treated as if they were a police authority, the police force maintained by that authority and the chief officer of police of that force respectively, and the reference in subsection (1) to "police functions" shall include the functions of that Squad.".

74. At the end of section 24 (mutual aid) there shall be added—

"(5) This section shall apply in relation to the Service Authority for the National Crime Squad, the National Crime Squad and the Director General of that Squad as it applies to a police authority, a police force and a chief officer of police respectively, and accordingly the reference in subsection (3) to section 10(1) shall be construed, in a case where constables are provided by the Director General of the National Crime Squad, as including a reference to section 56(1) of the Police Act 1997.".

75. At the end of section 53 (regulations as to standards of equipment) (which becomes subsection (1)) there shall be added—

"(2) The Secretary of State shall consult the Police Information Technology Organisation before making regulations under this section relating to information technology.

(3) In subsection (2) "information technology" includes any computer or other technology by means of which information or other matter may be recorded or communicated without being reduced to documentary form.".

76. In section 54 (appointment and functions of inspectors of constabulary), at the end of subsection (2) there shall be added "and the National Criminal Intelligence Service and the National Crime Squad".

77. In section 55 (publication of reports), after subsection (6) there shall be added—

"(7) Subsections (3) to (6) above shall apply in relation to a report relating to the National Criminal Intelligence Service or the National Crime Squad as if—

(a) the body to which the report relates were a police force,

(b) the Service Authority which maintains that body were the police authority which maintains that force, and

(c) the Director General of that body were the chief officer of police of that force.".

78.—(1) Section 57 (common services) shall be amended as follows.

(2) After subsection (3) there shall be inserted—

"(3A) Regulations under this section relating to all police forces may also require the National Crime Squad to use the specified facilities or services, or the facilities or services of a specified description, if the Secretary of State considers that it would be in the interests of the efficiency or effectiveness of the Squad for the Squad to do so.".

(3) In subsection (4), at the end of paragraph (b) there shall be added—

", and

(c) if the regulations relate to the National Crime Squad, the Service Authority for the National Crime Squad and the Director General of that Squad".

(4) After subsection (4) there shall be added—

"(5) The Secretary of State shall consult the Police Information Technology Organisation before making regulations under this section relating to information technology.

(6) In subsection (5) "information technology" includes any computer or other technology by means of which information or other matter may be recorded or communicated without being reduced to documentary form."

79. In section 59 (Police Federations), after subsection (7) there shall be added—

"(8) For the purposes of subsection (1)—

(a) the Director General of the National Criminal Intelligence Service and persons within section 9(2)(a) of the Police Act 1997 (former members of police forces) appointed as police members of the National Criminal Intelligence Service, and

(b) the Director General of the National Crime Squad and persons within section 55(2)(a) of that Act (former members of police forces) appointed as police members of the National Crime Squad,

shall be treated as members of a police force in England and Wales, and references in this section to police service shall be construed accordingly.".

80. In section 60 (regulations for police federations), after subsection (2) there shall be inserted—

"(2A) For the purposes of paragraphs (c) and (d) of subsection (2)—

(a) the Service Authority for the National Criminal Intelligence Service and the Service Authority for the National Crime Squad shall be treated as police authorities, and

(b) the Director General of the National Criminal Intelligence Service and the Director General of the National Crime Squad shall be treated as chief officers of police,

and the reference in paragraph (d) of that subsection to "police purposes" shall be construed accordingly.".

81. In section 61 (Police Negotiating Board for the United Kingdom), in subsection (1)—

(a) after paragraph (a), there shall be inserted—

"(aa) the Service Authority for the National Criminal Intelligence Service and the Service Authority for the National Crime Squad;"

, and

(b) after paragraph (b) there shall be inserted—

"(ba) the persons who are members of the National Criminal Intelligence Service within section 9(1)(a) or (b) of the Police Act 1997 or members of the National Crime Squad within section 55(1)(a) or (b) of that Act;".

82.—(1) Section 62 (functions of Police Negotiating Board) shall be amended as follows.

(2) After subsection (1) there shall be inserted—

"(1A) Before determining the terms and conditions on which a person is to be appointed under section 6, 9(1)(b), 52 or 55(1)(b) of the Police Act 1997, the Service Authority for the National Criminal Intelligence Service or, as the case may be, the Service Authority for the National Crime Squad shall—

(a) consult the Police Negotiating Board for the United Kingdom about any term or condition which relates to any of the matters mentioned in section 61(1) (other than pensions), and

(b) take into consideration any recommendation made by the Board.".

(3) In subsection (2), after "subsection (1)" there shall be inserted "or (1A)".

83.—(1) Section 63 (Police Advisory Boards) shall be amended as follows.

(2) After subsection (1) there shall be inserted—

"(1A) The Police Advisory Board for England and Wales shall also advise the Secretary of State on general questions affecting—

(a) members of the National Criminal Intelligence Service within section 9(1)(a) or (b) of the Police Act 1997 (other than members engaged with that Service on a period of temporary service to which section 38A(1)(ba) of the Police (Scotland) Act 1967 or section 21 of the Police Act (Northern Ireland) 1970 applies), or

(b) members of the National Crime Squad within section 55(1)(a) or (b) of the Police Act 1997.

(1B) The Police Advisory Board for Scotland shall also advise the Secretary of State on general questions affecting members of the National Criminal Intelligence Service engaged on periods of temporary service to which section 38A(1)(ba) of the Police (Scotland) Act 1967 applies.".

(3) In subsection (3), at the end of paragraph (b) there shall be inserted—

", or

(c) regulations under section 37, 39, 81, 83 of the Police Act 1997,".

84. In section 64 (membership of trade unions), after subsection (4) there shall be inserted—

"(4A) This section applies to members of the National Criminal Intelligence Service within section 9(1)(a) or (b) of the Police Act 1997 or members of the National Crime Squad within section 55(1)(a) or (b) of that Act (police members) as it applies to members of a police force, and references to a police force or to service in a police force shall be construed accordingly.

(4B) In its application by virtue of subsection (4A), subsection (2) shall have effect as if the reference to the chief officer of police were a reference to the Director General of the National Criminal Intelligence Service or, as the case may be, the Director General of the National Crime Squad.".

85. In section 88 (liability for wrongful acts of constables), in subsection (5)(b), after "or 98" there shall be inserted "of this Act or section 23 of the Police Act 1997".

86.—(1) Section 97 (police officers engaged on service outside their force) shall be amended as follows.

(2) In subsection (1), after paragraph (c) there shall be inserted—

"(ca) temporary service with the National Criminal Intelligence Service on which a person is engaged with the consent of the appropriate authority;

(cb) temporary service with the National Crime Squad on which a person is engaged with the consent of the appropriate authority;

(cc) temporary service with the Police Information Technology Organisation on which a person is engaged with the consent of the appropriate authority;".

(3) In subsection (6)(a) after "(c)," there shall be inserted "(ca), (cb), (cc),"

(4) In subsection (8) after "(c)" there shall be inserted ", (ca), (cb), (cc),".

87.—(1) Section 98 (cross-border aid) shall be amended as follows.

(2) In subsection (2)—

(i) after "Constabulary", in the first place it occurs, there shall be inserted "or the Director General of the National Crime Squad", and

(ii) after "Constabulary", in the second place it occurs there shall be inserted "or the National Crime Squad".

(3) In subsection (3)—

(i) after "Scotland" there shall be inserted "or the Director General of the National Crime Squad", and

(ii) after "Scottish force" there shall be inserted "or the National Crime Squad".

(4) After subsection (3) there shall be inserted—

"(3A) The Director General of the National Crime Squad may, on the application of the chief officer of a police force in Scotland or the Chief Constable of the Royal Ulster Constabulary, provide constables or other assistance for the purpose of enabling the Scottish force or the Royal Ulster Constabulary to meet any special demand on its resources.".

(5) In subsection (4)—
- (a) in paragraph (a) after "force" there shall be inserted "or the National Crime Squad",
- (b) in paragraph (b), for "or (3)" there shall be substituted ", (3) or (3A)", and
- (c) after "Constabulary" there shall be inserted "or the Director General of the National Crime Squad".

(6) In subsection (5)—
- (a) after "force" in the first place it occurs there shall be inserted "or the National Crime Squad",
- (b) after "Constabulary" in the first place it occurs there shall be inserted "or the National Crime Squad", and
- (c) after "Constabulary" in the second place it occurs there shall be inserted "or the Director General of the National Crime Squad".

(7) After subsection (6) there shall be inserted—

"(6A) For the purposes of subsection (6), the Service Authority for the National Crime Squad shall be treated as a police authority and the National Crime Squad as the police force maintained by it.".

Employment Rights Act 1996 (c 18)

88. In section 50 of the Employment Rights Act 1996 (right to time off for public duties), in subsection (2), after paragraph (c) there shall be inserted—

"(ca) the Service Authority for the National Criminal Intelligence Service or the Service Authority for the National Crime Squad,".

Housing Grants, Construction and Regeneration Act 1996 (c 53)

89. In section 3 of the Housing Grants, Construction and Regeneration Act 1996 (persons ineligible for grant under Chapter I of Part I of that Act), in subsection (2), for paragraph (g) there shall be substituted—

"(g) a police authority established under section 3 of the Police Act 1996, the Service Authority for the National Criminal Intelligence Service or the Service Authority for the National Crime Squad;".

90. In section 64, in subsection (7) (persons ineligible to participate in group repair schemes as assisted participants), for paragraph (e) there shall be substituted—

"(e) a police authority established under section 3 of the Police Act 1996, the Service Authority for the National Criminal Intelligence Service or the Service Authority for the National Crime Squad;".

Juries (Northern Ireland) Order 1996 (NI 6)

91. In Schedule 2 to the Juries (Northern Ireland) Order 1996 (persons ineligible for jury service), after the entry for members and staff of the Police Authority for Northern Ireland there shall be inserted—

"Members of the National Criminal Intelligence Service, members of the Service Authority for the National Criminal Intelligence Service and persons employed by the Authority.".

Justices of the Peace Act 1997 (c 25)

92. In section 66 of the Justices of the Peace Act 1997, in subsection (7), after paragraph (b) there shall be inserted—

"(ba) the Service Authority for the National Criminal Intelligence Service;
(bb) the Service Authority for the National Crime Squad;".

Definitions In the Police and Criminal Evidence Act 1984, as to "road check", see s 4(2) thereof.
In the Road Traffic Act 1988, for "under the other's control", see s 161(1) thereof.
In the Police Act 1996, for "chief officer of police", "police authority" and "police force", see s 101(1) thereof.

SCHEDULE 10

Section 134(2)

REPEALS

Chapter	Short title	Extent of repeal
1967 c 77	Police (Scotland) Act 1967	In section 39(4), the word "or" in the third place where it occurs.
1967 c 88	Leasehold Reform Act 1967	In section 28(5)(a), the word "and" in second place where it occurs.
1972 c 70	Local Government Act 1972	In section 146A(1A), the word "not". In section 223(2) the word "and".
1976 c 35	Police Pensions Act 1976	After section 11(2)(a), the word "and".
1976 c 57	Local Government (Miscellaneous Provisions) Act 1976	Sections 51(1A) and 59(1A).
1986 c 60	Finance Services Act 1986	Section 189.
		Schedule 14.
1987 c 22	Banking Act 1987	Section 95.
1989 c 5	Security Service Act 1989	Section 2(3B).
1990 c 31	Aviation and Maritime Security Act 1990	In section 22(4)(b), the words "who is a member of a body of constables maintained".
1991 c 40	Road Traffic Act 1991	Section 47.
1993 c 21	Osteopaths Act 1993	Section 39.
1993 c 39	National Lottery etc Act 1993	Section 19.
1994 c 17	Chiropractors Act 1994	Section 40.
1995 c 25	Environment Act 1995	In Schedule 22, paragraph 17(a).
1996 c 16	Police Act 1996	In section 62(1), at the end of paragraph (b) the word "or".
		In section 98(4), the word "or" in the sixth place occurs.
1996 c 35	Security Service Act 1996	Section 1(3).

Police Act 1997 (Commencement No 1 and Transitional Provisions) Order 1997

(SI 1997/1377)

Made 29 May 1997.

1 Citation, commencement and interpretation

(1) This Order may be cited as the Police Act 1997 (Commencement No 1 and Transitional Provisions) Order 1997.

(2) This Order shall come into force on 25th June 1997.

(3) In this Order "the Act" means the Police Act 1997.

2 Commencement on 25th June 1997

(1) The provisions of the Act which are listed in paragraph (2) below shall come into force on 25th June 1997.

(2) The provisions referred to in paragraph (1) above are—

(a) section 17, except subsections (1) and (6), (power to issue levies);
(b) section 44 (orders governing NCIS Service Authority);
(c) section 45 (orders and regulations);
(d) section 46 (interpretation of Part I);
(e) section 62, except subsections (1) and (6), (power to issue levies);
(f) section 89 (orders and regulations);
(g) section 90 (interpretation of Part II);
(h) section 128 (regulations for special constables and police cadets);
(i) section 129, except paragraph (a), (change of name or description of certain police areas);
(j) section 130 (members of RUC engaged on service outside their force);
(k) section 131 (regulations requiring use of specified facilities or services); and
(l) section 132 (expenditure by Secretary of State for police purposes).

3 Commencement on 25th June 1997 for certain purposes only

(1) Subject to the modifications set out in paragraphs (3) and (4) below, the provisions of the Act which are listed in paragraph (2) below shall come into force on 25th June 1997 for the purposes of the appointment, as soon as possible thereafter, of members of the Service Authority for the National Criminal Intelligence Service and members of the Service Authority for the National Crime Squad.

(2) The provisions referred to in paragraph (1) are—

(a) section 1 (the Service Authority for the National Criminal Intelligence Service);
(b) section 47 (the Service Authority for the National Crime Squad);
(c) Schedule 1 (appointment of members of Service Authorities); and
(d) Schedule 2 (other provisions about members of Service Authorities).

(3) In paragraph 13 to Schedule 1 for the words "clerk to a Service Authority" there shall be substituted "Secretary of State".

(4) Schedule 2 shall have effect as if there was inserted after paragraph 15 the following—

"**15A.**—(1) The first meeting of the Service Authority shall be—

(a) held within 21 days after appointments to it have been made under Schedule 1; and

(b) treated as being the annual meeting of the authority in the year in which it is held.

(2) The provisions of article 5 of the Police Act 1997 (Commencement No 1 and Transitional Provisions) Order 1997 shall have effect in relation to the first meeting of a Service Authority".

4 Commencement on 23rd July 1997

(1) The provisions of the Act which are listed in paragraph (2) below shall come into force on 23rd July 1997.

(2) The provisions referred to in paragraph (1) are—

(a) sections 1 and 47 and Schedules 1 and 2, for the purposes for which they are not already in force;

(b) section 6 (appointment of Director General);

(c) section 13 (officers and employees);

(d) section 14 (appointment of clerk);

(e) section 15 (appointment of persons not employed by the NCIS Service Authority);

(f) section 16 (NCIS Service Fund);

(g) section 18 (initial financing of the NCIS Service Authority);

(h) section 52 (appointment of Director General);

(i) section 58 (officers and employees);

(j) section 59 (appointment of clerk);

(k) section 60 (appointment of persons not employed by the NCS Service Authority);

(l) section 61 (NCS Service Fund);

(m) section 63 (initial financing of NCS Service Authority);

(n) section 88 (application to NCS Service Authority of local authority enactments), so far as it relates to paragraphs 3, 5 and 10 of Schedule 6;

(o) section 134 (minor and consequential amendments) so far as it relates to paragraphs 27, 40 and 88 of Schedule 9;

(p) paragraphs 27 and 41 of Schedule 9 (ineligibility for jury service of certain persons concerned with the administration of justice), so far as they relate to the members of the service authorities for the National Criminal Intelligence Service and the National Crime Squad;

(q) paragraphs 28 and 40 of Schedule 9 (disqualification in certain cases of justices who are members of local authorities); and

(r) paragraph 88 of Schedule 9 (right to time off for public duties).

5 First meeting of Service Authorities

(1) The first meeting of a Service Authority shall be convened, and held at a time and place appointed by the Secretary of State.

(2) The regulation of the proceedings and the business of the meeting shall be determined by the chairman.

Police Act 1997 (Commencement No 2) Order 1997

(SI 1997/1696)

Made 14 July 1997.

1 This Order may be cited as the Police Act 1997 (Commencement No 2) Order 1997.

2 Section 101 (code of practice in connection with authorisation of action in respect of property) of the Police Act 1997 shall come into force on 5th August 1997.

Police Act 1997 (Commencement No 3 and Transitional Provisions) Order 1997

(SI 1997/1930)

Made 1 August 1997.

1 Citation, commencement and interpretation

(1) This Order may be cited as the Police Act 1997 (Commencement No 3 and Transitional Provisions) Order 1997 and shall come into force on 1st September 1997.

(2) In this Order "the 1997 Act" means the Police Act 1997.

2 Commencement on 1st September 1997

(1) Subject to the modifications set out in paragraph (3) below, the provisions of the 1997 Act which are listed in paragraph (2) below shall come into force on 1st September 1997.

(2) The provisions referred to in paragraph (1) above are—

- (a) section 2(6), so far as it relates to any directions given under section 27;
- (b) section 3(2) to (4);
- (c) sections 25 to 27;
- (d) section 48(7), so far as it relates to any directions given under section 72;
- (e) section 49(2) to (4);
- (f) sections 70 to 72;
- (g) section 91, except subsection (10);
- (h) section 96, for the purpose of making orders;
- (i) section 109(1);
- (j) section 109(2), so far as it relates to paragraphs 1, (except sub-paragraph (6)), 2 (except sub-paragraphs (3)(e) and (f)), 4, 8(1), 9, 10 (except the reference to paragraph 1(3)(e) in sub-paragraph (1)(a) and the reference to paragraph 1(3)(f) in sub-paragraph (1)(b)), 11 and 18 of Schedule 8;
- (k) section 109(3) and (5), for the purpose of making orders;
- (l) section 111, except subsections (1)(c) and (d), (2)(d) and (e) and (3)(c) and (d);
- (m) Schedule 4;
- (n) paragraphs 3, 5 and 10 of Schedule 6;
- (o) paragraph 1 of Schedule 8; except sub-paragraph (3)(e) and (f);
- (p) paragraph 2 of Schedule 8, except sub-paragraph (6);
- (q) paragraph 4 of Schedule 8;
- (r) paragraph 8(1) of Schedule 8;

(s) paragraph 9 of Schedule 8;
(t) paragraph 10 of Schedule 8, except the reference to paragraph 1(3)(e) in subparagraph (1)(a) and the reference to paragraph 1(3)(f) in sub-paragraph (1)(b);
(u) paragraph 11 of Schedule 8;
(v) paragraph 18 of Schedule 8;
(w) section 134, so far as it relates to paragraphs 3, 8, 9, 28, 29(3), 41, 72, 81, 82 and 83 of Schedule 9;
(x) paragraphs 3, 8, 9, 29(3), 82 and 83 of Schedule 9.

(3) Notwithstanding the provisions of section 111 of the 1997 Act, in paragraph 1(2) of Schedule 8 to that Act the reference to "police authorities" shall not include the Police Authority for Northern Ireland and the reference to "chief officers of police" shall not include the Chief Constable of the Royal Ulster Constabulary.

3 Commencement on 8th October 1997

(1) The provisions of the 1997 Act which are listed in paragraph (2) below shall come into force on 8th October 1997.

(2) The provisions referred to in paragraph (1) above are—
(a) section 2(6), so far as it relates, to any directions given under Schedule 3;
(b) section 17(1) and (6);
(c) section 48(7), so far as it relates to any directions given under Schedule 5;
(d) section 62(1) and (6); and
(e) Schedules 3 and 5.

4 Transitional provision about Director General

(1) Prior to the Director General appointed under sections 6 or 52 of the 1997 Act taking up his post, the Secretary of State may designate a person to carry out the functions of the Director General of NCIS and the Director General of National Crime Squad.

(2) Sections 3(4)(a), 26(2)(b) and (f), 49(4)(a) and 71(2)(b) and (f) of; and paragraph 1(4)(a) of Schedules 3 and 5 to, the 1997 Act shall have effect as if the references to the Director General of NCIS and the Director General of the National Crime Squad were references to the person designated to carry out the functions of the Director General of NCIS under paragraph (1) above and the person designated to carry out the functions of the Director General of NCS under paragraph (1) above respectively.

Police Act 1997 (Commencement No 4 and Transitional Provisions) Order 1997

(SI 1997/2390)

Made 3 October 1997.

1 Citation, commencement and interpretation

(1) This Order may be cited as the Police Act 1997 (Commencement No 4 and Transitional Provisions) Order 1997.

(2) This Order shall come into force on 31st October 1997.

(3) In this Order "the 1997 Act" means the Police Act 1997.

2 Commencement on 31st October 1997

(1) Subject to articles 3 to 7 below, the provisions of the 1997 Act which are listed in paragraph (2) below shall come into force on 31st October 1997.

(2) The provisions referred to in paragraph (1) above are—

(a) section 4 (service plans);
(b) section 8 (Deputy Director General);
(c) section 9 (members of NCIS);
(d) section 19 (charges);
(e) section 21 (pensions and gratuities);
(f) section 22(4) to (8) (collaboration agreements);
(g) section 28 (Codes of Practice);
(h) section 37 (discipline regulations);
(i) section 38 (appeals), for the purpose of making orders;
(j) section 39 (complaints);
(k) section 50 (service plans);
(l) section 54 (Deputy Director General);
(m) section 55 (members of the National Crime Squad);
(n) section 64 (charges);
(o) section 66 (pensions and gratuities);
(p) section 73 (Codes of Practice);
(q) section 81 (discipline regulations);
(r) section 82 (appeals), for the purpose of making orders;
(s) section 83 (complaints);
(t) section 88 (application to NCS Service Authority of local authority enactments), so far as it relates to paragraphs 1, 2, 6, 9(e), 29 and 32 of Schedule 6;
(u) section 134 (amendments and repeals), so far as it relates to paragraphs 13, 14, 23, 38, 39, 43, 49 to 52, 55, 57, 66 to 68, 73, 86 and 91 of Schedule 9;
(v) paragraphs 1, 2, 6, 9(e), 29 and 32 of Schedule 6;
(w) paragraphs 13, 14, 23, 38, 39, 43, 49 to 52, 55, 57, 66 to 68, 72, 73, 81, 86, and 91 of Schedule 9.

3 Transitional provision about the Directors General

The references to the Director General of NCIS and the Director General of the National Crime Squad in sections 4(3), (4) and (5)(e), 8(1) and (2), 9(6), (8), (9)(b) and (10) (in the first place where it occurs), 50(3), (4) and (5)(e), 54(1) and (2), and 55(6), (8), (9)(b) and (10) (in the first place where it occurs) of the 1997 Act shall have effect as if they were respectively references to the person designated to carry out the functions of the Director General of NCIS and the person designated to carry out the functions of the Director General of the National Crime Squad under article 4(1) of the Police Act 1997 (Commencement No 3 and Transitional Provisions) Order 1997.

4 Transitional provision about the Deputy Directors General

Sections 8(1) and 54(1) of the 1997 Act shall have effect as if the references to a member of NCIS and a member of National Crime Squad appointed under section 9 and section 55 respectively were references to an appointment made which takes effect on 1st April 1998.

5 Transitional provision about collaboration agreements

(1) Section 22(5)(a) of the 1997 Act shall be omitted.

(2) Section 22(6) of the 1997 Act shall have effect as if "(1) or" were omitted.

(3) Section 22(7) of the 1997 Act shall have effect as if "(1)," were omitted.

6 Transitional provision about Local Government Act 1972

Paragraph 6 of Schedule 6 to the 1997 Act shall have effect as if, in section 146A(1AA) of the Local Government Act 1972 (application to police authorities of miscellaneous powers of local authorities), as inserted by sub-paragraph (4) of that paragraph, for the words from "shall" to the end there were substituted the words "shall be treated as a principal council for the purposes of section 120 above only and as local authority for the purposes of section 135 above only".

7 Transitional provision about the Local Government and Housing Act 1989

Paragraph 29 of Schedule 6 to the 1997 Act (definition of local authority for purposes of various provisions relating to their members, officers, staff and committees etc) shall have effect as if for the words from "inserted" to the end there were substituted the words "inserted" "or, in sections 7, 19 and 20 only, the Service Authority for the National Crime Squad.".

8 Repeals

Article 3(3) of the Police Act 1997 (Commencement No 1 and Transitional Provisions) Order 1997 is hereby repealed.

Index